# Teaching Handicapped Students in the Mainstream:

## Coming Back or Never Leaving

Second Edition

**Anne Langstaff Pasanella**
*Santa Barbara County Schools*

**Cara B. Volkmor**
*Consulting Associates in Education*

Charles E. Merrill Publishing Company
*A Bell & Howell Company*
Columbus   Toronto   London   Sydney

Published by Charles E. Merrill Publishing Co.
A Bell & Howell Company
Columbus, Ohio 43216

This book was set in Palatino.
Production Coordination: Judith Rose Sacks
Cover Design Coordination: Will Chenoweth
Cover Illustration: Jan Benham

Photo Credits: p. 6 Charles E. Merrill   p. 43 © 1981 Jack Hamilton   p. 123 Celia Drake   p. 207 Strix Pix   p. 262 © 1981 Jack Hamilton

Adapted model on p. 4 and quotation on pp. 8–9 are from:

Deno, E. Special education as developmental capital. *Exceptional Children*, 1970, 37 (3), p. 236.

Reprinted from *Exceptional Children* by permission of The Council for Exceptional Children, copyright © 1970.

**The first edition of this book was published under the title** *Coming Back ... Or Never Leaving: Instructional Programming for Handicapped Students in the Mainstream.* **Copyright ©1977 by University of Southern California.**

**Copyright ©1981 by University of Southern California and Bell & Howell Company. Copyright is claimed until 1986. Thereafter, all portions of this work covered by this copyright will be in the public domain.**

Portions of this work were developed under a contract with the U.S. Office of Education, Department of Health, Education, and Welfare. However, the content does not necessarily reflect the position or policy of that Agency, and no official endorsement of these materials should be inferred.

Library of Congress Catalog Card Number: 80–83604
International Standard Book Number: 0–675–08026–6
**Printed in the United States of America**
1  2  3  4  5  6  7  8  9  10—86 85 84 83 82 81

# Contents

**Preface** v

**Acknowledgments** vi

**1 Mainstreaming—A Social Issue** 1
*What the law intends concerning placement; toward a definition; a historical overview; service delivery strategies; mainstreaming and the dynamics of change; where do we go from here?*

**2 Getting It All Together: Process Steps and Techniques for IEP Teams** 33
*Model for educational decision making—an overview; shared responsibilities within the process*

**3 Identification and Referral** 51
*Characteristics of high risk learners; screening for identification; alternatives to formal referral; referral procedures*

**4 Assessment—Part One** 91
*Observation; assessment checklist: classroom environment, curriculum, methods, and materials; interviewing; school records; testing*

**5 Assessment—Part Two** 133
*Planning assessment—a systems approach; reporting assessment outcomes*

**6 Designing the IEP** 161
*Purpose and intent of the IEP; the IEP team; IEP components; the placement recommendation; the IEP form; some common concerns; the letter vs. the spirit of the law*

**7 Implementing the IEP** 181
*Understanding the handicapped: planning for social and instructional integration; hearing handicapped; visually handicapped; learning handicapped; physically handicapped; preparing classmates; the individual implementation plan; some*

*principles of good instruction; behavior management; teaching subject matter areas; evaluating student progress in the classroom; evaluating the IEP*

## 8 Making It All Work: Skills for Educational Decision-Makers 241

*School administrators; the role of the resource teacher; the regular classroom teacher; parents as team members—what they should know*

## 9 Making It All Work: Inservice Training, Service Delivery, and Program Evaluation 287

*Inservice training; planning a full service delivery system; evaluation of the instructional program; program review model*

# Index 339

# Preface

Since 1977, when the first edition of our text *Coming Back . . . or Never Leaving* (now entitled *Teaching Handicapped Students in the Mainstream*) was published, we have continued to work closely with groups of educators, both at home and abroad, whose commitment to quality programming for the handicapped we share. Among our favorite memories of these encounters is the occasion when we were introduced as the authors of *Mainstreaming: Getting There or Never Coming Back!*

In the past few years a tremendous amount of creativity and energy has gone into "getting there"—getting closer to the point where all handicapped students will have access to a quality education in our public schools and to the time when their right to such an opportunity is no longer questioned. And so, we are "coming back" to our readers with an expanded, updated and practical book on the "whys" and the "hows" of educating handicapped students in the mainstream.

The focus of this book is instructional programming for mildly and moderately handicapped students in regular classrooms. We are not talking about severely handicapped children whose problems are so obvious and so profound that they are unable to enter the mainstream when they begin school, though many of the techniques in this book are very effective with this group also. Rather, we are looking at two other populations of children:

1. those students who have been removed from regular programs and placed in special education because they are slow learners, have IQs below average, have not learned the basic skills, or are behavior problems; and
2. those students who are in the mainstream but who are potential candidates for special services.

We do not believe in a categorical approach to educating handicapped students; therefore, this book is not organized around the traditional categories. We do present some special tips for teachers which are unique to various handicapping conditions, but we feel that the educational approaches and instructional techniques described in this text are applicable to a wide range of learners.

It is our belief that a new future is emerging for the handicapped in our society and that the "know-how" to bring that future closer to today exists. We believe that to make the technology work, to change the lives of handicapped students, two critical components are necessary: a fair and systematic process for making educational decisions and a coordinated team approach to implementing such a process. Our book attempts to present both components of this process. We believe in the right of all mildly handicapped learners to be educated to the maximum of their ability.

# Acknowledgments

We are grateful to our California colleagues in regular and special education for their many insights and for their support. A special thank you goes to Rosella H. Jordan and Nikki Klauschie for preparation of the original manuscript; Karl Skindrud, Chair, Department of Special Education, California State University at Dominguez Hills, for his contributions to the content; and Marianne Taflinger, Special Education Editor at Charles E. Merrill Publishing Company, for her assistance in making this edition possible.

# 1

# Mainstreaming—A Social Issue

> Mainstreaming in the past, as well as today, cannot be seen as an educational problem or issue. It has always reflected the nature of the larger society, if only because deviancy or handicap are consequence of societal norms.   (Sarason & Doris, 1979, p. 373)

In order to appreciate the impetus for, and the implications of, that educational innovation of the 1960s and 1970s which we call *mainstreaming*, it is necessary to view it within the context of social change. This period in educational history may well go down as the "Years of the Laws" (Keogh & Levitt, 1976). The highlights included the passage of the Civil Rights Act in 1964 and then the Elementary and Secondary Education Act of 1965. This act (P.L. 89–10) came as a clear federal directive to attend to the inadequacies of an educational system in which significant numbers of children were not getting the compensatory help needed to offset the effects of "educational deprivation." Funds were authorized for programs to meet the special needs of such children; subsequent amendments to the act strengthened the federal effort to bring about improvement in the nation's schools. Finally, heralded by a series of far-reaching court decisions and new legislation in some states, came P.L. 94–142, the Education for All Handicapped Children Act of 1975. These laws forced society as a whole to confront the issue of individual rights and protections for the handicapped and other minority groups. Special education, therefore, became a target for change. The segregated nature of the majority of special education programming was called into question, and *mainstreaming* emerged as the watchword of a new era, characterized by decentralization of many of the large institutions for the handicapped, a movement toward "barrier-free" design, and a proliferation of programs offering alternatives to full-time placement in the special day school or classroom.

The new, and already implemented educational policies and procedures related to delivering appropriate services to handicapped students represent the positive impact of recent legislation and litigation. However, there remains a challenge for the 1980s and the years ahead: moving beyond compliance with the minimal standards set by law while pursuing quality programming for all the children, youth, and families we serve. It is our belief that a commitment to quality programming for the handicapped develops out of

1. A clear understanding of the intent of P.L. 94–142 and the climate which created it;
2. A perspective on what is being tried and its effectiveness;
3. An awareness of the dynamics of change.

The remainder of this chapter attempts to provide such understanding, perspective, and awareness with regard to the instruction of handicapped children in the context of the educational mainstream.

## WHAT THE LAW INTENDS CONCERNING PLACEMENT

> ... procedures to assure that, to the maximum extent appropriate, handicapped children, including children in public or private institutions or other care facilities, are educated with children who are not handicapped, and that special classes, separate schooling, or other removal of handicapped children from the regular educational environment occurs only when the nature or severity of the handicap is such that education in regular classes with the use of supplementary aids and services cannot be achieved satisfactorily ... (Public Law 94–142, 20 U.S.C. 1412 [5] [B])
>
> Unless a handicapped child's individualized education program requires some other arrangement, the child is educated in the school which he or she would attend if not handicapped. (45 CFR, Sec. 121 a. 552)

The preceding quotations, from the law and federal regulations governing the implementation of P.L. 94–142, spell out the meaning of the "least restrictive environment" placement mandate of the law. Similar language now appears in state law and education codes. As Gilhool so forcefully states:

> It is a new language that suggests a new conception of the handicapped citizen, a new conception of that citizen's place in our society, a new conception of those obligations owed to him by those who act in place of the society . . . It is now a question of justice. (1976, p. 21)

It is important to note at the outset that the word *mainstreaming* does not appear in P.L. 94–142, nor in the federal regulations governing the implementation of that law. In the words of Keogh and Levitt, "Mainstreaming refers to instruction of pupils within the regular education setting" (1976, p. 2). P.L. 94–142 is not a mainstreaming law. It does not mandate placement of handicapped pupils into regular classes. It does, however, mandate that whenever a student is placed in an educational setting other than the regular program, the proximity of that setting to the student's regular school and to nonhandicapped peers be considered. The law further calls upon educational agencies to make available a continuum of alternative placements to meet the special needs of handicapped students. Figure 1, an adaptation of Deno's "cascade model" (1970), is a graphic representation of such a continuum. It illustrates the meaning of the P.L. 94–142 concept of *least restrictive environment*—a concept originally applied to the institutionalized mentally retarded—which is now seen as having applicability to all persons classified as having exceptional needs. Stemming from the principle of a person's fundamental liberty, *least restrictive environment*, when applied to education, "means that among all alternatives for placement within a general education system, handicapped children should be placed where they can obtain the best education at the least distance away from mainstream society" (Molloy, 1974, p. 5). Such a system is designed to make available a full range of special educational services and environments which are appropriate for individual students at a given time. For students who require special placement, the goal is integration or reentry into the mainstream. "The concept is that there is one system of public education for *all* children, not one for the handicapped and another for everyone else" (Abeson, Burgdorf, Casey, Kunz, & McNeil, 1975). Such an approach to educational programming means that the majority of handicapped students (those with the least amount of learning handicap) will be served in regular classrooms where their program can be modified or supplemented to meet their individual needs. Students whose handicapping conditions are severe (a much smaller percentage of the handicapped population) will receive educational and support services in a protective setting—a special class, a hospital, or an institution. The cascade diagram also conveys that the appropriateness of any special education placement should be continuously evaluated with reference to the student's changing needs and that students should be returned to, or placed close to, the regular classroom when they acquire the social and academic competencies to function in less restrictive settings.

While the requirement of *least restrictive environment*, or *placement alternative*, applies to all students, regardless of the degree or complexity of their handicapping condition, our focus throughout this book is primarily on the delivery of special education services to handicapped students who now participate on a full-time or part-time basis in regular classrooms. These students comprise that segment of the school population traditionally identified as *mildly handicapped*—the educable mentally retarded, educationally handi-

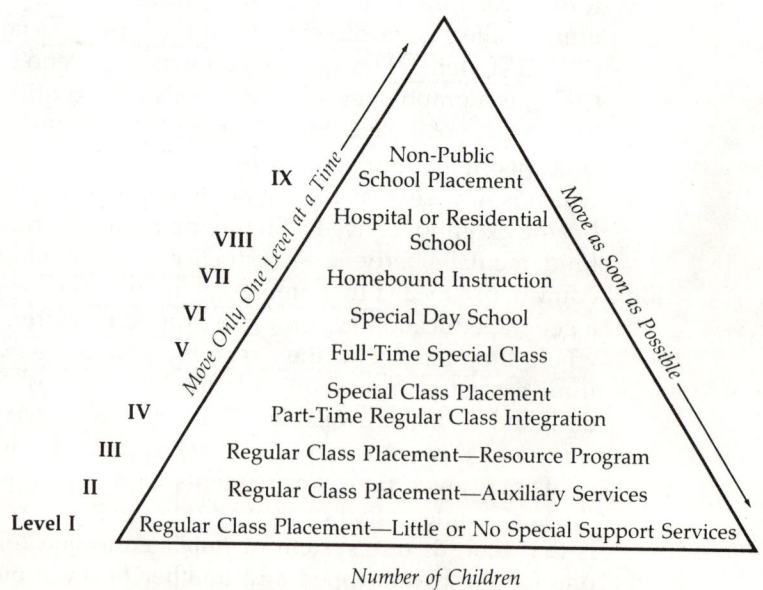

**Figure 1** *Continuum of Instructional Arrangements Available To Public School Handicapped Children*

capped, or learning disabled. They are the students who, in the past, were typically referred out of regular education and placed in special classes "because of some sort of teacher perceived behavioral or learning problem" (Lilly, 1970, p. 37). Now, based on the placement principle of least restrictive environment, these kinds of learners, and others with mild to moderate physical or sensory deficits, are returning to, or remaining in, the mainstream and are receiving needed special education services as a supplement to their regular class program. The content of this book, then, concerns meeting the needs of all handicapped students who can benefit from regular classroom placement for all or most of their school day, when they and/or their teachers receive specialized instruction, services, or support as necessary. With this perspective in mind, we turn now to a consideration of *mainstreaming*—the popularized, though imprecise, term for placement in the least restrictive environment.

## MAINSTREAMING—TOWARD A DEFINITION

MacMillan and Semmel (1977) point out that although no consensus definition of mainstreaming appears to have been reached by educators, most of the definitions offered fall into one of two categories: "(1) those which merely state something about desegregation and/or delabeling; and (2) those which feature some steps in which a child is assisted while in the regular education program" (p. 3). Definitions of the first type include Beery's (1972) observation that mainstreaming implies a continuum of programs, including reduction of programs which "pull" a student *out* of the mainstream and "Educational Specialists" who work much of the time in the regular classroom. Birch also speaks to desegregation in his 1974 definition of mainstreaming as an "amalgamation of regular and special education into one system to provide a spectrum of services for all children according to their learning needs" (1974, p.iii).

Kaufman, Gottlieb, Agard, and Kukic (1975) state that definitions such as those of Beery and Birch are elusive and that a more concise definition encompassing the many complexities of mainstreaming is necessary. These authors point out that

> ... definitions and comments pertaining to mainstreaming which appear in the literature have focused more on administrative considerations (e.g., the amount of time spent in regular classrooms) than on instructional variables (e.g., the instructional activities in

which the child should participate when he attends the regular class). Quite possibly, the emphasis on administrative concerns reflects the prevailing view among researchers and practitioners that mainstreaming is primarily an administrative arrangement and is only secondarily, if at all, an instructional approach. (p. 4)

Accordingly, Kaufman et al. define the structure of mainstreaming as encompassing three major components: (a) integration, (b) educational planning and programming, and (c) clarification of responsibility. *Integration*, as used in this definition, includes three interdependent elements—*temporal integration*, meaning time spent in the regular classroom; *instructional integration*, or sharing in the instructional environment of that class; and *social integration* and acceptance by classmates. The educational planning and programming component of mainstreaming is the ongoing cycle of assessment, instructional planning, and evaluating processes. Mainstreaming also involves articulated planning and programming by both regular and special educators at all levels of the system, and thus clarification and assignment of responsibilities is the third component.

Note that these three components of mainstreaming are interactive. *Integration*, while critical, is not synonymous with *mainstreaming*,

which, in the words of Kaufman et al., "represents one of the most complex educational service innovations undertaken to date by the educational system" (p. 11).

In a cautionary article proposing guidelines for mainstreaming the mildly retarded, MacMillan, Jones, and Meyers argue for the addition of the following elements to the Kaufman et al. definition:

1. The children being mainstreamed must be enrolled in a regular class or program roster and spend half or more of their time with that regular class or program.
2. The regular class teacher or teachers, regardless of any shared responsibility with other professionals for programming for the child, must be primarily, if not exclusively, accountable for the child's progress.
3. No categorical labels or classifications can be applied to any child to whom mainstreaming is applied; this is so for such formerly labeled but decertified EMR or other once segregated children as well as for those never previously labeled or segregated.
4. Mainstreaming is delimited to the educational strategies which can be applied in normalized educational service for children with learning handicaps where the handicaps are not so severe as to preclude the identification for and placement with a regular class or program. (1976, p. 3)

This final constraint on the use of the term mainstreaming succinctly distinguishes mainstreaming as a specific application, versus the total meaning, of the principle of least restrictive environment.

As will be noted in a later section of this chapter, lack of a precise, functional, and generally accepted definition of mainstreaming has hampered efforts to evaluate the outcome of the mainstreaming movement.

## MAINSTREAMING—A HISTORICAL OVERVIEW

Factors providing impetus to the mainstreaming approach to special education service delivery may be categorized as (a) the determination of professional educators, (b) court decisions, and (c) governmental policies. For an in-depth review of these factors and a greater historical perspective, the publications by Deno (1970), Gottlieb (1980), Hobbs (1975), Kaufman et al. (1975), Kirp, Buss, and Kuriloff (1974), Lilly (1970, 1971), Meyers, MacMillan, and Yoshida (1975), and Weintraub, Abeson, Ballard, and La Vor (1976) are helpful.

## Influence of Professional Educators

Criticism and concern about special education services are expressed in the literature as far back as the 1960s. Johnson's article (1962) questions the validity of segregated classes for educable mentally retarded students. Dunn's celebrated article (1968) may be seen as a turning point for special educators. He prefaces this article as follows:

> In my view, much of our past and present practices are morally and educationally wrong. . . . Let us stop being pressured into continuing and expanding a special education program that we know now to be undesirable for many of the children we are dedicated to serve. (p. 5)

Lilly (1970, 1971) extended Dunn's view. Motivated by his review of the current efficacy studies which he found to yield inconclusive and conflicting evidence concerning special programs, he recommended drastic changes to the special education delivery system. Solutions viable in the past were now seen by many critics as creating problems, and the forces of change began to move. Deno (1970) challenged special educators to face the issue of "whether they are justified in continuing to try to fix up the children that an inadequate instructional program has maimed so they will fit better into a system that should be adjusting itself to the learning needs of the children" (p. 231). She stated a belief that the special education system could serve as "developmental capital" in a major effort to upgrade all of public education. Her words are strong.

> It is suggested that the special education system abandon its long standing assumption that its success can be judged by how many more children are enrolled in special education programs this year than were enrolled last year or 10 years ago. We suggest judgment by criteria which indicate: (a) to what extent special education is serving those children who cannot reasonably be accommodated in a good regular education program and (b) how the children it serves are progressing toward socially relevant goals. We suggest that special education resources be mobilized to serve as an experimental cutting edge to help education move itself along the path toward truly individualized or personalized instruction so that chil-

dren who are different can be increasingly accommodated in a hospitable educational mainstream. (p. 236)

In an extremely comprehensive review of the literature on the efficacy of special class placement, Meyers et al. (1975) raise the question of failure to control for the teacher variable as a serious problem in the reported attempts to evaluate special classes. These authors take the position that "any particular low-IQ child placed with the 'right' teacher, regardless of the administrative arrangement, (special class, regular class) is likely to benefit," going on to add, "unfortunately the reverse is just as true" (p. 9).

The concern for the children who were being inappropriately and inadequately served in special classes brought with it a recognition that a worthwhile goal for special educators might be to enable regular teachers, through support and training, to become more self-sufficient in managing the instructional programs of the mildly handicapped. This is the philsophy underlying the previously cited concept of a "continuum" or "cascade" of educational alternatives.

Closely related to the "cascade" system which addresses the needs of the total range of exceptional individuals is Lilly's (1971) "zero reject" model, which places the responsibility for failure to educate the *mildly* handicapped on the teacher rather than on the taught. *Zero reject* means "that once a child is enrolled in a regular education program within a school, it must be impossible to administratively separate him from that program for any reason" (Lilly, 1971, p. 745). Problems must be dealt with by those most directly involved, and not referred to separate and isolated programs for treatment, though such services may still be the most appropriate for the severely handicapped.

The "Fail-Save" model, developed by Van Etten and Adamson (1973), focuses on how to keep a child with special needs from being held in a service plan that is ineffective and also provides an operational basis for Deno's (1970) "cascade" system. This model has four phases, beginning with consultant services to the regular classroom teacher and progressing to full-time special class or day school placement. The "Fail-Save" model limits the amount of time that a child can spend in any program phase, thus forcing program accountability and ensuring that individual students have every available opportunity to demonstrate success in the mainstream. A student cannot be moved away from the mainstream more than one phase at a time. With parents playing a vital role, placement decisions are made by a group of professionals who know the child. Success of the model depends more on the skill and dedication of trained personnel than on administrative design.

The necessity for collaboration between regular and special education service providers continues to be viewed as critical to effective programming for the mildly handicapped:

> In order to achieve success in school, many exceptional pupils need specialized, ongoing help as a supplement to regular instruction. Where the primary educational program for exceptional pupils is carried out within the mainstream, these specialized services must be available and functional in regular classes. In our opinion it is both reasonable and possible that these important supplemental services can be provided within the context of regular class instruction. It should be emphasized, however, that such services are often expensive and require coordination and cooperation of a number of professionals and paraprofessionals within the educational system. (Keogh & Levitt, 1976, p. 10)

## Court Decisions

Until very recently, the law offered parents of handicapped children relatively little assistance in resolving their most pressing educational problems. In increasing numbers, however, handicapped citizens and their parents have turned to the courts to secure their rights, to secure that which is due them under the law (Gilhool, 1976, McClung, 1975). Lawyers have assumed a very active role in disputes over the adequacy of educational programs for the handicapped. The essence of the movement, which began over 2 decades ago with civil rights activists, is a concern for individual rights in general. Resulting litigation has had a profound effect on educational goals and policy and is beginning to have a dramatic, practical effect on the lives of handicapped children and their parents. The problem areas most frequently addressed by the courts have been (a) exclusion of handicapped children from the public schools, (b) misclassification (labeling), and (c) inappropriate programming. While cases centering around the problem of exclusion from public education programs are less relevant to the present discussion of mainstreaming for the mildly handicapped than those cases dealing with misclassification and inappropriate programming, two such landmark cases will be included in the following brief account of recent litigation, since these cases demonstrate the impact which court decisions have had on the public school system.

The legal bases for the litigation involving the rights of handicapped children are the equal protection and due process clauses of the Fourteenth Amendment. The meaning of these terms as they relate to education is shown in Figure 2. Exercising their rights under the equal protection clause, 13 retarded children and the Pennsylvania Association for Retarded Children (PARC) went to court in January 1971 against the Commonwealth of Pennsylvania on behalf of every excluded child in that state. They went to Federal District Court to secure access to a free public education in a state where the law said that a proper education for all of its retarded children would be provided. On the other hand, the law also stated that children who were "uneducable" or "untrainable" could be excluded from public schools. The arguments of this group were based on the legal precedent set in a much earlier case, *Brown* v. *Board of Education* (1954), which established education as a right, and on the fact, attested to by expert witnesses, that all children are able to benefit from an education (Gilhool, 1976). In the PARC case, the state did not deny or try to defend the practices being challenged, and the agreement reached provided that all retarded children between the ages of 4 and 21 years be granted access to a program of free public education and training appropriate to their individual capacities. The court further ordered that access was to be accorded those children within the context of "least restrictive alternative," and with due process safeguards.

Similar results were obtained in the case of *Mills* v. *D.C. Board of Education* (1972) where the court extended the right to education to all students previously denied (including emotionally or physically handicapped and those with behavior problems), ruling that no child can be excluded from public education because of handicap. The decision also included due process hearings to determine classification and placement. Also of interest is the fact the court found as unacceptable the Washington, D.C. School District's claim of insufficient funds, asserting that funding limitations cannot burden handicapped pupils more than it does normal students.

The courts have also inquired into the quality and appropriateness of publicly supported programs for the handicapped. In *Wyatt* v. *Stickney* (1971), the judge of the northern district of Alabama ruled that citizens residing in state schools and hospitals have the right to a humane physical and psychological environment and the right to an educational program which is individually designed to meet their needs. Furthermore, the court ruled that these individuals have the right to receive this treatment in the least restrictive setting—in the community or in a public school, rather than in an institution.

The U.S. Supreme Court decision in the case of *Lau* v. *Nichols* (1974) was that the San Francisco schools' failure to provide Chinese-

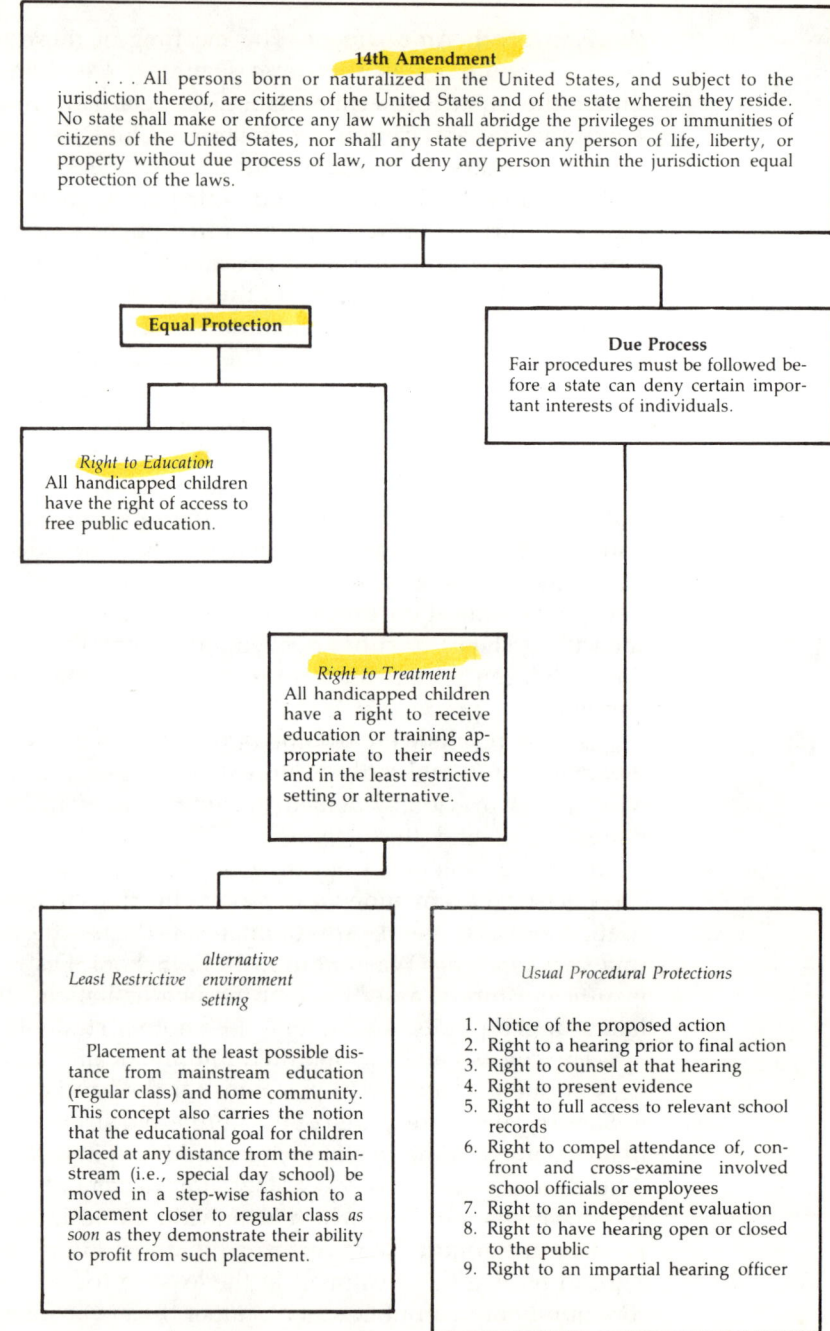

**Figure 2** *Educational Definition of Legal Terms*

speaking students with an education in Chinese or instruction in the use of the English language was a violation under the Civil Rights Act of 1964. The Court stated that equal treatment of unequals did not in this case result in equal protection, and an appropriate program should be made available to the Chinese children.

The problem of misclassification, which is very critical to programming for the mildly handicapped, is related to the criteria or standards used to determine special education placement and is therefore related to due process. Two California cases illustrate this issue as it relates to the placement of minority group children. The background for these cases is the demonstrated over-representation (meaning more highly represented in special classes than would be expected based on population statistics) of Black and Chicano students in special classes. Many of these children are so placed on the basis of their scores on IQ tests designed for the white, middle-class culture.

Beginning with the cases of *Diana* v. *State Board of Education* (1970) and *Larry P.* v. *Riles* (1972–1979) and followed by similar suits in other states, the courts have ruled (a) against the use of group IQ tests, (b) against the use of tests which are biased or culturally inappropriate for the child being tested, (c) that children be tested in their primary language, (d) that court approval be obtained prior to using any standardized intelligence tests for the identification and/or placement of Black children into classes for the educable mentally retarded, and (e) that students may not be assigned to special education without parental consent.

In both *Diana* and *Larry P.*, the legal arguments centered around the equal protection and due process provisions of the Fourteenth Amendment. As noted earlier, the *PARC* and *Mills* cases also relate to the right to due process of law. Due process, as stated in the definition given in Figure 2, provides individuals with the right to question official decisions. It is a tool for keeping officials accountable for their actions. Procedural protection, also listed in Figure 2, must now be afforded to handicapped students and their parents whenever special education placement is being considered. The procedure typically begins with the requirement that parents be notified that an assessment of their child's performance is going to be made by the school.

In summary, the courts have taken the position that the burden of proof rests with the school system to demonstrate that the exclusion of a child from participation with his/her peers in the educational mainstream is in the child's best interests and is not a violation of his/her personal rights. Specifically, schools have been required to conform to certain standards regarding the ethnic balance of students in special programs, to refrain from placing Black children in classes for the retarded on the basis of current IQ test scores, and to ensure due process of law in placement decisions.

## Legislation

At both state and federal levels, legislation has been enacted which attempts to remedy the problems of exclusion, inappropriate programming, and misclassification—legislation which therefore contributes to the rise of mainstreaming. For example, between 1969 and 1972 in California, a succession of legislative enactments which followed court mandates led to the reduction of registration in classes for the educable mentally retarded (EMR) within the state by over 11,000 cases. This reduction was based, not on educational need, but on legislated changes in the guidelines for cutoff IQ scores for admission to EMR programs. Most of the decertified EMR students were returned to regular classes. Most received, at least on a limited basis, "transition" assistance in the form of resource teachers or aides. Of note is the fact that "mainstreaming" was the descriptor used for these transitional programs. Meyers et al. (1975), in a document entitled *Correlates of Success in Transition of MR to Regular Class,* report on a large-scale project to investigate the current status of these decertified EMR students and to compare them with both normal peers and nondecertified EMR students. The report of Meyers et al. should be required reading for all educators responsible for, or involved in, mainstreaming of the mildly handicapped. It revealed that achievement scores of the average decertified student were below those of his/her matched "normal" classmates of the same sex and ethnicity, but *above* EMR students of the same age, sex, and ethnicity. The decertified students did not become "average" students.

> As an appraisal of mainstreaming, then, via the study of the transition program, we are able only to state that mainstreaming of these former EMR students did indeed work by the criterion that there were not wholesale droppings out of school. . . . By the criteria of achievement measures and marks awarded by teachers, the students were apparently surviving and learning nearly as well as the never-segregated regular class match cases. In that sense, whatever was done had to be deemed successful; one must keep in mind that some D (decertified) students had experienced no transition help at all, and perhaps some did not need it. (Meyers et al., p. 181)

California Superior Court Judge Richard A. Bancroft (1979) notes that in the year 1971 alone, 899 bills dealing with the education of the handicapped were introduced in state legislatures and 237 bills were enacted into law. The litigative movement described earlier appears to have spurred the passage of both federal and state special education laws. Numerous examples of legislation requiring least restrictive placement for handicapped are now found in state statutes which, in recent years, have paralleled or exceeded federal regulations concerning eligibility, range of supplementary services, and due process safeguards.

As mentioned in the opening of this chapter, P.L. 94-142 is the most significant federal attempt to date to improve the extent and quality of educational and related services delivered to handicapped children. This law is regarded as a permanent instrument. It has no expiration date, and it establishes four major rights and two important protections for all handicapped children (Friedman, 1978). The four *rights* are

1. Free appropriate public education.
2. Placement in the "least restrictive environment."
3. Supplementary aids and services.
4. Fair assessment of learning needs.

To ensure that these rights are extended to all children with exceptional learning needs, the law provides two *protections*:

1. A written Individualized Education Program (IEP).
2. Due process procedures.

Excerpts from the regulations pertaining to placement in the least restrictive environment have already been cited in this chapter. The goal and the mandate are these:

> Appropriate, individualized, non-segregated, non-discriminatory, quality education in a humane environment for all children in regular classes except for the few whose exceptionality is such that education in regular classes with the use of supplementary aids and services cannot be achieved satisfactorily. (Bancroft, 1979, p. 7)

## SERVICE DELIVERY STRATEGIES

The preceding discussion has provided a framework by which to examine the process of mainstreaming as well as a historical perspective and review of the major issues, both philosophical and legal, involved in this new special education delivery system. With the emphasis on providing special education services to the mildly handicapped *within* the regular school program came the need for a new kind of special educator—the resource teacher, or consultant teacher. Resource programs and consultant teacher models, as well as combinations of the two, have been developed and widely implemented in an attempt to more effectively meet the needs of mildly handicapped learners. Following an overview of the characteristics of such service delivery strategies, a summary of outcomes is presented from studies seeking to evaluate the effects of certain mainstreaming approaches.

## Resource Programs

Resource programs have developed rapidly in response to the trend towards keeping mildly handicapped students in the mainstream. While the role of the resource teacher is not well defined, program models generally are based on either a direct or indirect service delivery approach.

The direct or indirect services dimension of resource programs relates to the percentage of time the resource teacher—usually a special education teacher with advanced training—spends instructing students, as opposed to the amount of time spent consulting with and training regular class teachers. Direct service models are typically, although not exclusively, "pull-out" programs where students are assigned to regular classes for the majority of their school day and go to the resource room on a regularly scheduled basis. The resource room is the instructional setting for ongoing skills assessment and remediation. Programming is individualized, and the resource teacher works with students on a one-to-one basis and/or in small groups, providing needed tutoring, drill, and practice in core curricular areas such as reading and mathematics. Some programs also emphasize perceptual, motor, and psycholinguistic skills training. For some students, resource room instruction is combined with an array of other services—such as counseling, adaptive physical education, and speech therapy. The goal of such programs is to keep special education students integrated with their friends and age-mates, and at the same time to provide them with the intensive instructional support they need to grow educationally and personally in the mainstream. Under optimal conditions, the resource teacher in a direct service model keeps in close touch with each student's classroom teacher(s) so that there is articulation between instruction in the regular classroom and in the resource room. Several publications are available on setting up and managing a resource room program; among these are the works by Hawisher and Calhoun (1978) and Wiederholt, Hammill and Brown (1978).

Cooperation between regular and special education has already been mentioned in this chapter as a key to successful mainstreaming programs. One aspect of this needed cooperation is support for the regular classroom teacher who will carry the primary responsibility for instructing the mainstreamed student. Various program models focusing on the consultative role of the special educator are available; several are described below.

Lilly (1971), along with the "zero reject" concept described earlier, also proposed a training-based services model wherein special educators would function in a supportive role to regular teachers. Special educators, called instructional specialists, would provide these teachers with the necessary training to be self-sufficient—to be able to handle problem learners. These specialists would be available, upon request, to serve teachers who refer problem situations and would instruct the teachers in how to handle behavioral and academic problems in their classes. The instructional specialist's job would be to change the behavior of teachers—not to work directly with students. The instructional specialist would be skilled in educational diagnosis, individual and small group instruction, and behavior management techniques. In addition, they would act as a knowledgeable colleague of regular class teachers within a school.

Shaw and Shaw (1973) take Lilly's approach further, proposing a teacher-centered inservice program which focuses on those aspects of the teacher's classroom which she/he considers inadequate. Thus, inservice programs would be initiated at the teacher's request and then related to specific teacher needs. These authors see the teacher and the instructional specialist working very closely together on any or all of the following: (a) pinpointing the problem, (b) designing problem solutions, (c) implementation, and (d) evaluation. The teacher would actually experience the diagnostic-prescriptive process and begin to transfer learned skills to his/her work with other students, as opposed to being merely the recipient and implementor of an educational prescription prepared by an "expert." Acceptance of the instructional specialist would increase as the immediate usefulness of the inservice experience became apparent (by teacher satisfaction) and regular teachers would gradually become more self-sufficient in meeting the needs of handicapped students in their program.

Shaw and Shaw (1973, p. 65) emphasize that the validity of such an inservice strategy rests on three assumptions or conditions which must be present:

1. Teachers can change their teaching behavior.
2. They can become self-sufficient in teaching the basic skills.
3. They want to be competent in these areas.

A systematic application of Lilly's training-based services approach is seen in the work of Cartwright and Cartwright (1972); Cartwright, Cartwright, and Ysseldyke (1973); and Ward, Cartwright, Cartwright, Campbell, and Spinazola (1973). These authors propose two decision models: an identification model and a diagnostic teaching model. These can be followed by regular teachers in consultation with special educators to identify mildly handicapped students and to provide services to these children within the educational mainstream. The identification model specifies the competencies the teacher needs in order to be able to make informed decisions about students in his/her class: whether or not to request assistance from the special educator in order to maintain the student in regular class, or to refer the student for an alternative placement. The diagnostic teaching model specifies eight competencies.

1. Identify relevant attributes of the learner,
2. Specify learning objectives,
3. Select instructional strategies,
4. Select instructional materials,
5. Test the strategies and materials with students,
6. Evaluate performance,
7. Determine if the goal was met, and, if so,
8. Select the next goal and repeat the sequence.

This model can be used to train instructional specialists to provide regular teachers with the skills to handle learning problems in their own classes.

The Vermont Consulting Teacher (*see* Deno, 1973) model was developed in 1968 to facilitate the inclusion of mildly handicapped students in the regular classroom. Consultant teachers function as teacher trainers and are certified to provide University of Vermont course credit. They offer workshops and one-to-one consultation with regular classroom teachers on topics such as defining and measuring behaviors, specifying learner objectives, and designing, implementing, and evaluating appropriate teaching interventions. A helpful resource on the consultant teacher model is a book by Bagley (1977).

Notice that all of the above approaches are primarily aimed at extending the skills of the regular teacher so that the instructional responsibility for mildly handicapped students remains with that teacher. Such models have strong logical appeal: removal of the handicapped student from the regular class to the resource room without concurrent consultation, support, and training for the student's regular teacher does nothing to prepare the regular teacher to become more effective in meeting the future needs of that particular student or of other similar students. A disadvantage of the consultative approach to the delivery of resource program services is that consulting teachers sometimes experience a loss of credibility with some classroom teachers because they are not providing direct services to children.

Miller and Sabatino (1978) conducted a comparative study of the teacher consultant and resource room models of service delivery with mildly handicapped elementary level students. The task of the teacher consultants was "to convey best practice skills to the regular teacher, who then accepted the primary responsibility for implementation" (p. 87). In the resource room model, training of regular teachers was only incidental; resource teachers "participated in the familiar activities associated with this role: diagnosis, prescription, intensive clinical lessons, report writing, and so on" (p. 87). Academic achievement gains were found to be equal for both models; however, improvement in teacher behavior was slightly greater under the consultant model. The authors caution that the teacher consultant model is very time-consuming and that implementors must be aware of the need for continuous skills development on the part of the teacher consultant as well as adequate contact time with classroom teachers.

Regardless of the direct versus indirect services orientation, resource programs appear to have certain advantages over the traditional approach of providing special class placement. These advantages include

1. Students remaining in the educational mainstream and in their neighborhood school.
2. Students having the advantage of individualized instructional programming based on identified strengths and weaknesses.
3. More students being served than are served via special classes.

4. Early identification of learning problems. Resource program services can often prevent severe disorders later.
5. Placement based on educational need, not on diagnostic category. Therefore, labeling and the resulting stigma are minimized.

Along with all of the above positive features of resource programs, there are some problem areas. These include

1. Complexity of scheduling junior high and high school students into the program.
2. Lack of sufficient articulation between instruction in the resource room and in the regular classroom.
3. The role of the resource teacher in assessment which may be perceived negatively by school psychologists.
4. Lack of clear criteria for student entry and exit from program.
5. Resistance of regular class teachers and/or lack of administrative support.

Most of these problems can be minimized through intensive, relevant professional development programs and through consultation and support provided by skilled resource teachers. Skills and techniques related to the consultative role of the resource teacher are discussed in depth in the final chapter of this text.

## Evaluating the Mainstreaming Effort

To date, attempts to gather data on the effectiveness of mainstreaming as a service delivery alternative for mildly and moderately handicapped students have produced confusing and sometimes disappointing results. In a review of issues related to the evaluation of mainstreaming programs, the authors point out that "Integrated handicapped children appear to adapt socially about as well as their nonhandicapped peers. Yet their popularity tends to be considerably below average" (Jones, Gottlieb, Guskin, & Yoshida, 1978, p. 591). This conclusion was reached via examination of data collected in both large and small scale studies of educable mentally retarded children in regular and special classes and is based on the fact that classroom observations for peer interaction and sociometric testing produced opposite results. These same authors also note that the amount of time that handicapped children spend in the integrated setting, in and of itself, has no significant impact on the way their nonhandicapped peers feel about them. The social status of children mainstreamed for ten percent of the school day has been found to be virtually the same as that of children who spend 90% of their school day in regular classes. Keogh and Levitt conclude that

> mere physical placement in the regular classroom is not enough to ensure either academic achievement or social acceptance. Many exceptional pupils have specific needs which require accommodation and attention. Exceptional pupils are frequently behind their classmates in actual skill levels, requiring specialized and continuing remedial help. (1976, p. 9)

Several authors have reviewed the problems and issues surrounding the evaluation of mainstreaming programs (e.g., Jones et al., 1978; MacMillan & Semmel, 1977). Some of the problem areas attendant in researching the effectiveness of mainstreaming are listed below. These problems have contributed to the inconsistent and confusing data obtained so far:

1. Lack of agreement on a definition of mainstreaming. Program elements that must be present must be specified before outcomes can be predicted and measured.
2. Failure to look systematically at the quality of the instruction being provided to mainstreamed students.
3. Overlooking the fact that some regular classroom teachers are unwilling to modify their classroom environment and goals and/or are not equipped to teach to a wider range of behaviors.
4. Frequent lack of articulation between what is provided to the student in the regular classroom and what is provided by support services.
5. Differences in perception across roles. An administrator may say mainstreaming is good because it is cost-effective and parents are happy, while regular teachers in the same school view the program negatively because they have to cope with more problem behaviors than before.
6. Lack of appropriate instruments and techniques for assessing progress made by the learners being studied.
7. Ignoring the effects of mainstreaming on the achievement levels and social adjustment of regular class students.

In summary, it must be emphasized that the type of comprehensive evaluation needed to support or negate the validity of the mainstreaming approach to meeting the needs of certain handicapped students has yet to be undertaken. Yet it must be undertaken, for evaluation is a key feature of P.L. 94–142. Jones et al. offer some sound advice on what to do while waiting for the data to come in:

> Although conventional wisdom suggests that vigorous evaluation designs are necessary to determine the effectiveness of educational programs, teachers can play a critically important role in the evaluation of mainstreaming. It is the teachers, not the evaluators, who are in constant contact with the children, materials, and daily problems that arise. Whether or not mainstreaming will prove effective rests primarily in the hands of the teachers. The educational treatments they provide must at least be evaluated by them, however informally. There is nothing to be gained from ignoring this important source of information; moreover, teacher experiences and insights are likely to inform research and evaluation activities in a way that will make them much more useful than is presently the case. (1978, pp. 598–599)

## MAINSTREAMING AND THE DYNAMICS OF CHANGE

> There is a certain relief in change, even though it be from bad to worse! As I have found in travelling in a stage-coach, it is often a comfort to shift one's position, and be bruised in a new place. (Irving, 1865, p. 15)

As the educational system seeks to avoid the errors of the past and to serve handicapped students in more appropriate ways, many school administrators, teachers, support personnel, and parents have been "bruised in a new place." School principals, who once faced frustrated and confused parents of handicapped pupils with the news that their child did not "fit in" on a regular school campus, now oftentimes have to confront parents of "normal" children who question whether exposure to "those kinds of kids" will be positive for the regular class students. Teachers, who once waited months for the psychologist's report verifying what they had known since September ("Johnny is functioning in the educable mentally retarded range"), now find that referrals are processed much more quickly but that more "problem children" end up remaining in regular classrooms. Some parents, whose hopes were dashed when their child was turned away from the neighborhood school, now fear that their child will be ridiculed or even harmed if he is returned to the company of nonhandicapped peers. These examples are not intended to suggest that mainstreaming is not working, or that it cannot work in the best interests of children, parents, and educators; rather, the intent is to illustrate that educational change or reform is typically complex and difficult, bringing with it new problems to be solved.

A recently completed 4-year study of federal programs supporting educational change, conducted by the Rand Corporation (Berman & McLaughlin, 1975, 1977; McLaughlin & Marsh, 1978), identified four clusters of variables as critical to successful implementation and continuation of school change. These clusters are

1. institutional motivation.
2. project implementation strategies.
3. institutional leadership.
4. teacher characteristics.

Each of these clusters will be examined briefly in terms of its relevance to the nature of the educational changes implicit in the least restrictive environment mandate.

## Institutional Motivation

Institutional motivation refers to the reasons for which schools or individual educators become involved in projects requiring change. The reason or motivating factor, for initiating a new approach is not always the same at all levels of the system. A school district, for example, may decide to make policy changes in response to community pressure; teachers in the district may not all agree with the changes but participate because they are "told to" (McLaughlin & Marsh, 1978). The institutional motivations that characterize a planned change effort significantly influence both project implementation and the extent to which project methods and strategies are eventually incorporated into regular school or district practice (McLaughlin & Marsh, 1978, p. 72).

In most instances, the motivation for mainstreaming has not come from schools or teachers: it has come from the top—from the law. As a result, many teachers who must assume new responsibilities for educating handicapped children have not been involved in the necessary collaborative planning to ensure support of the mainstreaming concept at all levels. Feeling ill-prepared to handle their new responsibilities, these teachers have been unable to envision any intrinsic professional reward to be derived from teaching handicapped students in regular classes and so have appeared resistant or indifferent to the mainstreaming effort.

## Project Implementation Strategies

> The [Rand] study found that well-conducted staff training and staff training support activities improved project implementation, promoted student gains, fostered teacher change, and enhanced the continuation of project methods and materials. These training and support variables alone accounted for a substantial portion of the variation in project success and continuation. (McLaughlin & Marsh, 1978, p. 76)

Although P.L. 94–142 requires a Comprehensive System of Personnel Development structured to offer information dissemination and training to all educators who work with handicapped students, such a system is a massive undertaking for most states and school districts. Often, the handicapped child arrived in the regular classroom before the teacher had even heard about the law, much less had been inserviced in methods and techniques for meeting the child's instructional, personal, and social needs. Some teachers were required to attend inservice sessions which gave them nothing more than a notebook of forms and procedures to be followed and the distinct impression that the heavy hand of the law was upon them. Too often, there was no program or person who could respond to their fears and anxieties concerning special education students in their class. To enable regular teachers to change their instructional approach and to increase their teaching repertoire, there must be specific skill training *and* ongoing support until the new ways are internalized. Without such training and support, the "instructional integration" component of Kaufman et al. (1975) cannot be met.

## Institutional Leadership

The Rand studies showed that the attitude of the site principal toward changes being made in the school was extremely critical in ensuring long-term results of change projects (McLaughlin & Marsh, 1978). This finding is very relevant to the success of mainstreaming. Effective principals play the role of instructional leaders in their schools: when special education students are integrated on regular school campuses, this instructional leadership role takes on broader dimensions. Even though many principals have no firsthand experience in working with handicapped students, they are expected to guide teachers in doing so, to chair meetings where the special education student's program is being designed, and to be a knowledgeable resource for parents of special education students. This is a difficult position to operate from. Some principals have responded by giving away some of their administrative responsibility to resource teachers and other special educators; a few have been satisfied with perfunctory performance of their role in relationship to special education students. Administrators, as well as teachers, must receive relevant inservice in how to perform competently in their new role. Without knowledge of the techniques that are effective in meeting the needs of a wider range of learners, and without expertise in using team-building and problem-solving procedures, regular education principals cannot exert the kind of leadership influence necessary to create a school climate where learners with special needs are accepted and valued.

## Teacher Characteristics

The Rand study also examined the influence of teacher attitudes, abilities, and experience on the outcomes of planned change efforts. Again, the findings have import for mainstreaming programs.

> The most powerful teacher attribute in the Rand analysis was teacher sense of efficacy—a belief that the teacher can help even the most difficult or unmotivated students. . . . Teacher sense of efficacy was positively related to the percent of project goals achieved, the amount of teacher change, total improved student performance, and the continuation of both project methods and materials. Teacher attitudes about their own professional competence, in short, appear to have major influence on what happens to change-agent projects and how effective they are.   (McLaughlin & Marsh, 1978, p. 85)

How do teachers develop and maintain a view of themselves as competent professionals able to promote learning in a wide range of students who have varying educational needs and learning styles? Three answers are obvious: through opportunities to participate in policy planning and decision making, through specific training in classroom methods, and through strong staff support systems.

## WHERE DO WE GO FROM HERE?

Mainstreaming is a social issue. It involves changing our views and our attitudes. It involves trying new ways of working with students and our professional colleagues and new ways of interacting with handicapped persons in our community. The remaining chapters of this text provide a base of information and methodology which can be used by regular and special educators to make these changes happen. To conclude this chapter on the intent of the law and the dynamics of change, we offer the following list of success strategies for mainstreaming.

1. Take into account the power structure of the total educational system.
2. Create administrative arrangements and staffing patterns which permit communication and interface between regular and special educators at all levels.
3. Enlist the support of building administrators. Build their role as change agents and educational leaders.
4. Employ personnel from the educational mainstream as supervisors and coordinators of new programs to provide special education services.
5. Focus on external variables in the system or in the learning environment which can be changed, not on defects in the students.
6. Design programs which allow exceptional pupils to truly participate in the instructional and social activities of the mainstream.
7. Remember that the degree to which all exceptional children can be integrated is more a function of the adaptability of the curriculum, instructional materials, and teaching procedures than of handicap.
8. Allow the regular and special education staff to cooperatively design and make decisions on local policies and procedures for mainstreaming. They will have an investment in its success.
9. Do a needs assessment prior to initiating inservice.
10. Use creative, innovative faculty members for leaders in building-level inservice programs.
11. Give the school staff a detailed description of how the mainstreaming program will work. *Before* the program begins, handle concerns of both regular and special educators, such as "How will my professional responsibilities change?"
12. Give regular teachers inservice *before* you give them the exceptional students. Help them understand that handicapped students will only be placed in their class with their full understanding and agreement.
13. Build the confidence and competence of the regular class

teachers so that they do not greet the atypical learner with rejection.
14. Remember that the regular class teachers will be more willing to accept handicapped students when they know that they will get support and can also refer nonhandicapped pupils with learning problems.
15. Provide help with the social and emotional development of exceptional children to insure that these students will be better accepted by the regular teacher and ready for academic instruction in the mainstream.
16. Keep the *responsibility* for the education of children with learning disabilities with the regular class teacher.
17. Alert teachers to the value of early detection and prevention of learning problems.
18. Make the teacher a central member of the treatment team.
19. Improve the capacity of the regular teachers to provide for the diversity of children's needs by showing them effective ways to individualize instruction.
20. Be aware that the attitudes of special educators toward mainstreaming influence the reactions of regular educators.
21. Encourage resource persons to take into account at all times the "real world" of the student's regular classroom.
22. Provide opportunities for cross-fertilization so that teachers may share experiences, exchange ideas, and visit other classrooms within and across school district boundaries.
23. Make record keeping, monitoring of pupil progress, and reporting of program results as simple as possible—communication will be enhanced.
24. Respect and protect the rights of individual children, parents, and teachers.

## Study Questions and Activities

1. Discuss the assumptions underlying traditional segregated placement of the mildly handicapped. How do these assumptions differ from those underlying the service delivery strategies presented in Chapter 1? (See the description of Deno's "cascade" model, and the Van Etten and Adamson "Fail-Save" model in Chapter 1.)
2. Kaufman (1975) and his colleagues see "instructional integra-

tion" as a more critical component of mainstreaming than "temporal integration." What do they mean by "instructional integration"? What are the implications of such integration for the regular classroom if instruction is to serve both regular and special pupils?

3. Visit a neighboring school district. Interview the director of special education and outline the special services provided for the mildly, moderately, and severely handicapped. Compare these services to the continuum of services described in Chapter One. (See the adaptation of Deno's "cascade" model and the "Fail-Save" model.) Identify any major gaps between the services offered and the services required under Public Law 94–142 for placement in the least restrictive alternative.

4. Visit a special education resource room operated by an experienced resource teacher. Ask permission to interview the teacher regarding the following: (a) criteria for placement of pupils in the resource program, (b) assessment of pupils for instructional planning, (c) coordination of instructional planning and evaluation with the pupil's regular teacher and parents, (d) consultation and/or inservice training provided regular teachers regarding learning and behavior problems, (e) reevaluation and placement of pupils following one year in the resource program, and (f) the attitude of regular teachers and parents toward the resource program.

# References

Abeson, A., Burgdorf, R. L., Casey, R. J., Kunz, J. W., & McNeil, W. Access to opportunity. In N. Hobbs (Ed.), *Issues in the classification of children* (Vol. II). San Francisco: Jossey-Bass, 1975.

Bagley, M. T., *Teacher consultant.* Woodcliff Lake, N. J.: Educational Consulting Associates, 1977.

Bancroft, R. A., From litigation to social policy. Paper (mimeo) prepared for the California State Department of Education, Office of Special Education, 1979.

Beery, K. (Ed.), *Models for mainstreaming.* Sioux Falls, S. Dak.: Dimensions (division of Adapt Press), 1972.

Berman, P., & McLaughlin, M. W. *Federal programs supporting educational change, Vol. IV: The findings in review.* Santa Monica, Calif.: The Rand Corporation (R–1589/4–HEW), April 1975.

Berman, P., & McLaughlin, M. W. *Federal programs supporting educational change, Vol. VII: Factors affecting implementation and continuation.* Santa Monica, Calif.: The Rand Corporation (R–1589/7–HEW), April 1977.

Birch, J. W. *Mainstreaming: Educable mentally retarded children in regular classes.* Reston, Va.: The Council for Exceptional Children, 1974.

*Brown v. Board of Education.* 347 US 483, 493; 74 S Ct 686; 98 L Ed 873 (1954).

Cartwright, G. P., & Cartwright, C. A. Gilding the lilly: Comments on the training based model. *Exceptional Children,* 1972, *39* (3), 231–234.

Cartwright, G. P., Cartwright, C. A., & Ysseldyke, J. E. Two decision models: Identification and diagnostic teaching of handicapped children in the regular classroom. *Psychology in the Schools,* 1973, *10* (1), 4–11.

Deno, E. Special education as developmental capital. *Exceptional Children,* 1970, *37* (3), 229–237.

Deno, E. (Ed.). *Instructional alternatives for exceptional children.* Reston, Va.: The Council for Exceptional Children, 1973.

*Diana v. California State Board of Education,* Civil Action No. C–70–37 RFP (ND Cal 1970).

Dunn, L. M. Special education for the mildly retarded—Is much of it justified? *Exceptional Children,* 1968, *35* (1), 5–21.

Friedman, T. Overview of law on education of handicapped children. Los Angeles: Western Center on Law and Poverty, 1978, mimeo.

Gilhool, T. K. Education: An inalienable right. In F. J. Weintraub, A. Abeson, J. Ballard, & M. L. LaVor (Eds.), *Public policy and the education of exceptional children.* Reston, Va.: The Council for Exceptional Children, 1976.

Gottlieb, J. (Ed.) *Educating mentally retarded persons in the mainstream.* Baltimore: University Park Press, 1980.

Hawisher, M. F., & Calhoun, M. L. *The resource room: An educational asset for children with special needs.* Columbus: Charles E. Merrill, 1978.

Hobbs, N. (Ed.). *Issues in the classification of children* (Vols. I & II). San Francisco: Jossey-Bass, 1975.

Irving, W. *Tales of a traveler.* N.Y.: Putnam, 1865.

Johnson, G. O. Special education for the mentally handicapped—A paradox. *Exceptional Children,* 1962, *29* (2), 62–69.

Jones, R. L., Gottlieb, J., Guskin, S., & Yoshida, R. K. Evaluating mainstreaming programs: Models, caveats, considerations, and guidelines. *Exceptional Children,* 1978, *44* (8), 588–601.

Kaufman, M. J., Gottlieb, J., Agard, J. A., & Kukic, M. B. Mainstreaming: Toward an explication of the concept. *Focus on Exceptional Children,* 1975, *7* (3), 1–12.

Keogh, B. K., & Levitt, M. L. Special education in the mainstream: A confrontation of limitations. *Focus on Exceptional Children*, 1976, *8* (1), 1–11.

Kirp, D. L., Buss, W., & Kuriloff, P. Legal reform of special education: Empirical studies and procedural proposals. *California Law Review*, 1974, *62* (1), 40–155.

*Larry P. v. Riles*, 1979— F.—Supp.—*West Federal Case News*, 2 (45), 23.

*Lau v. Nichols*, 94 S Ct 786 (1974).

Lilly, M. S. Special education: A teapot in a tempest. *Exceptional Children*, 1970, *37* (1), 43–49.

Lilly, M. S. A training based model for special education. *Exceptional Children*, 1971, *37* (10), 745–749.

McClung, M. The legal rights of handicapped school children. *Educational Horizons*, 1975, *54* (1), 25–32.

Meyers, C. E., MacMillan, D. L., & Yoshida, R. K. *Correlates of success in transition of MR to regular class*. Final Report, Grant No. OEG–0–73–5263, U.S. Office of Education, Bureau of Education for the Handicapped, Nov. 1975.

MacMillan, D. L., Jones, R. L., & Meyers, C. E. *Mental Retardation*, 1976, *14* (1), 3–10.

MacMillan, D. L. & Semmel, M. I. Evaluation of mainstreaming programs. *Focus on Exceptional Children*, 1977, *9* (4), 1–14.

McLaughlin, M. W., & Marsh, D. D. Staff development and school change. *Teachers College Record*, 1978, *80* (1), 70–94.

Miller, T. L., & Sabatino, D. A. An evaluation of the teacher consultant model as an approach to mainstreaming. *Exceptional Children*, 1978, *45* (2), 86–91.

*Mills v. Board of Education of the District of Columbia*, Civil Action No. 1939–71; 348 F Supp 866; (DC Cir 1972).

Molloy, L. *One out of ten: School planning for the handicapped*. New York: Educational Facilities Laboratories, 1974.

*Pennsylvania Association for Retarded Children v. Commonwealth of Pennsylvania*. Civil Action No. 71–42; 343 F Supp 279 (ED Pa 1972).

Sarason, S. B., & Doris, J. *Educational handicap, public policy, and social history*. New York: The Free Press, 1979.

Shaw, S. F., & Shaw, W. The inservice experience plan: Changing the bath without losing the baby. In Evelyn N. Deno (Ed.), *Instructional alternatives for exceptional children*. Reston, Va.: The Council for Exceptional Children, 1973.

United States Office of Education, Title 45 of the Code of Federal Regulations, *Implementation of Part B of the Education of the Handicapped Act,* 1977.

United States Public Law, P. L. 89–10, *Elementary and Secondary Education Act of 1965,* as amended, 1965.

United States Public Law, P. L. 94–142, *Education for All Handicapped Act,* 1975.

Van Etten, G., & Adamson, G. The fail-save program: A special education service continuum. In Evelyn N. Deno (Ed.), *Instructional alternatives for exceptional children.* Reston, Va.: The Council for Exceptional Children, 1973.

Ward, M. E., Cartwright, G. P., Cartwright, C. A., Campbell, J., and Spinazola, C. *Diagnostic teaching of preschool and primary children.* University Park, Pa.: Pennsylvania State University, 1973.

Weiderholt, J. L., Hammill, D., & Brown, V. *The resource teacher: A guide to effective practices.* Boston: Allyn and Bacon, 1978.

Weintraub, F. J., Abeson, A., Ballard, J., & La Vor, M. L. *Public policy and the education of exceptional children.* Reston, Va.: The Council for Exceptional Children, 1976.

*Wyatt v. Stickney,* 344 F Supp 387 (MD Ala 1971).

## Resources

Council for Exceptional Children. *PL 94–142: The Education for All Handicapped Children Act.* Reston, Va.: Council for Exceptional Children, 1976. Three filmstrips and accompanying tapes detailing PL 94–142: I, "Introducing PL 94–142," hits the silent issues covered by PL 94–142, e.g., labeling. II, "Coping with PL 94–142," concerns the legally binding responsibilities of local and state educational agencies and the US Commissioner of Education. III, "PL 94–142 Works for Children," covers parent due process procedures and rights using three case-study examples.

Reynolds, M. C., & Birch, J. W. *Teaching exceptional children in all America's schools: A first course for teachers and principals.* Reston, Va.: Council for Exceptional Children, 1977. A text that examines the currents of change in the educational system, reviews critical issues related to mainstreaming, and discusses recent trends in the education of special needs students.

Special Learning Corporation. *Readings in mainstreaming.* 42 Boston Post Rd., Guilford, Conn. 06437, 1978. A compendium of 47 recent articles organized around the following topics: (a) Concept of mainstreaming: a perspective, (b) Controversy and debate: Special classes vs. integration, and (c) Future trends in educational services for exceptional children.

# 2

# Getting It All Together: Process Steps and Techniques for IEP Teams

> The nature of educational change is a complex process requiring the involvement of many individuals. Shared policy requires shared input. Educational personnel in both central administration and at the school building level have responsibilities in planning, implementing, and monitoring mainstreaming. (Paul, Turnbull, & Cruickshank, 1977, p. 46)

The previous chapter presented several critical factors involved in successfully implementing the "least restrictive environment" mandate. It should now be evident that developing individualized education programs for handicapped students and providing these programs within the educational mainstream cannot be viewed as isolated changes in the delivery of services to the handicapped. Rather, both are steps within a multi-step decision-making process that is responsive to the educational needs and rights of all students.

Chapter 2 is divided into two main parts. The first section overviews the model for educational decision-making that undergirds the remaining chapters of this text. The concept of shared responsibility for decision-making is the focus of the second section.

# MODEL FOR EDUCATIONAL DECISION-MAKING—AN OVERVIEW

## Process Steps

A Special Education Decision-Making Process, Figure 3 (pp. 36–37), graphically presents the 11 interrelated process steps in our special education decision-making model. The process begins with screening of all students to identify those potentially in need of special education services and continues on through IEP development, implementation, and annual review. Most states have established time lines for completing each process step; these time lines protect the rights of all involved. Only those students who need, and who receive, special education services will be involved in the total process. Various decision points within the process are noted in the figure. Each process step is defined below.

*Step 1.0: Screen students.* Locate and screen all students within the school or school district for the purpose of identifying those students with unmet learning needs and determining appropriate service alternatives, within regular education where possible.

*Step 2.0: Make appropriate referral.* Refer students who potentially need special education services, or those requiring reassessment and/or review of IEP, to school assessment team.

*Step 3.0: Analyze referral.* Gather and review relevant data and information on referred student, via examination of existing records and/or direct observation, for the purpose of

1. structuring the information received from the referring person and other sources.
2. determining if the student should be assessed by the team for possible special education placement or if other service options should be considered.
3. pinpointing areas where more information is needed.

If the decision is not to conduct assessment, return the referral to its source with an explanation.

*Step 4.0: Plan assessment.* Develop, with input from parents, a detailed assessment plan and time line for student assessment. Specify who will participate on the assessment team, what types of assessment will be done, and what instruments and techniques will be used. Inform parents of proposed assessment and possible outcomes, and request their consent for assessment. Assessment cannot begin until written parental consent is obtained.

*Step 5.0: Conduct assessment and analyze results.* Conduct assessment (or reassessment if the student is already receiving special education services) based on specified plan. Analyze and interpret results to determine eligibility for special education and/or other services. If special education services are needed, proceed to step 6.0.

*Step 6.0: Hold meeting with parents to design IEP.* Conduct team meeting, with the student's parents, to discuss assessment outcomes, design an IEP for the student, and make placement recommendations.

*Step 7.0: Place student in special education.* When the IEP is completed, request parent consent for placement, then place the student in the selected program or class. Arrange for needed services, as specified in the IEP, and for transportation, if required.

*Step 8.0: Develop plan to implement IEP.* Provide needed technical assistance and support to teachers and other professionals in developing a plan for implementing the student's IEP: task-analysis of short-term objectives; instructional methods and materials; and so on.

*Step 9.0: Implement and monitor IEP.* Provide needed follow-up assistance to IEP implementors, as they instruct student and monitor student progress.

*Step 10.0: Review IEP.* Review the student's IEP at least annually to evaluate progress toward stated objectives, and to determine if

1. the student can benefit from an alternative placement.
2. the IEP should be modified and continued.
3. reassessment is needed.

*Step 11.0: Continue special education services.* Deliver program and services as defined on the IEP.

Once a student has been referred, assessed, and placed in special education, the process recycles through the necessary steps until such time as a determination is made that the student no longer requires special education services. Subsequent chapters of this book provide detailed discussion of critical issues and practical techniques attendant to each process step. Steps 1.0, 2.0, and 3.0 are covered in Chapter 3; Chapters 4 and 5 deal with Steps 4.0 and 5.0.

**Figure 3** *A Special Education Decision-Making Process*

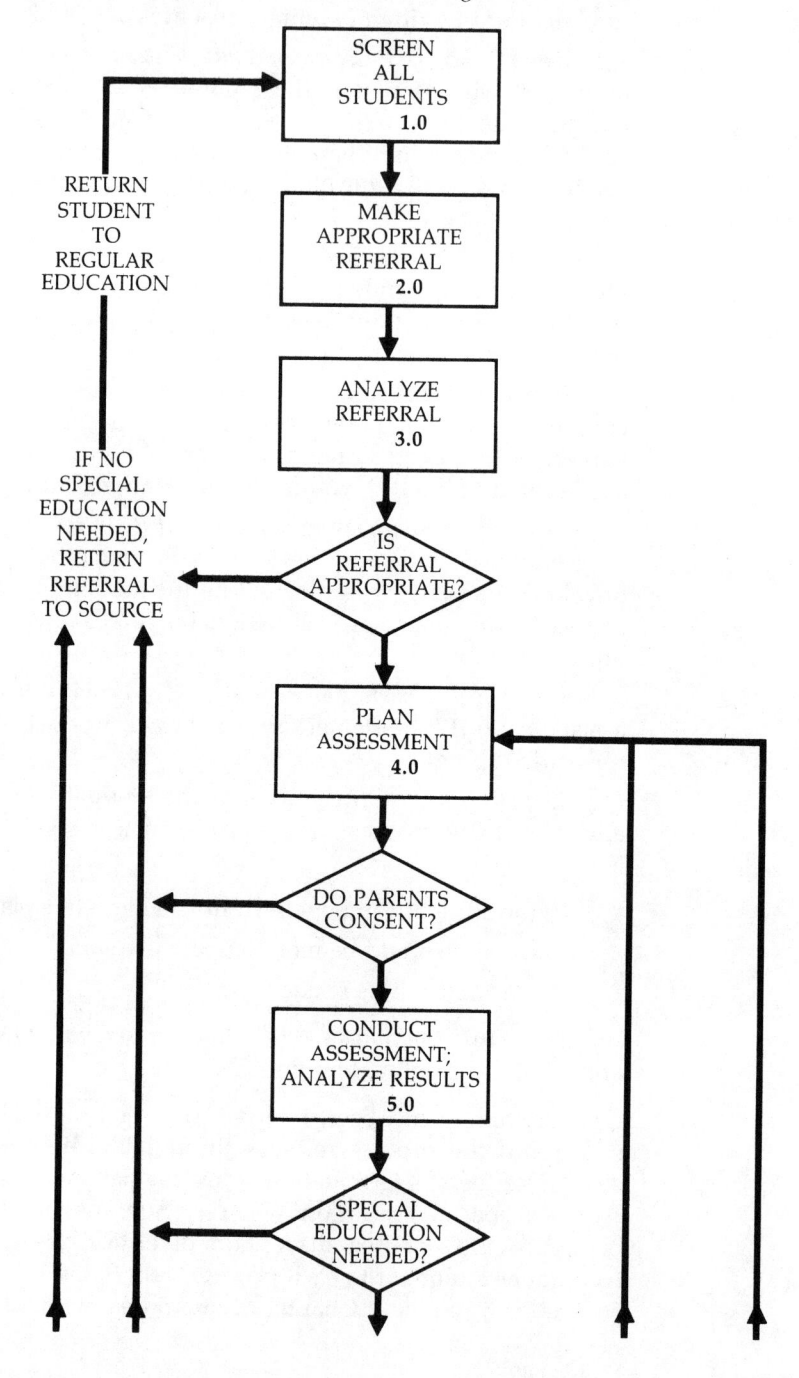

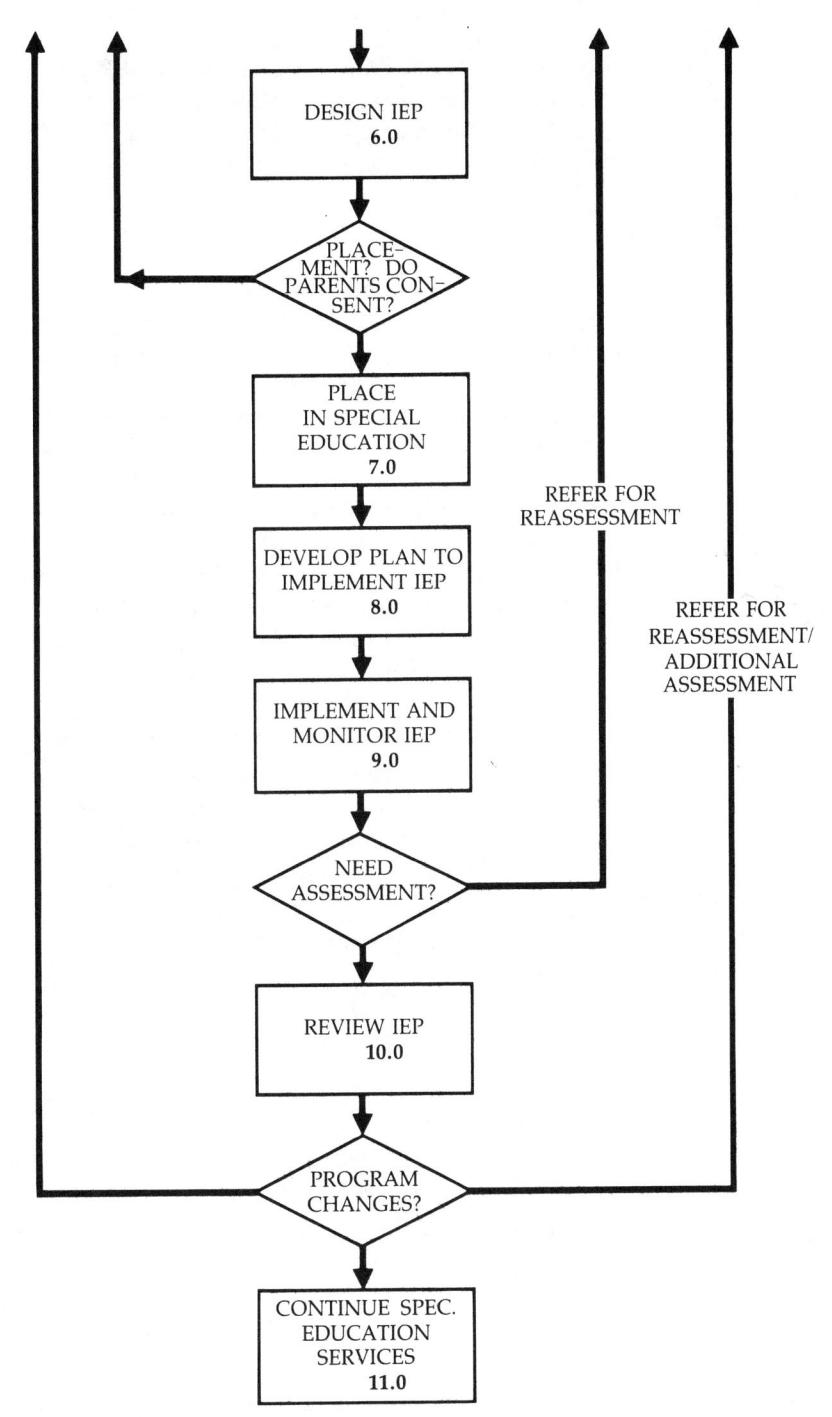

```
                    ┌─────────────┐
                    │  DESIGN IEP │
                    │     6.0     │
                    └──────┬──────┘
                           ▼
                    ◇ PLACEMENT? DO
                      PARENTS CONSENT? ◇
                           │
                           ▼
                    ┌─────────────┐
                    │   PLACE     │
                    │ IN SPECIAL  │
                    │ EDUCATION   │
                    │    7.0      │
                    └──────┬──────┘
                           ▼                    REFER FOR
                    ┌─────────────┐            REASSESSMENT
                    │DEVELOP PLAN TO│
                    │IMPLEMENT IEP │
                    │    8.0      │             REFER FOR
                    └──────┬──────┘            REASSESSMENT/
                           ▼                    ADDITIONAL
                    ┌─────────────┐            ASSESSMENT
                    │IMPLEMENT AND│
                    │MONITOR IEP  │
                    │    9.0      │
                    └──────┬──────┘
                           ▼
                    ◇    NEED      ◇
                      ASSESSMENT?
                           │
                           ▼
                    ┌─────────────┐
                    │  REVIEW IEP │
                    │    10.0     │
                    └──────┬──────┘
                           ▼
                    ◇   PROGRAM    ◇
                       CHANGES?
                           │
                           ▼
                    ┌─────────────┐
                    │CONTINUE SPEC│
                    │ EDUCATION   │
                    │  SERVICES   │
                    │    11.0     │
                    └─────────────┘
```

Source: Adapted from *A Handbook for Culturally Appropriate Assessment*. Los Angeles: CRRC, 1977, p. 2.

Steps 6.0 and 7.0, Development of the IEP and placement are the content of Chapter 6; IEP Implementation and Monitoring Strategies, Steps 8.0 and 9.0, are found in Chapter 7, along with Steps 10.0 and 11.0, Annual Review and Continued Services.

## Procedural Safeguards

In Chapter 1 we mentioned due process procedures as one of the major protections provided under P.L. 94–142. Due process—once a term used only by lawyers—is becoming a part of our everyday lives and vocabulary. Due process is a safeguard provided by the Fourteenth Amendment. It refers to the procedures which protect the rights of every person, and insures that every person is treated fairly. Due process has a special meaning for educators and for parents of handicapped children. In education, procedural due process is necessary *when and if significant changes are made, or even proposed, in a student's identification, assessment, educational placement, or the provision of a free appropriate public education.* Remember, due process is a safeguard for everyone involved—the student, the parents, and the schools. Listed below are some of the important things you should know about due process and procedural safeguards as they relate to the educational decision-making model just described:

1. *Parents must be notified whenever the school plans to conduct a special assessment of a child; or wants to change a child's identification, assessment, educational placement, or the provision of a free, appropriate education to the child.*

2. *Parent consent must be obtained before the school conducts the assessment or makes a placement.*

3. *Parents have the right to obtain an independent educational assessment of their child.*

4. *Parents must be informed by the school of their right to examine school records which relate to their child's identification, assessment, and educational placement.*

5. *Parents must receive a full explanation from the school of all of the procedural safeguards provided by the law.*

6. *Parents have the right to participate in the meeting when their child's educational program is designed.*

7. *Parents have the right to an impartial hearing if they disagree with the decision of the school. The schools also have the right to request a hearing.*

8. *Parents and the schools have certain rights in hearing procedures.*

## Teacher Rights

As noted attorney Reed Martin points out, "There is an unfortunate perception that recent federal laws take something away from teachers and special educators and give it to the parents so parents can club educators over the head" (1978, pp. 4–5). In reality, the same laws actually provide rights for professionals. Following is a summary list of teacher rights drawn from the work of Martin (1978) and Turnbull and Turnbull (1979). According to these authorities, teachers have the right to

1. *participate in system-wide planning of special education programs and services.*
2. *have a student adequately assessed to identify educational needs.*
3. *receive the necessary resources to assist in meeting the student's special education needs.*
4. *contribute to the assessment phase and participate on the IEP team when the student's program is being developed.*
5. *receive support from other professionals in meeting student needs.*
6. *receive assistance from parents in supporting their child's school program at home.*
7. *receive inservice training in new methods and techniques.*

By knowing and exercising their rights, educators can be more effective in the decision-making process for special education students. In the next section the responsibilities of various professionals will be reviewed.

## SHARED RESPONSIBILITIES WITHIN THE PROCESS

While each State Department of Education and their special education divisions have the overall responsibility of fulfilling the state's mandate to provide a free, appropriate, and public education to all handicapped children aged 3 to 21 years in the state, school districts or local Education Agencies (LEAs), are primarily responsible for providing appropriate programs. Within a LEA there is generally a director or coordinator of special education who has a leadership role in developing and improving the special education programs and services of the district. This person is responsible for implementing state policies and regulations and for developing consistent district-wide local policies and procedures. In most school districts, however, it is the building principal who has the direct responsibility for ensuring the provision of needed and appropriate services to handicapped children in the school through a process similar to that described above. All teachers, including resource teachers and itinerant teachers who serve the handicapped, and support personnel (counselors, school psychologists, nurses, therapists, social workers, and speech and language pathologists, and other specialists) also have responsibilities at various steps of the special education decision-making process. Specific responsibilities of building principals, teachers, and support personnel are identified below.

School Principals

1. coordinate and administer special education services in the school.
2. supervise educational personnel serving handicapped children in the school.
3. designate and implement educational programs for handicapped children in the school, in accordance with approved policies, procedures, and guidelines of the LEA and of the State Department of Education.
4. promote attitudes of school personnel and parents that encourage the acceptance and inclusion of handicapped children in regular classes and interaction with regular students.
5. receive referrals of students with suspected handicapping conditions from teachers, parents, and others.
6. arrange for appropriate assessment of those students referred for assessment as a result of a screening procedure.
7. supervise the maintenance of child records at the school level and protect the confidentiality of these records.
8. receive teacher requests for assistance and provide or arrange for specialized assistance.
9. implement due process procedures.
10. plan for special education programs in the school and make budget recommendations to the superintendent.
11. participate in LEA plan for special education services.

Teachers Serving Handicapped Students

1. participate in the referral and assessment processes, as appropriate.
2. cooperate and participate in the development of IEPs.

3. develop individual instruction plan for each child, including activities leading to the achievement of IEP goals and objectives.
4. provide appropriate instruction to handicapped students.
5. request support and assistance from specialized resource personnel as necessary to meet the needs of handicapped children.
6. provide consultation assistance to other educational personnel, as appropriate.
7. monitor student progress and update individual instructional plan.
8. maintain continuous progress report on student achievement of specified objectives.
9. participate in and conduct periodic reviews of student progress.
10. hold and attend regular parental conferences, and conduct home visits to students and their parents, as appropriate.
11. participate in annual review meeting for handicapped students.

Support Personnel

1. participate in the referral, assessment, and placement processes, as appropriate.
2. assist in the development and implementation of IEPs for each handicapped student.
3. provide necessary supportive services for handicapped children.
4. provide consultative services to other educational personnel.
5. participate in periodic reviews of student programs. (Adapted from National Association of State Directors of Special Education, 1976, pp. 17–20).

A major responsibility, shared by *all* educators who serve handicapped students, is participation in a team approach to identifying, planning, and delivering instructional programs and services to these students. In the next section several important dimensions of the team approach to educational decision-making are discussed.

# Team Approach to Educational Decision-Making*

A team approach to planning and programming for handicapped students is not new; interdisciplinary teams have been functioning in special education for many years. What *is* new since P.L. 94–142 went into effect is (a) the required minimal membership of an educational planning team, (b) what that team's responsibilities are with regard to the educational decision-making, and (c) some techniques for realizing that intent.

## Who Are the Team Members?

Federal law requires that meetings be held to develop and to review and revise the IEP for each student who requires special education services. Each of these meetings must include

1. a special education administrator or program supervisor, other than the child's teacher,
2. the child's teacher,
3. the child's parent(s),
4. the child, where appropriate.

This group of persons is known by a variety of names, depending on the particular state or school district. In some places the term *Special Services Committee* is used; in others this group may be known as the *School Appraisal Team*. The word *team* most strongly conveys the function of this group, and so throughout this book it will be referred to as as the IEP team.

The persons listed above constitute the *minimum* membership of the IEP team. For example, other persons—speech and language specialists, psychologists, nurses, social workers, counselors, resource teachers, and pediatricians—may participate in the meetings if their expertise is determined to be needed by either the school or the parents. In addition, when a student has been assessed for special education for the first time, one of the persons who conducted the assessment, or someone who is knowledgeable about the procedures and results, must be present at the meeting. Good practice suggests, however, that assessment be conducted by a multidisciplinary team and that all of the people who conducted the assessment should be at the IEP meeting. Ideally, IEP team composition is structured so that there are two or more permanent members.

---

*The content of this section is based on Pasanella (1980).

The site level team usually has the school principal and resource teacher as permanent members. This allows for continuity and consistency within the process steps of referral, identification, assessment, and instructional planning and review. Typically, one member of the team functions as case manager, seeing that all due process procedures and time lines for completing the assessment and instructional planning are met.

## How Should the Team Function?

The intent of the law is clear. Decisions about special education placement and programming must not be made unilaterally: they must be based on the informed opinion of those persons best qualified to identify the child's educational needs and to provide the services that can meet these needs. In this context, a team may be defined as "a unified group of people with special individual skills and expertise who join together in a cooperative problem-solving process to reach a shared goal" (Starr-Anderlini, 1979, p. 23). Each member of the IEP team has unique contributions to make based on his instructional, parental, administrative, or support personnel role.

It is the teacher's responsibility to come to the meeting thoroughly prepared to accurately describe the way the student functions in the learning situation and to make suggestions regarding the type of classroom or program in which the student will learn best. Often it will be the teacher who has had the most contact with the child's parents and who can, therefore, help them prepare for the IEP meeting and encourage their active participation. Teachers can assist the team in designing an IEP which is manageable and realistic for the student being considered.

For parents, the IEP meeting is an opportunity to share what they perceive to be realistic goals and objectives for their child and to match these against the data provided by other members of the team. Parents are responsible for contributing information about how their child performs at home and in the community and for providing a perspective on their child's developmental and educational history. They should also be willing to learn how they can support their child's school program at home.

The administrator on the team must be responsible for determining that all the necessary information for making sound educational decisions is available, and that the right people are in attendance at the IEP meeting. This person must have a thorough knowledge of existing programs and services and must be able to commit the necessary resources for the provision of an appropriate educational program for the student. The administrator also has the responsibility to ensure that due process safeguards are upheld throughout the entire decision-making process. The administrator (or designee) usually chairs the meeting and in this capacity must keep the team focused on the primary task of designing the IEP before discussing specific educational placements, methods, and materials.

In addition to the responsibilities defined by occupational role, each person has responsibilities either as team leader or participant. Leadership responsibilities, identified by Daniels (1980), are to

1. provide an agenda for the meeting.
2. structure the participation of group members (who will be present and who will do what at the meeting).
3. establish the feeling of equal influence among members.
4. select and use appropriate group procedures (for example, problem analysis, brain-storming, decision matrix).
5. provide a "memory system" (for example, flip-chart) so the group can all see what has been considered and decided.

Two types of participant responsibilities, or functions, are described by Daniels (1980). *Task-related functions* are the things that group participants do that are directly related to processing the information of the group to achieve the end-product or goal. *Maintenance functions* are the things participants do to assist in maintaining equality of influence within the group. According to Daniels, there are seven basic task-related functions and four basic maintenance functions.

In task-related functions, participants

1. *Initiate*—get things "off the ground" and present initial ideas for group consideration.
2. *Provide information and opinions*—come to the meeting prepared and with a sense of obligation to do this in areas relevant to the group's task.
3. *Ask for information and opinions*—draw on the expertise of group members.
4. *Clarify*—question, restate, and test until the information presented is clear.
5. *Elaborate*—point out extensions and implications of an idea.
6. *Summarize*—recap what has been discussed or decided.
7. *Compromise*—find a position that unifies opposing viewpoints.

In maintenance functions, participants

1. *Gate-keep*—turn attention to a person who seems to need help in getting a chance to speak.
2. *Harmonize*—getting the group to recognize that their feelings are getting in the way of accomplishing the group task.
3. *Test the group's "norm state"*—make an effort to bring to the group's attention something that is working against the state of equal influence among members.
4. *Encourage*—remind the group of the benefits of staying on a task when the group is feeling frustrated or at a loss.

Generally, it is the administrator (or his or her designee) on the team who performs the leadership function. The leader must also perform participant responsibilities to keep the group working as a team until the group task is accomplished. There may be times when the team does not reach a consensus and then the administrator must offer a recommendation, prefacing it with the rationale on which it is based. Group decision-making is not easy; it requires patience and practice. Considering the empirical evidence that groups can out-think individuals, the team approach is a goal worth striving for by all who are committed to improving educational and life opportunities for handicapped students. Further discussion of team process techniques is found in Chapter Eight.

Since federal law leaves much up to the discretion of local school districts, there is wide variation in the functioning of IEP teams. There are, however, some universal problems or concerns.

- Reports indicate that often students are not included on the IEP team when they should be.
- Guidelines are lacking to indicate how many other professionals are to be included on the IEP team (beyond required members).
- It is often not determined what to do when there is disagreement among team members.
- It is not determined which teacher(s) should be present at the meeting (the referring teacher or the teacher who may receive the student in his or her class).
- Decisions are not made about how regular educators share with special educators the responsibility to educate handicapped students.
- How to bring about the positive involvement of parents as members of the team is an important concern.
- And how to get the whole group to function as a team.

Next we consider some thoughts and suggestions on how these concerns can best be approached. There are seven tips for effective IEP team meetings.

*Student participation*—When appropriate to the student's age and level of understanding, the student should be contacted personally and invited to the IEP meeting. The student should receive an explanation as to what will happen—that this will be a meeting to make a decision about his/her life and that he/she is being given a chance to share in that decision. Often, the outcome is a greater investment in the decision on the part of the student.

*Participation of additional team members*—The key is to include only those persons who are able to contribute *significant*, current information which impacts on the development or review of the student's IEP. Try to keep the group as small as possible without sacrificing the comprehensiveness of the data base on which decisions are to be made. Frequently, there are people who express interest in a particular case and who want to attend even though they have little concrete information to contribute. Since this is often disruptive to the team process, the attendance of such persons should be discouraged. One strategy that works is to inform all professionals who want to attend that they must come to the meeting prepared to share their reports on their findings about the student's performance, and be able to put those reports into written form for inclusion in the student's file. It is not a question of *how many* people to include, but one of determining who is *essential* to making the best possible decision for the student. Keep in mind that representatives of various community service agencies may have valuable contributions to make and their participation should be planned for and encouraged.

*Handling disagreement*—Differences of opinion are to be expected. Productive challenging of the opinions of others can be healthy if it is done with the student's best interest in mind, rather than out of self-interest. The chairperson should let each team member have a fair chance to express his or her viewpoint, attempt to summarize what has been said, and, if necessary, set a time limit for reaching consensus. When consensus cannot be obtained, the majority recommendation may prevail, but only with parent consent. Persons who dissent may file a statement of their opinions.

*Teachers on the team* should be those who know the student best. There is also the question of ensuring the commitment of the receiving teacher who will be responsible for implementing the IEP. This is a tricky problem, since the presence at the IEP meeting of the receiving teacher may open the door for accusations that the team has already determined the child's placement before the meeting. In instances where the possible placement options appear to be limited to one or two choices, the teachers from those programs may be invited to the meeting.

*Regular and special education collaboration*—When a student is referred from a regular class, or when the student will likely be placed in regular education for some part of the school day, the IEP team should include representation from the regular education staff. If this person does not attend, a team member should be assigned to report back the results of the meeting. We should no longer be thinking of a "two-box" model with special education and regular education functioning as two systems. It is time to work toward *one* system—one that provides a continuum of placement options; one in which responsibility for educating *all* students is shared by regular and special educators. On another level, this collaboration between regular and special education is essential to protect the rights of regular class students and teachers.

*Parent involvement* in educational decision-making is a critical requirement. It is not enough merely to invite parents to the IEP meeting and then proceed as though they weren't there or had nothing to contribute. While it is actually the responsibility of the team to help parents prepare for the meeting and to fully understand the proceedings, one person on the team must assume a primary role in ensuring that this is done. Parents often need specific guidance on what materials to review and/or bring to the meeting, on what kinds of questions to ask, and on what to do if they disagree with the suggestions being made about programming for their child. Parents should not only be informed of their rights but also taught how to exercise their rights. Some parents still do not know that they may ask for time to consider a placement recommendation before granting consent, or that they may request a review of their child's IEP if they are not satisfied with their child's progress.

*Getting the group to function as a team* is actually the essence of realizing the intent of the law. IEP teams should be characterized by their ability to use shared decision-making procedures and by their capacity for creating and maintaining a communication system between the school and the home. To become a team and to function effectively, the group must (a) clearly understand the group task or goal, (b) keep channels of communication open, (c) be clear about the responsibilities of individual members, and as individuals, (d) carry out responsibilities. Effective team performance does not *just happen*. It is highly dependent upon skilled leadership of the group—a role that appropriately falls to the administrator or team leader. Here are some things that the administrator or team leader can do to increase the effectiveness of meetings.

- Be sure that meeting procedures are established and clearly explained at the start.
- Start the meeting on time and keep it moving—keep the team on the task.
- Monitor the feeling and tone of the group—strive for a relaxed, supportive, professional atmosphere.
- Give each person a chance to voice his or her opinions and concerns and to react to the comments of others.
- Discourage the use of educational jargon. Verify with parents, through discussion, their understanding.
- Ensure that the group carefully considers all possible alternatives for the student's placement and programming.
- Appoint someone to keep minutes of the meeting—without a

permanent record, ideas or decisions can be lost or misinterpreted.
- Bring the team to consensus whenever possible.
- Summarize the outcomes of the meeting.

*Conclusion.* The IEP team is responsible for identifying a student's educational needs, matching these needs with the most appropriate resources, and providing support. The intent of the team approach is to make educational decisions for students that are more sound then if members made decisions without team support. When every person on the team is clear about this goal, and is participating actively in each step of the process, then the commitment to the educational decisions that are made will be greater. The team approach to educational decision-making is a prerequisite to quality programming for the handicapped.

## Study Questions and Activities

1. Compare the special education decision-making process described in Chapter 2 with the one used in a local school district. Note any additional steps or procedures as well as time lines for completing the various process steps.
2. Interview several parents of special education students to learn their views on parental rights and responsibilities within the special education decision-making process.
3. Find out how due process hearings are initiated and conducted in your state.
4. Form small groups and brainstorm techniques for increasing IEP team participation skills.

## References

Daniels, W. R. *The manager's playbook: Procedures for effective teamwork in meetings.* Mill Valley, Calif.: American Consulting and Training, 1980 (Mimeo).

[Martin, R.] The teacher's rights in P.L. 94–142: A conversation with attorney Reed Martin. *Journal of Learning Disabilities,* 1978, *11* (6), 4–14.

National Association of State Directors of Special Education. *The Prince William model: A planning guide for the development and implementation of full services for all handicapped children.* Washington, D. C., 1976.

Pasanella, A. L., Persselin, L., Sales, T. B., & Volkmor, C. B. (Eds.). *A handbook for culturally appropriate assessment.* Los Angeles: California Regional Resource Center, 1977.

Pasanella, J. A team approach to educational decision making. *Exceptional Teacher*, 1980, 1 (8), 1, 2, 8.

Paul, J. L., Turnbull, A. P., & Cruickshank, W. M. *Mainstreaming: A practical guide.* Syracuse, N.Y.: Syracuse University Press, 1977.

Starr-Anderlini, L. *Facilitator's manual for Module Two, the team approach to educational decision-making: Increasing the effectiveness of IEP teams through team dynamics and team skills.* Los Angeles: California Regional Resource Center, 1979.

Turnbull, A., & Turnbull, R. P.L. 94–142: Who says teachers have no rights? *Exceptional Teacher*, 1979, 1 (1), 1, 2, 7.

## Resources

Dyer, W. *Team building: Issues and alternatives.* Reading, Mass.: Addison-Wesley Publishing Co., 1977.

Fenton, K. S., Yoshida, R. K., Maxwell, J. P., & Kaufman, M. J. *Role expectations: Implications for multidisciplinary pupil programming.* Hartford: Connecticut State Dept. of Education, n.d.

Schmuck, R., Runkel, P., Arends, J., & Arends, R. *The second handbook of organization development in schools.* Palo Alto, Calif.: Mayfield Publishing Co., 1977.

*The IEP: Team Planning.* Columbus, Ohio: Charles E. Merrill Publishing Co. Videotape (or 16mm film). Color, 16 minutes.

Turnbull, A. P., Strickland, B. B., & Brantley, J. C. *Developing and implementing individualized education programs (2nd Edition).* Columbus, Ohio: Charles E. Merrill, in press.

Yoshida, R. K. and Gottlieb, J. A model of parental participation in the pupil planning process. *Mental Retardation*, 1977, 15 (3), 17–20.

Yoshida, R. K., Fenton, K. S., Maxwell, J. P., & Kaufman, M. J. *Ripple effect: Communication of planning team decisions to program implementors:* Hartford: Connecticut State Dept. of Education, 1977.

Yoshida, R. K., Fenton, K. S., Maxwell, J. P., & Kaufman, M. J. *Group decision making in the planning team process: Myth or reality?* Hartford: Connecticut State Dept. of Education., n.d.

# 3

# Identification and Referral

> Few teachers are so well and so broadly prepared that they can solve every kind of problem which is encountered in schools on their own. What is needed is training that will give teachers the skills to detect actual or potential problems, determine whether the solutions to the problems are within their professional competency, and, if not, permit the referral of the problem for help or solution. (Reynolds, 1979, p. 17)

This chapter is designed to assist regular classroom teachers to become more sensitive to learning problems or characteristics in their students that signal the need for program modification or for referral for an indepth assessment of the student's learning needs. Characteristics of high risk learners and techniques to identify them are briefly reviewed, alternatives to formal referral are presented, and suggestions are made regarding when and how to refer a student.

## CHARACTERISTICS OF HIGH RISK LEARNERS

Children constantly generate behavioral data in the classroom. When this data is precisely observed and analyzed, it enables us to detect deviations that are, or may become, learning handicaps. There are two basic determiners of what constitutes a learning problem: (a) the extent to which the child's behavior deviates from what may be considered "normal" or typical for children of his/her age or grade level, and (b) the teacher's tolerance for and ability to deal with behavioral and academic differences.

The emphasis here is on observable behaviors that may indicate or provide an initial description of learning problems* requiring attention. While it is beyond the scope of this book to present information on developmental stages and norms for various skill areas, several excellent resources on these topics are listed at the end of this chapter. Since identical behaviors may be demonstrated by children with different handicaps, and since a certain handicap may produce different behaviors in different children (Cartwright & Cartwright, 1972), knowing the etiology of a problem does not necessarily facilitate effective instructional planning. Therefore, we have not organized the information on behavioral characteristics according to the traditional handicap categories. Also, one child may display one or more of these characteristics and not require special services, while another child may. Finally, many children with potential or actual learning problems display various combinations of characteristics. Hewett and Forness (1974) have observed that

> The normal child succeeds in school because he looks and listens, readily tries, follows established routines, has learned about the physical properties of the environment, gains the approval of others, and acquires knowledge and skill. The exceptional child assumes his educational uniqueness because he falters along one or more of these behavioral dimensions. (pp. 219–220)

Accordingly, the following examples of behavioral characteristics are those associated primarily with the areas of information processing, storage and retrieval, as well as language, perceptual-motor, speech, vision, hearing, and social-emotional functioning.

## 1. Evidences of Information Processing, Storage, and Retrieval Problems**

learns slowly
learns at levels below age expectancy

---

*The term *learning problems* as used in this book refers to behaviors which interfere with the student's functioning in the educational setting; it is not intended to be synonymous with, or limited to "learning disabilities."

**Behavioral descriptors in sections 1–7 were adapted from Cartwright and Cartwright (1972), Haring (1978), and Heward and Orlansky (1980).

# Identification and Referral

forgets quickly
does not transfer a learned skill or concept to a new situation where it is also appropriate
unable to stay on task
performs concrete tasks better than abstract ones
does not profit from incidental learning
performs poorly on tasks related to verbal learning
has difficulty establishing a "learning set"—tackling problems in a systematic manner

## 2. Evidences of Language Problems

has limited vocabulary for age
has difficulty with verbal learning tasks—receptive and/or expressive
has difficulty in organizing words to express an idea
has inability to understand what has been said
has difficulty with written language tasks
has difficulty with verbal sequences (saying days of week in order) words often pronounced correctly in isolation, but incorrectly in sentences
runs words together
uses unusual vocal rhythms or volume
has speech problems (see Section 4): emphasis on gestural, rather than vocal expression
uses tenses or plurals incorrectly
exhibits poor oral reading ability, but good comprehension of what is read

## 3. Evidences of Perceptual-Motor Problems

is unable to correct errors spontaneously
reversals, inversions, and rotations in writing words, letters, and numbers
is awkward physically
is unable to discriminate shapes, sizes (visual perception)
is unable to differentiate sounds (auditory perception) or to blend sounds into words
has poor visual memory
has poor auditory recall
has poor handwriting
is a poor reader (reads one word at a time, loses place, skips words, lines, and so on)

has difficulty with fine or gross motor tasks (cutting, tracing, catching a ball)

4. **Evidences of Speech Problems**

    articulation errors (omissions, substitutions, distortions—as opposed to pronunciation)
    stutters
    uses inappropriate pitch, loudness, and quality of voice
    is nonfluent

5. **Evidences of Vision Problems**

    exhibits poor or awkward motor coordination
    exhibits physical tension of the body
    tilts head to one side or thrusts head forward
    moves head excessively when reading
    cries, becomes ill or feigns illness, is tense, is unwilling to participate when called upon for tasks requiring good vision
    is unable to distinguish colors
    Shows physical abnormalities of eyes (crossed, red, swollen, drooping lids) when present over a long period of time and/or in combination

6. **Evidences of Hearing Problems**

    has difficulty understanding faint or distant sounds
    says frequently "What?" "Pardon?"
    shows speech problems
    makes inappropriate or inconsistent responses
    shows unusual concentration on speaker's face
    is shy
    makes bizarre or silly responses

7. **Evidences of Social-Emotional Problems**

    is disorganized in thought and in attempts to carry out meaningful actions
    bizarre or inappropriate responses occur frequently or consistently
    has short attention span
    exhibits inconsistent behavior
    loses control—fighting, temper tantrums
    exhibits mood swings
    is hyper- or overactive
    is lethargic

has unrealistic or negative self-concept
excessive complaints about health
overreacts to fear or has irrational fears
shows delayed speech or speech problems
verbalizes excessively
relates poorly to other children and/or adults
shows poor academic achievement
exhibits nail-biting, thumb-sucking, or facial twitching
cries frequently
shows excessive dependance on others

It is obvious that these categories are not mutually exclusive, nor are they inclusive of all samples of problem behavior. Extreme caution should be used in interpreting behavior. It is the frequency, intensity, and clustering of discrete behaviors that provide evidence of a problem. These characteristics are intended only to *alert* you to potential learning problem areas.

# SCREENING FOR IDENTIFICATION

## Screening Process

As Deno observes, "Virtually every teacher has at least one student who might variously be described as 'a behavior problem,' 'inattentive,' 'hyperactive,' 'acting out,' or 'disruptive' " (1980, p. 396). Such students are noticed immediately by the teacher, but learning difficulties of other students are not so easily identified. Effective educational decision making depends on surveying all students in the class to identify those who display behaviors interfering with present learning (inattention, poor self-concept, inadequate study habits), as well as those students who are deficient in the basic skills (reading, math, social interaction) required for future learning. A variety of screening instruments and techniques are available for this purpose; some are discussed below. Many school districts now have set up routine screening models to "filter out" those students in the general school population who may need extra help or special education services in order to develop to their maximum potential—those students who are having difficulty achieving success in the regular classroom. Organizing and implementing a screening process typically involves:

1. selecting procedures and/or instruments to be used
2. assuring parent notification and community acceptance of the screening program

3. training teachers and other school personnel in the use of procedures,
4. ensuring confidentiality in data collection and use,
5. scheduling the screening,
6. gathering and analyzing results,
7. developing and implementing procedures for providing follow-up services.*

Note that when all students in a school, grade level, or classroom are screened, parental consent is not required. However, parents must be advised of the purpose of the screening and the procedure being used.

## Screening Techniques

Checklists and rating scales are the two most common approaches to educational screening. Educators should be knowledgeable about the characteristics of both types of instruments so that the most appropriate screening tool may be selected. Checklists provide the maximum amount of observer structuring: the behaviors to be noticed are established at the time the checklist is constructed. The observer simply checks those items listed that are descriptive of a particular child. Note that checklists are necessarily limited to those specific aspects of behaviors upon which observers can readily agree. Brandt (1972) points out that they are "especially appropriate when the behavior alternatives with respect to a given problem are somewhat limited, mutually exclusive, and readily discernable to observers" (p. 95). For example, some observations might be "reads at grade level," "counts by tens," and "responds when name is called." Checklists allow us to quickly and systematically examine a wide range of behaviors. The extent to which the checklist items are behaviorally stated increases its usefulness as a screening device.

Rating scales are a more discriminating type of checklist since they call for observer interpretation of behavior. In completing a rating scale, the observer must make judgments about the presence, absence, or extent of certain characteristics. The observer may be required to assign a numerical value, according to a high-to-low scale, to a specific trait, such as "dependence," or simply to mark the appropriate word to describe the frequency of a given behavior (always, sometimes, never).

---

*Adapted from G. Gurski, *Identification*. A Trainer's Guide developed for the California State Department of Education, Sacramento, 1978.

It should be noted that rating scales suffer some inherent weaknesses. One is the ambiguity of the characteristics or traits being rated—what one person judges to be dependent behavior, another does not. Another problem is the "halo" effect. When a rater feels positive toward an individual, he tends to rate that person high on positive attributes and to play down the person's negative traits. Finally, some judges tend to avoid both extremes when rating, giving every person an average rating. This tendency precludes the identification of individual students who deviate from the group. Preferred rating scales are those that include operational definitions of the trait to be rated. Also, it is good practice to rate all students on the same item before moving on to the next item or variable. For example, the teacher would individually rate all students on item 1—"asserts own opinions"—before going to item 2—"enjoys trying new things". This procedure minimizes the halo effect.

Brandt (1972) notes that "The difference between checklist data and ratings is primarily a matter of the kind of judgment required of the observer. With checklists, he classifies behavioral events. His judgment is qualitative. . . . In contrast to this type of judgment, ratings represent a quantitative assessment of the degree to which some quality is present" (p. 118). However, both checklists and rating scales are imprecise tools, and the probability of bias is significant (Foster, Ysseldyke, & Reese, 1975; Ysseldyke & Foster, 1978). Such instruments should only be used to obtain organized descriptions or impressions of behavioral functioning that can later be verified through systematic observation.

Direct observation and recording of student behavior is likely to be the most objective and useful approach to screening. It is critical that the teacher routinely and systematically observes how students are functioning in the classroom setting. The most effective procedure is to set up a continuous schedule whereby each student is studied every few weeks. Classroom observation methods include:

1. Anecdotal records.
2. Frequency or event recording.
3. Duration recording.
4. Time sampling.
5. Placheck (Planned Activity Check).
6. Precision teaching.

Each of the above methods is discussed in Chapter 4. It is often the responsibility of the resource teacher, or other special educator, to assist classroom teachers in the selection and use of a particular observation technique to study individual students.

## Considerations in the Screening Process

1. The purpose of the screening process is prevention—not diagnosis or labeling. Since learning problems tend to be cumulative, early identification is essential.
2. The most powerful approach to screening is to focus on behaviors that are relevant to school success and also to examine the demands of the classroom environment on the student.
3. Before selecting a screening instrument for classroom use, review it carefully to determine whether it is suited to your purpose. Some screening devices are quite broad while others attend to a narrow range of behaviors. Determine whether the instrument is expedient to administer, score, and interpret. Consider whether the instrument is appropriate for children from culturally and/or linguistically different backgrounds.
4. A successful screening process should result in identifying most, if not all students who need special consideration—i.e., the process should not lead to over- or underidentification.
5. Not all students who are "screened out" should be referred as potential candidates for special education services. The range of follow-up options should include alternative interventions.

## ALTERNATIVES TO FORMAL REFERRAL

One of the important outcomes of the movement to identify all handicapped students and to provide them with programs and services appropriate to their unique learning needs has been the confrontation of the question, where does the responsibility of special education begin and where does that of regular education end? As Larsen (1975) points out:

> Perhaps the most frequently held assumption regarding children who exhibit school-related problems is that they are somehow disabled or disordered and, therefore, are significantly different from 'normal' students. While this belief may have some relevance to more severely involved children, its application to students who merely fail to read at grade level or are mild behavior problems is largely superfluous.  (p. 11)

Larsen also states that acceptance of the assumption that a child does have some type of disorder or deficit frequently leads to the

# Identification and Referral

belief that the regular educator cannot be held accountable for the student's lack of success in school. "Obviously, this assumption implies that the failure is primarily the fault of the child and is not due to inadequacies in the instructional techniques or interactional patterns utilized in the classroom" (Larsen, 1975, p. 11).

The factors Larsen describes are precisely those that are leading many school districts to develop more stringent guidelines for making referrals to special education and for establishing more specific criteria regarding which students are deemed eligible to receive special education services. Providing consultation and other support services to teachers of students identified as having actual or potential learning problems is becoming widely advocated. Such services may be provided by the principal, resource teacher, psychologist, counselor, or program consultant on a formal or informal basis.

## Consultation and Indirect Services

Teachers differ in their ability to determine what behavioral differences fall within normal limits, how their own classroom management or instructional style may interfere with the style of certain learners, and which social and cultural factors may be playing in a child's school problems. Together, the teacher and the consultant or resource person should review the screening results and/or discuss the teacher's concerns about the student's performance in order to consider alternatives for action. Alternatives may include:

1. Continue in present program but make more frequent progress checks; set a date for review.
2. Make modifications in regular program.
3. Utilize other program options or services.
4. Request administrative interventions.
5. Make formal referral for assessment.

Examples of alternatives 2, 3, and 4 are shown below.

    A. *Modifications of Regular Program**
        1. Modify instructional materials/methods.
          • shorter assignments or learning tasks

---

*Adapted from Santa Barbara County Special Education Services Region Criteria of Eligibility for Services: Learning Handicapped (Draft, Proposed Guidelines, March, 1980).

- change instructional content focus or level
- change type of materials (worksheets, books, audio-visual)
- provide immediate feedback
- create opportunities for active learning
- use timed tasks and untimed tasks

2. Modify classroom management techniques.
   - implement a contingency management system
   - use student contracts
   - vary grading system
3. Modify classroom environment.
   - change the room arrangement
   - change student groupings
   - reschedule class activities
4. Use additional instructional assistance.
   - inter-teacher exchange for academics
   - cross-age or peer tutoring
   - classroom aide or volunteer
5. Increase home-school cooperation.
   - parent-teacher conferences
   - parent tutoring

B. *Other program options or services*
   - Health/safety program
   - Reading specialists
   - Math specialists
   - Bilingual program
   - Title I (Elementary and Secondary Education Act)
   - Community agencies

C. *Administrative interventions*
   - Change in classroom or grade
   - Adjustment of school day

Which of the five alternatives should be selected as the best course of action for an individual student at a particular point in time depends on several variables—competency and commitment of the teacher, availability of support services, and the nature or severity of

# Identification and Referral

the student's problem. If modification to the regular program, utilization of other programs or services, or administrative interventions are deemed appropriate, the specific use and resulting outcomes of these strategies must be carefully documented. In addition, parents should be informed of the changes in their child's program via parent-teacher conferences. In some instances, ongoing consultation and/or skills training will be needed by the classroom teacher responsible for implementing alternative strategies (see Chapter 8). To summarize, the provision of consultation and indirect services to classroom teachers should consist of the following steps.

1. If a child has been identified as a result of a formal or informal screening process, the resource person determines, in conjunction with the home-room teacher, whether the child does indeed evidence exceptional needs. If there is an indication of exceptionality, the resource person goes on to #2. If there is no such indication, no further action is taken, and the child's name and screening records are removed from the list of children identified as possible candidates for special education services.

2. The resource person clarifies the problem situation with the child's teacher, using the consultation process.

3. The resource person provides additional information about the child on a general basis (e.g., child development data, cultural/linguistic data, and so forth) which will assist the teacher in interacting with and planning for the child.

4. Using existing materials the resource person assists in planning to modify the regular classroom program.

5. The resource person provides additional assistance in the form of suggested alternative materials and techniques that can be incorporated within the regular classroom structure.

6. The resource person provides for reasonable *follow-up* consultation. If the follow-up consultation and quantifiable data indicate that appropriate adjustment has been accomplished, no further action is taken, and the child's name and screening records are removed from the list of children identified as possibly requiring special education services. If the modification of the regular program has not proven to be satisfactory in meeting the child's needs, and further consultation is not indicated, a formal referral for assessment is completed (Adapted from Gurski, 1978).

## REFERRAL PROCEDURES

In addition to referrals made on the basis of screening and follow-up consultations, direct referrals may be made by parents, teachers, other professionals, or the student. Regardless of the source, referral should include:

1. Completion of a written referral form.
2. Routing of referrals to the person responsible for logging them in and initiating the next procedural step.
3. Analyzing the referral to determine its appropriateness and completeness.
4. Development of an assessment plan or return of the referral to its source.
5. Parent conferencing prior to submission of a referral is a most desirable extra step.

## The Referral Form

A referral form represents a statement of concern about a student's rate of learning. The referral statement is often the initial basis of communication between the classroom teacher and the specialist. The referral form should be clear, concise, and easy to complete. Hammill and Wiederholt (1972) emphasize that referral forms should not be too demanding of the teacher, either in terms of assessment skills or in terms of time needed to complete. If the referral form is too sophisticated and detailed, some teachers will feel inadequate and will fail to refer children who really need additional help. These authors suggest:

> The forms should instead request information on such factors as the child's level of performance in basic academic skills, his ability to benefit from group instruction, and his classroom behavior, and should include a section for any comments the regular classroom teacher might care to make. (p. 52)

The resource teacher should provide regular teachers with specific information and guidance on how to complete referral forms. The following five items are basic:

1. *The child's presenting problem should be stated precisely.* Expressions such as "decreasing academic ability", "low academic achievement", and "displays social problems" are vague and generalized and do not zero in on the problem. Referral

# Identification and Referral

statements should be specific and should attempt to delimit the problem, for example: "reading achievement scores have dropped over the past 18 months while math scores remain at or near grade level"; "achievement in all basic skill areas is below age and grade level expectation although language skills have shown improvement recently"; "refuses to join in group activities and frequently cries when classmates tease him."

2. *Include specific comments on learner strengths.* This places the emphasis on the positive aspects of the learner's behavior, and can provide valuable ideas for planning remediation.

3. *Avoid making inferences as to why the child behaves in a certain way; include descriptions of what the child actually does (not your interpretation).* Saying that a student is "hyperactive," "aggressive," or that she/he is "suspected to have mild cerebral palsy involvement" does not describe the actual behaviors that concern us as teachers. When a student is being referred for assessment, every attempt should be made to describe his/her behavior in functional terms: "does not sit at desk for more than two minute intervals; talks while others are talking; starts an activity before directions have been given; punches children on the playground; talks loudly; always tries to be first in line, or to use equipment; speaks in a halting manner, has difficulty using pencil, scissors; frequently requires help with buttoning, shoelaces." These are examples of *behavioral* descriptions of students' problems.

4. *Provide as much supportive documentation of the problem statement as possible (test scores, baseline performance data, tried materials and methods, and so on.* The extent to which the problem statement is supported by data which the teacher has gathered will help to point to specific assessment strategies and avoid duplication of effort.

5. *Include accurate identifying information: age, birthdate, date of referral, date testing was done, and so forth.* This may seem an obvious point, but it is amazing how often referrals are submitted without these data being completed. Since the referral form will become part of the student's file, it is important that careful records be kept.

## Sample Referral Forms

Sample A, which follows, is an example of a completed referral form which illustrates many of the points discussed above. Notice that the reason for referral is stated in fairly precise terms and is supported by actual test scores. The referring teacher has also commented on the student's strengths. The form itself provides the teacher with a structure for quickly recording referral information.

Compared to sample A, sample B (page 65) is much less structured. The teacher is not directed, by the form, to supply *specific* data on the student's performance. Lack of structure in the design of the referral form contributes to the reporting of vague information which is of little value in formulating an assessment plan.

**Sample A**  *Student Referral Form**

Name: Thomas Barton    Birthdate: 6/15/71 C.A. 8:5   Date of Referral 11/17/79

School: Starlight Elementary    Teacher: Mrs. Sharon Lake    Grade: 3

PARENT/GUARDIAN: Mrs. Nettie Thomas    ADDRESS: 1214 E. Walnut

PHONE: 737-2102

*Reason for referral:* Reading and math skills are below grade level; Tommy seems to try hard but gets few results. He very seldom responds in group situations and is kind of a "loner." I'm concerned about his reading comprehension and social adjustment.

*Describe program and materials used with student in the classroom:*
Lately Tommy has been using the manipulative materials in the math center with some success. I have tried some reading drill techniques but Tommy gets tense and seems confused.

*Areas of strength:* Tommy is very attentive; he follows directions and seems motivated to try hard. He enjoys drawing and painting and is very interested in cars.

*Math—Text and Skill Level:* Greater Cleveland; SRA Achievement Test (arithmetic) given 9/24/79 grade placement score = 2.5. Errors in reading numbers and writing answers were noted.

*Reading—Text and Skill Level:* Bank Street Reader—California Reading Test, Upper Primary (9/19/79) score = 2.4. Comprehension skills are weak.

*Social Adjustment:*
Tommy is new in our school this year. He does not seem to have many friends and usually plays alone at recess or stands watching a group of kids. He responds well to adult attention.

*Health:*
Generally good though Tommy frequently appears tired and listless. Vision and hearing are normal.

*Parent's Cooperation:*
Mrs. Thomas seems very concerned about Tommy's school performance and says

---

*Adapted from a form used in Humboldt-Del Norte Master Plan Project, Humboldt County Office of Education, Eureka, California.

## Identification and Referral

**Sample A** continued

she would like to help but she is working on shifts and does not see Tommy when he comes home from school. Father is not in the home.

*Other agencies involved with child:*
None at present. I have suggested to Mrs. Thomas that she contact "Big Brother."

**Sample B** *Student Referral Form*

Name ____Sandra Storia____ Birthdate __2/8/73__ Age _____

Referral Date ____11/17/79____ School __Camelia__ Grade __1__

Referred By ____Mrs. Doolittle_____

Parent or Guardian ____Mr. and Mrs. Storia_____

Address ____939 Buttonwood____ Phone _____

1. *Reasons for Referral:*
   Very disruptive in class, possible dyslexia

2. *Where in class is student deficient?*
   Reading and behavior

3. *What do you want to know about the student?*
   Why she can't learn to read

4. *Background Information:*
   a. *Past school history:* was in kindergarten in Martindale last year.
   b. *Family structure:* mother; father; two siblings and a grandmother.
   c. *Other information:* I have talked to the mother and she says they have a lot of trouble with Sandra at home, too.

The next three referral forms, Samples C, D, and E, are examples of more structured and detailed formats. The following features should be noted in the examples.

Note in *Sample C:*
1. provides a space to indicate the student's primary language.
2. suggests that the parent be notified that the referral is being made.
3. asks the teacher to complete a screening checklist and prioritize problem areas.
4. encourages referrals from persons who know the student outside of the school situation.

|  |  |
|---|---|
|  | 5. asks for behavioral descriptions and test scores. |
|  | 6. asks for comments on student's strengths. |
| Note in *Sample D:* | 1. requests baseline data (test scores). |
|  | 2. provides a checklist of behaviors, though the items are not all directly observable behaviors. |
|  | 3. allows the teacher to include personal impressions and observations of the student. |
| Note in *Sample E:* | 1. asks for use of behavioral terms to describe behavior. |
|  | 2. requests test results when available. |
|  | 3. provides behavior checklists in critical areas, focusing on both positive and negative behaviors. |
|  | 4. can be used both for screening and for informal follow-up evaluation. |

**Sample C**  *Student Referral Form For School Appraisal Team*\*

REFERRED BY: _____ DATE _____
NAME/POSITION

STUDENT'S NAME _____ BIRTHDATE_____
CHRONOLOGICAL AGE _____ SCHOOL_____
GRADE _____ TEACHER/COUNSELOR _____ SEX _____
NAME OF PARENT (or guardian) _____
ADDRESS _____ TELEPHONE _____
LANGUAGE SPOKEN AT HOME:          ☐ ENGLISH    ☐ SPANISH
☐ BOTH    ☐ OTHER _____

I SPECIFY REASON FOR REFERRAL:
PARENT NOTIFIED: ☐ YES        PARENT AGREES: ☐ YES
                 ☐ NO                         ☐ NO

\*Developed by Santa Barbara County Comprehensive Plan for Special Education, Santa Barbara County Schools, Santa Barbara, California, 1975.

# Identification and Referral

### Sample C   continued

II  DESCRIBE ANY ATTEMPTED INTERVENTIONS (Educational, Psychological, Medical, etc.)

III  KNOWN SIGNIFICANT HEALTH PROBLEMS:

IV  OTHER AGENCIES INVOLVED WITH STUDENT:

V  PAST AND/OR CURRENT SPECIAL EDUCATION PLACEMENTS:

Where referral is initiated from outside of school, principal/designee contacts students' classroom teacher and/or counselor to complete the following section:

#### CLASSROOM TEACHER/COUNSELOR

PLEASE COMPLETE CITES SCREEN AND ANSWER FOLLOWING QUESTIONS:

1. CHECK, RATE, AND PRIORITIZE FOLLOWING AREAS OF CONCERN:
   A. Check areas of concern.
   B. For each area identified, assign a "1" or "2" rating.
   C. When all areas of concern have been checked and rated, go back and assign a priority number for each area.

| AREA | A | B | C |
|---|---|---|---|
| 1. Speech and Verbal Communications | | | |
| 2. Visual Behaviors | | | |
| 3. Visual Perception | | | |
| 4. Auditory Behaviors | | | |
| 5. In-Class Social Behavior | | | |
| 6. Out-of-Class Social Behavior | | | |
| 7. Work Habits | | | |
| 8. General Motor Behaviors | | | |
| 9. Discrepancy Classwork & Test Score Data | | | |
| 10. Attentional Behaviors | | | |
| 11. Absenteeism/Tardiness | | | |
| 12. Conformity to Values | | | |

2. INDICATE SPECIFIC OBSERVED BEHAVIORS FOR ABOVE AREAS CHECKED:

3. DESCRIBE PROGRAM AND MATERIALS USED WITH STUDENT:

**Sample C**  continued

4. CURRENT GRADE LEVEL AT WHICH STUDENT IS FUNCTIONING:

READING: _____ MATH: _____

5. CURRENT TEST INFORMATION:

6. AREAS OF STRENGTH AND/OR INTEREST OBSERVED IN STUDENT:

_____
TEACHER'S/COUNSELOR'S SIGNATURE                   DATE

**Sample D**  *Referral for Special Services**

It is the desire of the special services staff to have the most complete picture possible of the student referred in order to better understand the problem and to provide assistance as soon as possible. This form has been made succinct and therefore must be filled in *completely* before services can be provided.

DATE _____ SCHOOL _____

STUDENT _____ ADDRESS _____

AGE _____ BIRTHPLACE _____

PARENT _____ PHONE NO. _____

GRADE _____ REPEATED GRADE _____

RECENT TEST SCORES:
| NAME OF TEST | DATE OF TEST | SIGNIFICANT RESULTS |
|---|---|---|
| _____ | _____ | _____ |
| _____ | _____ | _____ |
| _____ | _____ | _____ |

SPECIFIC AREA OF ACADEMIC WEAKNESS:
| SUBJECT | DESCRIPTION OF PROBLEM |
|---|---|
| _____ | _____ |
| _____ | _____ |
| _____ | _____ |
| _____ | _____ |

REMEDIAL ASSISTANCE AND APPROACHES I HAVE TRIED:
_____
_____
_____

* Adapted from *The resource room: An access to excellence.* South Carolina Region V, Educational Services Center, 1975, pp. 167–69.

# Identification and Referral

## Sample D  continued

CHECK THE SPACE BESIDE THE STATEMENTS THAT BEST DESCRIBE THE STUDENT:

### ADJUSTMENT:

- __ well poised
- __ at ease
- __ courteous
- __ cooperative
- __ cheerful
- __ tense
- __ anxious
- __ exictable
- __ easily upset
- __ unhappy
- __ moody
- __ hostile
- __ eager for praise
- __ sensitive
- __ needs frequent reassurance
- __ lazy
- __ shy
- __ cries often
- __ depressed

### RESPONSIVENESS:

- __ alert
- __ prompt responses
- __ industrious
- __ hyperactive
- __ impulsive
- __ confused
- __ indecisive
- __ withdrawn
- __ hesitant
- __ deliberate
- __ daydreams
- __ irrelevant or bizarre response

TEACHER OPINIONS—BEHAVIOR OBSERVATIONS: (Please comment on student's personality and general adjustment as you know him/her)

_____
_____
_____

### RELATIONS WITH OTHERS:

- __ outgoing: good natured
- __ has many friends
- __ has few friends
- __ seeks attention
- __ enjoys group activities
- __ plays alone
- __ high degree of conformity to peer group expectations
- __ conscientious
- __ friendly
- __ independent
- __ patient
- __ tolerant
- __ jealous
- __ tactful

### EFFORT, APPLICATION:

- __ careful
- __ gives up easily
- __ careless
- __ works at rapid tempo
- __ distractible
- __ works at slow tempo
- __ readily fatigued
- __ spontaneous
- __ creative

### SELF-CRITICISM:

- __ extremely critical of self
- __ healthy recognition of own mistakes
- __ downplays own inadequacies
- __ boastful, in spite of lack of success
- __ does not seem bothered by poor efforts

### ATTENTION:

- __ listens carefully
- __ waits until instructions are completed before beginning task
- __ begins to work impulsively without listening to instructions
- __ inattentive to most instructions
- __ seems to understand most instructions

**Sample D** continued

PERSEVERANCE:
— works constructively on long tasks
— distracted only by unusual circumstances
— easily distracted after short periods of concentration
— does not complete many tasks

MOTIVATION:
— eager
— indifferent
— resistant, sullen
— apathetic
— guarded, suspicious
— excessive concern with results

VERBALIZATION:
— talkative
— expresses him/herself well
— difficulty in expressing him/herself
— offers frequent comment

SELF-CONCEPT:
— seems self-centered
— lacks self-confidence
— seems self-confident
— forceful
— submissive

How do you see this child? _____

_____

_____

_____

_____
Signature of Person Initiating
Referral and Position

**Sample E**  *Teacher Referral Statement**

Name of Student _____ C.A. _____ Report Date _____
School _____ Birthdate & Grade _____
Teacher(s) _____ Consultant _____

   I. Achievement Data
   Describe the student's typical performance in each area. Use behavioral terms so that the description is precise. Cite any available test results. If not observed or sampled, mark N/O.
   A. Oral Language _____
   _____

   Written Language _____
   _____

   B. Reading Comprehension _____
   _____

   Word Analysis Skills _____
   _____

*Adapted from Cartwright and Cartwright, 1972, pp. 308–15.

# Identification and Referral

**Sample E** continued

    C. Mathematical Comprehension _____

       Computation Abilities _____

    D. Other _____

II. Learning Behaviors Checklist

Place a check mark next to the statements which describe behavior *usually* exhibited by the student. Use the comment space to elaborate on your choice and to provide supporting information.

A. Behavior Related to Inputs
- __ is attentive during most activities
- __ is attentive only during his/her favorite activities
- __ rarely pays attention
- __ indicates a preference for material received through the
    - __ auditory channel
    - __ visual channel
    - __ combination
- __ is able to use tactile sensations
- __ exhibits unusual behavior during activities which require good hearing
- __ exhibits unusual behavior during activities which require good vision

Comment: _____

B. Behaviors Related to Information Processing
- __ organizes tasks and materials so that time is used efficiently
- __ has short-term retention for most learning areas
- __ has long-term retention for most learning areas
- __ can recall information for only some selected learning areas
- __ does not remember information
- __ discriminates between sounds
- __ discriminates between shapes and figures
- __ discriminates between letters, numbers, words
- __ can make associations
- __ can recognize associations
- __ can make generalizations
- __ can differentiate between generalizations and specific facts
- __ translates from concrete experiences to abstractions
- __ is able to profit from incidental learning
- __ finishes (or attempts to finish) tasks s/he starts
- __ is easily distracted regardless of task
- __ follows instructions directed to a group

**Sample E** continued
    __ follows instructions directed to him/her individually
    __ follows one direction but not a sequence of directions

Comment: _____
_____

C. Behaviors Related to Outputs
- __ volunteers comments, answers, etc. during group activities
- __ speaks spontaneously on a one-to-one basis to other child and/or adults
- __ speaks only when called on or when conversation is initiated by another person
- __ must be urged to speak
- __ shows specific speech problem (describe)
- __ performs gross motor skills in coordinated fashion
- __ performs fine motor skills in coordinated fashion
- __ is clumsy and awkward in most motor activities
- __ exhibits involuntary repetition when making a motor response
- __ exhibits involuntary repetition when making a spoken response
- __ uses a vocabulary typical of older children
- __ uses a limited vocabulary typical of children his/her age
- __ uses a limited vocabulary
- __ uses only simple sentences
- __ uses single words and some phrases, but not complete sentences
- __ reverses some letters and/or numbers when writing
- __ prefers right hand for most activities
- __ prefers left hand for most activities
- __ uses either hand with about equal dexterity

Comment: _____
_____

D. Behaviors Related to Feedback
Place a check mark next to the events which are rewarding for the student.
- __ tangible rewards such as tokens which can be traded for free time
- __ physical attention such as a hug, a pat on the back
- __ symbolic rewards such as grades, stars
- __ competitive rewards such as being named the winner
- __ comments of approval (verbal praise) from an adult
- __ comments or indications of approval from peers
- __ opportunities to pursue activities of his/her own choosing
- __ knowledge of results such as being told an answer is correct

# Identification and Referral

**Sample E** continued

Place a check mark next to statements which apply to the student.

___ exhibits a strong preference for a certain type of reward; if so, specify _____

___ does not display a preference for any one type of reward but works well for a variety of rewards

___ needs to be rewarded several times during completion of a task

___ can delay receiving reward until competion of task

___ can delay receiving reward until several tasks are completed

Comment: _____
_____
_____
_____

III. Physical Symptoms Checklist

Place a check mark next to the statements which apply to the child. Use the comment space to elaborate and provide supporting information. Attach any medical reports which are available.

___ is often absent
___ is usually tired
___ is overly active
___ is listless, lethargic
___ is underweight
___ is overweight
___ complains of headaches, dizziness
___ has unusual posture when doing visual tasks
___ has unusual posture when standing
___ has unusual gait
___ appearance of eyes is abnormal
___ has frequent earaches

Comment: _____
_____
_____
_____

IV. Social-Emotional Behaviors Checklist

Place a check mark next to the statements which apply to the child. Use the comment space to elaborate and provide supporting information.

___ prefers working with others
___ prefers to work by himself
___ exhibits about equal willingness to work with others and alone
___ gets along with others in work situations
___ gets along with others in play situations
___ refuses to participate in group activities

**Sample E** continued

    __ adapts easily to changes
    __ needs to be carefully prepared and gradually introduced to change
    __ behavior in group activities is predictable
    __ is more easily excited than others his age
    __ has temper tantrums (kicks, screams, beats on floor, etc)
    __ makes a deliberate attempt to be by himself
    __ exhibits an unusual amount of persistence
    __ gives up and moves to another activity when he experiences difficulty
    __ is aggressive (fights, kicks, hits, verbal insults, etc.)

Comment: _____

_____

_____

_____

Resource teachers often receive informal referrals from teachers in their school(s) who desire a "second opinion" or some specific teaching suggestions for a student in the regular program. Sample F is the type of form which could be adapted for use in this situation.

In summary, we feel it is important to structure referral forms very carefully so that the teacher, or other referring agent, is encouraged to provide precise information about the student's performance that is based on observable behavior. When descriptions of what the student *can* do and what efforts (methods and materials) have been made by the teacher to meet the student's needs are provided, this information, analyzed in relation to the problem statement, enables the resource teacher to make preliminary suggestions for program modifications. The process of actually filling out the referral form allows the teacher to check whether the information about the student is adequate and complete. It is also important that resource persons convey to teachers that making a referral does not mean transferring ownership of a problem to a specialist: it is a way of getting into partnership with a colleague who may be able to offer help (Reynolds, 1979, p. 17).

**Sample F**    *Diagnostic/Prescriptive Teacher Program\**
             *Referral Form*

Student's Name _____ Age _____ Sex _____
Grade/Team/Subject _____ Room No. _____
Date of Referral _____ Referring Teacher _____

---

*The Diagnostic/Prescriptive Teacher Program, The George Washington University.

# Identification and Referral

**Sample F** continued

Please complete this form and return both copies to the Diagnostic/Prescriptive Teacher's mailbox.

1. What is the specific behavior that led to this referral?

2. What methods have you tried to solve the problem?

3. What do you see as the student's particular strengths?

4. When is a convenient time for us to talk?

_____
Referring Teacher

### Routing of Referrals

Usually referrals are processed through the building administrator or chairperson of the IEP team, who can then keep track of the number of referrals, and which teachers are referring, and/or over-referring. This person should establish a system for monitoring referrals to ensure that each referral is considered in a timely manner. It is helpful if one staff person (often the resource teacher) is assigned the responsibility of acting as a case coordinator who checks to see that all necessary forms are completed, that contacts are made with parents, and that meetings are called to make decisions regarding the disposition of each referral.

## The Process Checklist

As soon as a referral is received, a Process Checklist should be initiated. This checklist becomes a permanent record, documenting that all the procedural safeguards and requirements for a pupil's assessment, IEP, placement, provision of service, review, and reassessment are met within established time frames. A sample Process Checklist, accompanied by instructions for its completion, is shown below. A discussion on referral analysis follows.

**Sample Process Checklist**

A. *REFERRAL*
   Pupil                    Date               Coordinator
   Name _____        Rec'd _____    Name _____
   Referral Analysis     Date Completed _____

**Sample Process Checklist**  continued

    Disposition of Referral (Check one):
    _____ Recommendation for Assessment
    _____ Returned to   _____ Follow-up
    Source                                     Consultation _____
    Assessment Plan   _____

B. *PARENT CONTACTS*
    Parent Interview   _____
    Notification of
      Due Process   _____
Request for Assessment/Release of Information _____

C. *ASSESSMENT/REASSESSMENT*
    Written Parental
      Consent   _____   _____
    Assessment Conducted _____   _____
    Meeting Scheduled   _____   _____
    Parents Notified of
      Meeting   _____   _____
    Meeting Results
      (Check one)   _____   _____
      _____ IEP Designed/Modified
      _____ Additional Assessment Planned
      _____ Special Education not Needed

D. *PROVISION OF SERVICES*
    Parent Consent   _____
    Student Placed/
    Services Initiated   _____

E. *REVIEW*
    Meeting Scheduled   _____
    Parents Notified
      of Meeting   _____
    Meeting Results
      (Check one):   _____
      _____ Continue IEP
      _____ Revise IEP
      _____ Return to Regular Education
      _____ Reassessment Planned

# Identification and Referral

## Instructions for Completing Process Checklist

A. Upon receiving the written referral, set up a case folder and initiate the checklist as follows:
1. Record pupil's name.
2. Record date referral was received.
3. Record name of case coordinator.
4. Complete Referral Analysis and record date.
5. Check whether assessment was recommended or if a decision was made to return referral to source. If referral was returned, note date, and date of follow-up consultation, if any.
6. If assessment was recommended, record date when assessment plan was completed.

B. 1. Indicate dates of all parent contacts.

C. 1. Record date when parent consent is received.
2. Record date when assessment was completed.
3. Note date when plans for team meeting were completed.
4. Record date when parents were notified of team meeting.
5. Note meeting results and completion date.
6. Repeat above steps if additional assessment was done following completion of initial assessment plan.

D. 1. Record dates when parental consent to placement was received and when services were begun.

E. 1. Note date when plans for annual review were completed.
2. Record date when parents were notified of this meeting.
3. Note meeting results and completion date.

## Analyzing Referrals

Since students cannot receive special education services without prior assessment of their learning needs, quick turn-around time from initial referral to making an assessment decision is essential. In planning for mildly handicapped students, an accurately completed referral form, submitted by the teacher, is the first step. The second step is for the responsible person (often the resource teacher who is sometimes assisted by other members of the team) to review the referrals and respond to the referring teacher. This is best accomplished by conferring with the teacher and by arranging to observe the student in the classroom. At this time, the student's teacher and the resource teacher can discuss how, together, they may try to deal with the identified problem behavior, and a detailed plan can be begun for more indepth assessment if necessary.

To assist in the process of analyzing referrals and planning assessment strategies, the Referral Analysis Chart (Gurski, 1978), shown on pages 79–80, may be used. A blank form has been included as well as a sample referral form and the resulting Referral Analysis.

General Directions for Completing the Referral Analysis Chart

1. Begin with the box in the upper left corner—"Baseline Information: Referring Agent," and complete the top row of boxes.
2. Complete the boxes in column A, taking information from the referral form itself.
3. Continue with column B. In column B, write any other relevant information known about the student.
4. In column C, write questions to be checked out in order to determine specifically the *what, when, where,* and *how* of the student's academic and/or behavioral characteristics.
5. In column D, write a method for investigating the questions listed in column C. Who will investigate? What methods (e.g., interviewing) or materials (tests, etc.) will be used?

More detailed instructions have been listed on the chart itself.

# Referral Analysis Chart

Case Coordinator: _____

Date: _____

| | A. Baseline Information | B. Other Information Known | C. Questions to be Explored | D. Persons, Materials, Strategies for Investigating Questions |
|---|---|---|---|---|
| 1. Identifying Information: Referring Agent | In this box list that information which identifies the person making the referral (i.e., name, grade level, subject matter taught, etc.) as listed on the referral form. | Add here any information which you, through past experience, know about the referring agent (i.e., preferred teaching style, interest, etc.). Also, add information about school/classroom environment that may be contributing to the present situation. | In this box list any information which you might need in order to interact with the referring person effectively and to modify the classroom environment. | In these boxes list those resource persons who can provide the necessary assessment data for answering the questions of column C: If you are the resource person for a particular question, list the strategies you would use in obtaining the assessment data. |
| 2. Identifying Information: Pupil Referred | Enter here that information which identifies the pupil referred (i.e., name, grade level, age, etc.) as listed on the referral form. | In this box add any information which you, through your experience, know about the pupil (i.e., home, family, health/medical info, cultural/linguistic factors, etc.). If you do not know the student personally, this box is not applicable. | List here questions about the pupil and his home environment which are relevant to the pupil's needs/presenting problems. | Same as above |

**Referral Analysis Chart**  continued

| | A. Baseline Information | B. Other Information Known | C. Questions to be Explored | D. Persons, Materials, Strategies for Investigating Questions |
|---|---|---|---|---|
| 3. Educational Needs | In this box list the functional description of the pupil's presenting educational problems/needs, as provided by the referral. | In this space, summarize any supporting data about the pupil's needs that may be listed on the referral or of which you are aware. Also enter significant educational information which may be contributing to aspects of the pupil's behavior. | Enter here any questions that need to be investigated in order to develop an effective plan for defining the pupil's needs in the educational domain. List any other information you would want to know about this pupil's learning/academic progress that can result in an effective educational plan. | Same as above |
| 4. Behavioral Needs | List here the functional description of the pupil's presenting behavioral problems/needs, as provided by the referral. | In this box summarize any supporting data about the pupil's presenting problems in the behavioral domain that may be listed on the referral or of which you are aware. Also enter significant behavioral info. that contributes to his/her difficulties. | In this box list any questions that need investigating in order to develop an effective plan for defining the pupil's needs in the behavioral domain. List other information you want to know that can result in an effective educational plan. (re. behavior) | Same as above |
| 5. Other Information | In this box list any other information about the pupil provided by the referral. | List here any additional information you know about this pupil's learning/behavioral (preferred learning style, interests, habits, etc.) which may have relevance for instructional planning. | List here any additional information you might want to know about the pupil in order to develop an effective educational plan. | Same as above |

# Referral Analysis Chart

SAMPLE COMPLETED

Case Coordinator: _____

Date: _____

|  | A. Baseline Information | B. Other Information Known | C. Questions to be Explored | D. Persons, Materials, Strategies for Investigating Questions |
|---|---|---|---|---|
| 1. Identifying Information: Referring Agent |  |  |  |  |
| 2. Identifying Information: Pupil Referred |  |  |  |  |

**Referral Analysis Chart**  *continued*

|  | A. Baseline Information | B. Other Information Known | C. Questions to be Explored | D. Persons, Materials, Strategies for Investigating Questions |
|---|---|---|---|---|
| 3. Educational Needs | | | | |
| 4. Behavioral Needs | | | | |
| 5. Other Information | | | | |

# Identification and Referral

*Student Referral Form For School Appraisal Team**

REFERRED BY: __J. Bates   Classroom Teacher__   DATE __9/30/79__
                              NAME/POSITION

STUDENT'S NAME ____Richard A.____   BIRTH DATE __6/1/69__
CHRONOLOGICAL AGE __11:4__   SCHOOL ____Cordova____
GRADE __5__   TEACHER/COUNSELOR ____J. Bates____
Sex __M__   NAME OF PARENT (or guardian) __Mr. and Mrs. A.__
ADDRESS __1876 Hollister Ave.__   TELEPHONE __964-2811__
LANGUAGE SPOKEN AT HOME:   ☒ ENGLISH   ☐ SPANISH
                                                      ☐ BOTH   ☐ OTHER _____

I. SPECIFY REASON FOR REFERRAL:
Richard performs significantly below grade level expectation in both reading and spelling. He has great difficulty with all academic areas related to reading. In 2 years he has shown less than a year's growth in reading. This seems to affect his feelings about himself; he worries about his poor reading.

PARENT NOTIFIED:  ☒ YES        PARENT AGREES:  ☒ YES
                               ☐ NO                              ☐ NO

II. DESCRIBE ANY ATTEMPTED INTERVENTIONS (Educational, Psychological, Medical, etc.)
Richard has been receiving extra help in reading since last fall, but is not making progress. Receives medication to control attention and behavior; this seems to help.

III. KNOWN SIGNIFICANT HEALTH PROBLEMS: None

IV. OTHER AGENCIES INVOLVED WITH STUDENT: None

V. PAST AND/OR CURRENT SPECIAL EDUCATION PLACEMENTS:
Regular class

Where referral is initiated from outside of school, principal/designee contacts students' classroom teacher and/or counselor to complete the following section:

CLASSROOM TEACHER/COUNSELOR

PLEASE COMPLETE CITES. SCREEN AND ANSWER FOLLOWING QUESTIONS:

1. CHECK, RATE, AND PRIORITIZE FOLLOWING AREAS OF CONCERN:
   A. Check areas of concern.
   B. For each area identified, assign a "1" or "2" rating.
   C. When all areas of concern have been checked and rated, go back and assign a priority number for each area.

*Form developed by Santa Barbara County Comprehensive Plan for Special Education, Santa Barbara County Schools, Santa Barbara, California, 1975.

| AREA | A | B | C |
|---|---|---|---|
| 1. Speech and Verbal Communications | | | |
| 2. Visual Behaviors | | | |
| 3. Visual Perception | ✓ | 1 | 1 |
| 4. Auditory Behaviors | ✓ | 2 | 1 |
| 5. In-Class Social Behavior | | | |
| 6. Out-of-Class Social Behavior | | | |

| AREA | A | B | C |
|---|---|---|---|
| 7. Work Habits | | | |
| 8. General Motor Behaviors | | | |
| 9. Discrepancy Classwork & Test Score Data | | | |
| 10. Attentional Behaviors | | | |
| 11. Absenteeism/Tardiness | | | |
| 12. Conformity to Values | | | |

2. INDICATE SPECIFIC OBSERVED BEHAVIORS FOR ABOVE AREAS CHECKED:

Has difficulty remembering names of people and things; reads in a halting manner. Word attack skills are poor, does not seem to hear beginning sounds.

3. DESCRIBE PROGRAM AND MATERIALS USED WITH STUDENT:

Sullivan; SRA

4. CURRENT GRADE LEVEL AT WHICH STUDENT IS FUNCTIONING: READING: _____2_____ MATH: _____4_____
5. CURRENT TEST INFORMATION:

Wide Range Achievement 5/27/79: Reading = 2.5; Spelling = 2.9; Arithmetic = 4.2

6. AREAS OF STRENGTH AND/OR INTEREST OBSERVED IN STUDENT:

Richard is an active participant in sports during the physical education program and in after school sports. He has many friends and his peer group admires him tremendously.

_____*J. Bates*_____   _____9-30-79_____
TEACHER'S/COUNSELOR'S SIGNATURE    DATE

# Referral Analysis Chart

**SAMPLE COMPLETED**

Case Coordinator: __B. Miller__

Date: __10/12/79__

| | A. Baseline Information | B. Other Information Known | C. Questions to be Explored | D. Persons, Materials, Strategies for Investigating Questions |
|---|---|---|---|---|
| 1. Identifying Information: Referring Agent | Bates—5th grade teacher | Arranges for extra help in reading; highly structured learning environment | What extra reading help is provided? What are teacher's goals for Richard? Instructional methods? | Teacher consultation. |
| 2. Identifying Information: Pupil Referred | Richard A. CA = 11.4 5th grade pupil | Lives with father, mother older brother. Older than most 5th graders | Ethnic/language factors involved in learning problem? Are parents willing to help him at home? | Home interview. Teacher consultation |

**Referral Analysis Chart** continued

| | | | | |
|---|---|---|---|---|
| 3. Educational Needs | Extra help in reading but no progress, below grade level in reading and spelling; has difficulty with all academic areas related to reading; less than 1 yr. growth in 2 yr. Math = 4.2 (WRAT 5/27/79) difficulty remembering names of people and things | Difference between reading and math achievement *might* suggest language problems | Retained in the past? Test results prior to 1979 Retest? Language assessment? Is he more successful with concrete-type tasks and work? | Cum folder Informal assessment Diagnostic testing Classroom observation Talk with student |
| 4. Behavioral Needs | Reads in halting manner; poor word attack skills; Lacks progress in reading; seems to affect feelings about self. Worries about poor reading. On medication to control attention and behavior—seems to help | Parents evidently sought medical help. | What indicators are there of lowered self-concept; worries? What medication? How long? | Classroom observation Teacher consultation Home interview Talk with student |
| 5. Other Information | Active participant in sports Many friends; admired by peer group | Shows strengths which could facilitate success in regular program | Does teacher select reading materials related to sports? How can peer reinforcement be used? | Teacher consultation Cum folder |

# Identification and Referral

## Decision Point

The purpose of completing the referral analysis is to make a determination as to whether the student's case should be reviewed by the assessment team for possible special education services. In some cases, the appropriate action will be to return the referral to the teacher (or other referring agent) with an explanation as to why the student is not being assessed, and to give specific suggestions on how to deal with the behavior of concern. As noted earlier, follow-up consultation and classroom observation may be needed. If assessment is recommended, the next step is to contact the assessment team members and schedule a meeting to discuss the assessment plan, a plan that will be based on the results of the referral analysis. At this point, parents should be contacted and informed of their legal rights.

No individual assessment for possible special education placement may be conducted without parent consent. Parents have the right to be notified of the purpose of the assessment, the tests or procedures to be used, and the right to receive an explanation of all of the procedural safeguards available to them under the law. If the referral was made by the child's parents and the school refuses to initiate the assessment, parents must be notified of the reasons. Suggestions on developing the assessment plan and involving parents are included in Chapter 5.

## Study Questions and Activities

1. Using the Referral Analysis Chart shown in the text, analyze sample referral forms A and B in Chapter 3. What specific questions were generated by your attempts to behaviorally define the descriptive terms of each referral? Which of the referral forms was easier to translate into behavorial terms? Why?
2. Outline an inservice workshop for regular classroom teachers explaining how to identify pupils with special learning and/or behavior problems and how to prepare appropriate referrals for special services.
3. Mrs. James, a fifth-grade teacher, habitually refers one-third of her class for special services. By contrast, Mr. Perez, the other fifth-grade teacher, has yet to submit his first referral. (There are no differences in the composition of Mrs. James' and Mr. Perez' classes.) How should a resource teacher deal with the problems of over- and under-referral noted here?

4. Develop a referral form from the samples presented in Chapter 3. As a class project, interview a half dozen regular class teachers and complete referral forms on two of their most difficult learning and/or behavior problems pupils (anonymous referrals, of course). Meet to analyze the referrals and recommend a course of action.

5. Conduct a small survey among resource teachers to get ideas for extending the list (given in Chapter 3) of possible ways to modify a student's program within the regular classroom.

6. Interview one or two school principals to learn about their site-level screening and referral processes. Compare your findings with the procedures recommended in Chapter 3.

# References

Brandt, R. M. *Studying behavior in natural settings.* New York: Holt, Rinehart and Winston, 1972.

Cartwright, G. P., & Cartwright, C. A. *Computer assisted remedial education: Early identification of handicapped children.* University Park, PA.: Computer Assisted Instruction Laboratory, College of Education, the Pennsylvania State University, 1972.

Deno, S. L. Direct observation approach to measuring classroom behavior. *Exceptional Children,* 1980, 46 (5), 396–399.

Foster, G. G., Ysseldyke, J. E., & Reese, J. H. I wouldn't have seen it if I hadn't believed it. *Exceptional Children,* 1975, 41 (7), 469–473.

Gurski, G. *Identification: A Trainer's guide developed for the California State Department of Education.* Sacramento, 1978.

Hammill, D., & Wiederholt, J. L. *The resource room: Rationale and implementation,* Philadelphia, PA: Buttonwood Farms, 1972.

Haring, N. G. (Ed.) *Behavior of Exceptional Children* (2nd ed.). Columbus, Ohio: Charles E. Merrill, 1978.

Heward, W. L. & Orlansky, M.D. *Exceptional Children: An Introductory Survey to Special Education.* Columbus, Ohio: Charles E. Merrill, 1980.

Hewett, F. M., & Forness, S. R. *Education of exceptional learners.* Boston: Allyn and Bacon, 1974.

Larsen, S. The influence of teacher expectations on the school performance of handicapped children. *Focus on Exceptional Children,* 1975, 6 (8), 1–14.

Region V Educational Services Center. *The resource room: An access to excellence.* Lancaster, S. C.: Region V Educational Services Center, 1975.

Reynolds, M. A common body of practice for teachers: The challenge of

Public Law 94–142 to teacher education. (mimeo) Paper presented at Conference on Dean's Projects, San Francisco, September 1979.

Ysseldyke, J. E. & Foster, G. G. Bias in teachers' observations of emotionally disturbed and learning disabled children. *Exceptional Children,* 1978, *44* (8), 613–615.

## Resources

Hiltbrunner, C. L. & Vasa, S. F. Watch the children: Precision referring. *Academic Therapy,* Winter 1974–75, X (2), 167–170.

Kauffman, J. M. *Characteristics of children's behavior disorders.* Columbus, Ohio: Charles E. Merrill, 1977.

Kurtz, D. P., Neisworth, J. T. & Laub, K. W. Issues concerning the early identification of handicapped children. *Journal of School Psychology,* 1977, *15* (2), 136–140.

# 4

# Assessment—Part One

> Without meaningful assessment information, educational decisions may be useless or even harmful. . . . *Assessment* is the step between 'identification' of the student who may need special intervention, and 'educational planning' for the student. Data collected in the assessment stage about the student's physical, cognitive, social/emotional development, and educational performance are used in making decisions about the student's eligibility for special education and recommendations for general instructional programming. (National Association of State Directors of Special Education, 1978, p. 2)

This statement of the purpose of educational assessment points to the need for changes in both the content and methodology of assessment. While we must still conduct individual assessment to determine if a handicapping condition is present and if special education is needed, the goal of the assessment phase has been broadened to extend beyond diagnosis and placement. Educational assessment must be viewed as a continuous process that provides the rationale for specific planned instruction; instruction itself provides a vehicle for further assessment. The assessment and instructional planning phases flow on into evaluation*—the process of

---

*P.L. 94–142 and implementing regulations use the term evaluation to mean both the collection of initial child performance data *and* progress data.

gathering measures of student progress to determine the extent to which IEP goals and objectives are being met. Given the intimate relationship between assessment and instructional planning, it is difficult conceptually to separate them; we do so in this book only to permit an indepth discussion of both these steps in the instructional programming process.

In this chapter and the next we review specific assessment techniques and present the components of an assessment plan. An overview of the basic requirements in educational assessment, as stipulated in P.L. 94–142, is presented first.

You will recall from Chapter 1 that fair assessment of learning needs is one of the basic guarantees of the federal law. P.L. 94–142 provides certain safeguards to protect the rights of children, parents, and educators during the assessment phase. These protections include

1. a full, individual assessment of learning needs *before* initial placement of a student in a special education program and a reassessment at least every three years (or more frequently if requested by the student's teacher or parents).

2. informed parental consent, in writing, to the proposed assessment.

3. administration of tests and other assessment procedures in the child's native language or other mode of communication (for example, sign-language).

4. use of assessment instruments and techniques that are valid for the specific purpose.

5. inclusion of tests and other assessment materials designed to determine the student's specific areas of *educational need* (as contrasted to devices designed to produce a general I.Q. score).

6. selection and administration of tests to ensure accurate measures of student performance rather than mere reflection of impaired sensory, manual, or speaking skills.

7. selection and administration of assessment materials that are not racially or culturally discriminatory.

8. assessment conducted in all areas related to the suspected disability (appropriate assessment of health, vision, hearing, social, emotional status, general intelligence, academic, communication, and motor performance).

9. educational programming decisions based on data from multiple sources—not on results of a single procedure or a score on one test.

10. assessment conducted by trained personnel who use the assessment materials as instructed by test authors or publishers.
11. assessment conducted by a multidisciplinary team, or group of persons, that includes at least one teacher or other specialist with expertise in the area of the student's suspected disability.
12. independent assessment obtained at the discretion of the student's parents. This means an assessment conducted by a qualified person who is not employed by the educational agency responsible for the student. (The independent assessment may be at public expense if the parent disagrees with the assessment conducted by the school; the school may, however, prove the appropriateness of its assessment via a fair hearing. The parent still has the right to an independent assessment, but not at public expense. Regardless of who pays for the independent assessment, the results must be considered when making any decision about the student's education.)

These due process procedures are intended to reduce, if not to eliminate, misclassification and mislabeling of children and to ensure that students who really do have special needs that cannot be met successfully in regular education, receive a program that is tailor-made for them. Mandated procedural safeguards during the educational assessment phase have highlighted several critical factors related to assessment methodology—parent involvement, the role of the classroom teacher, and the inherent bias of many assessment devices and techniques, especially when used with students from culturally and/or linguistically different backgrounds. These factors are addressed throughout the sections of this chapter and the following one that deals with planning and conducting assessment.

As noted in Chapter 3, the analysis of a referral on a student leads to a decision as to whether assessment by the team is needed, and if so, to the development of a detailed plan for carrying out the assessment. Planning for individualized assessment can only be done by persons who have a thorough knowledge of assessment methods and their respective strengths and limitations. Accordingly, the next section reviews a variety of methods, including (a) observation, (b) interviewing, (c) examining school records, and (d) testing (both norm and criterion-referenced).

Since this book is addressed to meeting the needs of the mildly handicapped, we are concerned in this chapter with those assessment techniques most appropriate for the local school assessment team. You will note, therefore, a heavy emphasis on the use of the more *informal* procedures as opposed to the standard diagnostic measures. In particular, we have stressed the use of observation and interview methods, focusing both on the student and on environmental events—often neglected areas of assessment. Many of these assessment techniques may also be used during instruction and in the evaluation of instructional outcomes.

## OBSERVATION

> To observe is to take notice, to pay attention to what children do and what they say. (Almy, 1959, p. 25)

Observation is a fundamental assessment technique that involves "systematically looking at and recording behavior for the purpose of making instructional decisions" (Cartwright & Cartwright, 1974, p. 3). By definition, observation occurs when someone, other than the student, notices and documents student behavior. In this way observation differs from testing—a situation in which the student makes his/her own record (writing answers on a test). There are many behaviors exhibited by students about which we might want to gather information and which cannot be studied through testing; for example, showing respect, sharing, playing with a group of peers. Direct observation methods allow us to assess such variables as:

- group participation and responsiveness
- individual behavior in a group
- attitudes toward academic work
- peer dynamics
- classroom structure and organization
- teaching methods and materials
- teaching style
- learning environment
- student-teacher interactions
- learner's history of success (entry behaviors).

Observation also plays a critical part in evaluation where the focus is on recording evidences of student achievement of objectives, and of the success of instructional interventions. Although it is not by any means a sufficient approach in all cases, observation has several distinct advantages over other assessment methods:

1. Observation provides us with a direct measure of behavior in natural settings; unlike psychological test results, observation data "speaks for itself" and does not need to be "translated" for the teacher.
2. The observer's attention is focused on facts as opposed to impressions and judgments.
3. Observation is an assessment process which can be conducted during ongoing instruction in the classroom.
4. The success of intervention techniques, educational methods and materials can be assessed on the basis of observation data; thus observation can increase teaching effectiveness.
5. Observation can itself be an intervention, bringing about change in student behavior.
6. Observation can result in a very precise assessment of student performance relative to the behaviors we expect the student to transfer to everyday situations. This is often a more reliable form of diagnosis than is psychological testing since the learner is usually performing without distraction or interruption.
7. While observing a particular target behavior, we may recognize previously unnoticed problems or side-effects.
8. Observation can provide teachers with hunches as to how learning may be facilitated.

Semmel (1975) argues that if we are to be able to select the teaching activities and conditions that are most likely to be effective in modifying the behavior and performance of a particular student, we must be able "to discriminate the state of a classroom or pupil at a given point in time during an educational interchange" (p. 258). For this reason, the starting point for the assessment process should be classroom observation, unless this has been thoroughly covered in the identification phase.

The classroom teacher is in a position to observe more of a student's learning behavior than anyone else on the assessment team and should therefore be seen as a primary contributor to and interpreter of assessment results (Hammill, 1971). With a little training and practice, we can all learn to observe behavior more objectively and precisely, thus becoming more able to interpret behavior diagnostically rather than judgmentally. Observation has a very long history in the field of child study; there are many very sophisticated methods, some old, some new, which can be used, including film, video, and/or audio tape techniques. Such methods are not reviewed here since they are too complex and time-consuming for typical classroom situations. The intent of this section is to provide information which will increase the skill of classroom teachers as educational decision makers. Simple systems for gathering information—anecdotal records, participation charts, frequency and time sampling—will be discussed, as well as additional uses for checklists and rating scales. Guidelines for selecting an observation approach and some cautions regarding the limitations of observation approaches, along with suggestions for off-setting these, are presented. First, let's outline some basic skills or prerequisites to the use of any particular observation method.

## Observation Skills

Although there are definite situations where one approach is appropriate and another not, the effectiveness of all observation methods depends on the skill of the observer. Here are some suggestions:

1. *Select and define the target behavior.* If a student is "screened out" and referred for further assessment, it means that there is a general category of behavior (often several behavioral areas) of concern to the teacher. Focus at first on the most critical in the perception of the teacher. Define, or describe, that behavior precisely and in such a way that most people would be able to agree that they had seen an instance of it. Saying that Todd is "constantly trying to attract attention" doesn't tell us much about what Todd does that really bothers us. What does Todd actually do? Does he "make faces," shout answers when it's not his turn, bring presents to the teacher, or crawl under his desk? Todd's actual observable behaviors must be listed in order to define "attracting attention."

2. *Note the setting for, and events following, the demonstration of target behavior.* This may be difficult at first, but through practice in immediately recording what you see it becomes easier. Analysis of Todd's behavior might reveal, for example, that Todd resorts to attention-seeking behavior following verbal reprimands from the teacher, or only in large group situations. Noticing the events that repeatedly follow the behavior, such as peer approval or teacher recognition, may suggest ways to control or change the target behavior. The setting includes such things as time of day, date, classroom activity, work assignment, people and materials involved, and behavior of others. Awareness of any or all of

these items may help you determine what triggers the behavior being studied. Since the classroom teacher is so close to the situation it will often be necessary for a member of the school assessment team to assist in identifying the significant variables surrounding the behavior being studied.

3. *Be thoroughly informed about the purpose underlying the observation.* This will influence your choice of observation method and recording procedure.

4. *Be as unobtrusive as possible.* Your presence may alter the behavior being observed.

5. *Try to get lots of observation data.* Choose a variety of settings for data collection—the playground, independent study, group situations, and so on. Usually behavior patterns do not become evident in a short span of time. To notice change or growth, observational records must be kept over time. Remember there are cycles and trends in behavior; some observations will merely reflect a temporary deviation and we must look at a larger sample of behavior to determine what is typical for the student.

6. *Select or design appropriate data-recording procedures.* Recording should be quick, efficient, and easily understandable by another person.

7. *Experiment with the procedure and forms.* Practice various observation techniques several times before data gathering. Observe several learners in the same situation for comparison.

8. *Be precise.* Lack of precision in information-gathering leads to misinterpretation of data and faulty instructional decision making.

9. *Do a reliability check.* Have another person observe the same student; compare your records. The teacher and the resource teacher, for example, should "exchange notes."

10. *Interpret your data cautiously.* Avoid the temptation to try to determine "cause" and the pitfall of circular reasoning (saying that a child who does not pay attention or sit still is "hyperactive," and then later explaining to his/her parent or teacher that the problems of inattention and restlessness are caused by hyperactivity). Make tentative inferences about process variables (such as feelings and attitudes) *only* on the basis of accumulated evidence (patterns or clusters of specific behaviors). Above all, don't jump to conclusions!

## Types of Observation

1. *Anecdotal records* are reports of informal teacher observations of students and are primarily used to provide a qualitative picture of certain aspects of social functioning or adjustment (Thorndike and Hagen, 1955). Observations of unanticipated behaviors or incidents should be recorded in the anecdotal format. By recording a behavioral event immediately after it occurs we gather dependable data that cannot become warped or distorted in our memory. "A set of such records provides stable evidence on which later appraisals can be based" (Thorndike & Hagen, 1955, p. 484). We can look for recurring patterns and progressive changes in a student's behavior and relate the anecdotal data to other information known about a student. Note that comments in "cum" folders are *not* anecdotal records since they are not based on direct and immediate observation; rather, they are subjective appraisals of the student.

Thorndike and Hagen (1955) state that a well-prepared and useful anecdotal record has the following features:

1. It provides an accurate description of a specific event.
2. It describes the setting sufficiently to give the event meaning.
3. If it includes interpretation or evaluation by the recorder, this interpretation is separated from the description and its different status is clearly identified.
4. The event it describes is one that relates to the child's personal development or social interactions.
5. The event it describes is either representative of the typical behavior of the child or significant because it is strikingly different from his usual form of behavior. If it is unusual behavior for the child, that fact is noted (p. 486).

At first you may find that your behavioral descriptions are too lengthy. Try not to be discouraged; your observation reports will become more concise as you gain skill in identifying the critical elements of behavior.

Two helpful resources on the use of observation methods are the books by Almy (1959) and Cartwright and Cartwright (1974) referenced at the end of this chapter. Anecdotal records I and II are examples drawn from these books.

Note the precise format used. Interpretations can be added, if desired, beneath the factual report of the incident. These two examples, when part of a sequence of such behaviors, can be interpreted

# Assessment—Part One

**Anecdotal Record I**

| Name: | Bryan G. | Date: | 10/17/79 |
|---|---|---|---|
| Observer: | T. Melchor | Time: | 10:30 a.m. |
| Setting: | Math | | |

Incident: When it was time for Bryan to work with a group in the Math Center, he said, "I want to stay at my own desk."

**Anecdotal Record II**

| Name: | Bryan G. | Date: | 10/20/79 |
|---|---|---|---|
| Observer: | T. Melchor | Time: | 1:30 p.m. |
| Setting: | Recess | | |

Incident: The whole class was out on the playground, engaged in various games and activities. Bryan stood by himself beside the swings where the younger children were playing.

to mean that the student, Bryan, avoids situations involving peer interaction.

Almy provides an example (A, which follows) of anecdotal data where the teacher has tried to describe a student's behavior clearly and without allowing her interpretation of it to creep into the report. She contrasts this with example B, following.

*Example A:*

> Helen came into the room today and took her seat without speaking to anyone in the room. She maintained an attentive attitude throughout the class period but took no part in the class discussion. When asked for a contribution once during the period, she flushed, shook her head, and remained silent. She picked up her books when the bell rang and left the room alone. (Almy, 1959, p. 49)

*Example B:*

> Helen is a shy, reticent, unsocial girl who does not make friends easily, who does not participate in class discussions, and who is alone much of the time. (Almy, 1959, p. 50)

2. *Observations involving measurement.* Several approaches to observational recording which involve numerical outputs will be briefly described here. Included are: frequency (event) recording, duration recording, time sampling, and the "placheck" method. These techniques can be used efficiently and effectively in school situations to obtain baseline data—the measure of a behavior under a set of stable conditions. Gathering baseline data on the target behavior is essential if we are to accurately measure and to evaluate behavioral changes that result from implementing various teaching strategies.

2.1 *Frequency or event recording* is simply a count of the *number of times* the target behavior occurs. The teacher might count and add up the number of times the student responded to verbal questions, or left his/her seat during a school morning or day. Counting devices, such as a wristband golf-counter, may be used, or simple tally marks written on a piece of paper will suffice. Frequency recording is used for counting behaviors which are single units: push-ups, talk outs, thank-yous said, and hitting. Many behaviors of this type occur at a very high rate and are of short duration, making it difficult for us to recall their frequency when we rely on memory alone. Systematic recording can help us find out if Todd *really* gets out of his chair excessively, or if it only *seems* that he does. Low rate behaviors are those which occur more infrequently and which are more difficult to describe in discrete observable units (such as temper outbursts and stealing). To get information on low rate behaviors we would rely not on frequency recording, but, rather, on teacher reports or interviews with the student, teacher, and parents.

Frequency counts made on a regular basis also enable us to notice small improvements in behavior—and remember, behavior changes *slowly*. Day to day comparisons can be made even if the target behavior is observed for different amounts of time each day. To convert frequency data into rate data, simply divide the number of occurences of the target behavior by the amount of time it was observed each day. Precision Teaching is an observation and data-gathering system based on frequency counts that is particularly appropriate for assessing behavior change, and is one that students can learn to use to monitor their own behavior. Information sources on Precision Teaching are included at the end of this chapter.

2.2 *Duration Recording* is a method for use when we are concerned with *how much time* is spent in a particular behavior. The amount of time a student is "on-task" might be of interest—or the length of time a preschooler engages in parallel play. To record these behaviors, a conventional watch or clock can be used (a stopwatch, if available, adds precision). During any given observation period we simply note the time the behavior starts and when it stops, then record the elapsed time. We might, for example, observe a student for a total of 20 minutes each day for 5 days (100 minutes), recording the duration of each display of "on-task" behavior, and totaling the amount each day. Our data might look something like this:

*Total minutes on task*

Student: Richard    Day 1   5
                                   2   7
                                   3   5
                                   4   8
                                   5   8
                            Total   33

We would then have some evidence to show that the student is "on-task" only about one-third of the time. Duration recording is very time-consuming for the observer, but can be used efficiently when the teacher is assisted by a resource teacher or an aide.

2.3 *Time sampling* is a technique which, like frequency recording, is very useful in observing high rate behaviors. The observation period is divided into equal time intervals—a 30-minute observation session might be divided into ten three-minute intervals—and the observer only records behavior at the *end* of the interval or, in this instance, every 3 minutes. What happens in the minute before or after is not recorded. In the following example, the observer recorded "out-of-seat" behavior every 3 minutes for 30 minutes, marking a + (plus) when the behavior was occurring at the end of a 3 minute period and − (minus) when it is not.

+ = out-of-seat

− = in-seat

| − | + | + | + | + | − | + | − | + | + |
|---|---|---|---|---|---|---|---|---|---|
| 3 | 6 | 9 | 12 | 15 | 18 | 21 | 24 | 27 | 30 |

minutes

The data show that the student was "out-of-seat" 70% of the time the observer sampled the behavior.

The time sampling method is especially useful for teachers in that it does not require their constant attention. In time sampling, shorter intervals generally lead to more accurate data; the observer must decide, however, on predetermined time periods within which to observe, based on past experience with the particular target behavior.

2.4 *Placheck* (Planned Activity Check) is a recording technique originally developed by Risley (1971), that is useful for teachers interested in observing *groups* of students. As described by Hall (1971), the procedure is as follows:

1. The observer scientifically defines the behavior (planned activity) he wishes to record in a group of children.
2. At given intervals (e.g., each ten minutes) the observer counts as quickly as possible how many individuals are engaged in the behavior, recording the total.
3. The observer then counts and records as quickly as possible how many individuals are present in the area of the activity.
4. The number of pupils present can then be divided into the number of pupils engaged in the behavior. By multiplying the result by 100, the observer finds the percent of those engaged in the behavior at a particular time. (p. 4)

Hall provides the following example of how the "Placheck" method works.

> Suppose a shop teacher wants to check on what portion of his class is working on an assigned woodworking project during a 50 minute period. Each ten minutes he quickly counts how many are working on the project. He then counts the number of pupils present. Let's suppose that during the first part of the period he finds that 10/20 and 15/20 are working. During the second part of the period, ten boys who had been excused to work on another project return to the class. He then finds 15/30, 30/30 and 20/30 of those present working on the assigned project. That is, 50 percent, 75 percent, 50 percent, 100 percent and 67 percent, or a mean of 68 percent worked on the assigned project during the class period. (p. 4)

The book by Hall is a practical resource on observing and recording behavior in school settings.

3. *Checklists and rating scales.* Several of the instruments mentioned in Chapter 2 under screening devices, can be used to systematically record observed behaviors of individual students. A frequently neglected source of relevant data for instructional planning is the *environment,* or situational context, in which the behavior is displayed —the classroom, school, and home. Following are some specific approaches to observing the classroom and environmental events within it. We feel that the use of such approaches is extremely

critical in the assessment and determination of techniques to maximize the handicapped child's effective interaction with the regular curriculum, subject matter, peers, and adults.

Teachers of young children may find the *Evaluation Checklist* developed by Harms (1972) useful to identify strengths and weaknesses in their own classroom environment. This checklist consists of lists of questions organized into four categories: physical environment, interpersonal environment, activities to stimulate development, and schedule. Sample questions include, "Can quiet and noisy activities go on without disturbing one another?" "Do the adults show children how to help themselves?" "Do children do real things like cooking, planting seeds, caring for animals?" "Are children involved in suggesting and planning activities?" (pp. 383–85).

## ASSESSMENT CHECKLIST: CLASSROOM ENVIRONMENT, CURRICULUM, METHODS, AND MATERIALS

The checklist which follows can be used to determine some of the environmental demands made on learners in a particular classroom. Individual student behavior can then be analyzed within the context of the environmental arrangements characteristic of the learning situation; this may produce many new insights about student performance. Each question on the checklist is answered "yes," "no," or "undecided." The more "yes" variables present, the more likely it is that the environment facilitates learning. "No" answers may indicate the need for change in the way the learning environment is set up; variables marked "undecided" can suggest areas where more observation is needed. Two additional forms for organizing classroom observation data follow.

**Assessment Checklist\*: Classroom Environment, Curriculum, Methods, Materials**

| A. *Curriculum* | Yes | No | Undecided |
|---|---|---|---|
| 1. Is the child a source of curricular objectives? | | | |
| 2. Is the curriculum relevant to the child's experience? | | | |
| 3. Are there hierarchies of skills within the curriculum? | | | |
| 4. Do objectives shape toward more difficult tasks? | | | |
| 5. Do curricular objectives include high-level as well as rote-level skills? | | | |

\*Adapted from R. M. Smith, J. T. Neisworth, & J. G. Greer. 1978. *Evaluating educational environments.* Columbus, Ohio: Charles E. Merrill Publishing Co.

**Assessment Checklist**  continued

|     | | Yes | No | Undecided |
|---|---|---|---|---|

6. Are objectives for group lessons applicable to the range of children within the group?

B. *Learning Environment*
7. Are both homogeneous and heterogeneous groupings used to enhance learning through modeling?
8. Are instructional groups small enough to ensure that all children have adequate access to the teacher?
9. Are modeling effects considered in planning seating arrangements?
10. Are environmental prompts used to assist children in discriminating what behaviors are expected of them?
11. Have an appropriate time and place been designated and assigned for all activities?
12. Is there a variety of places where different sized groups can meet and work?
13. Are there special places that individual children can go

> for isolation
> for rest and quiet
> to let off steam
> to reward themselves
> for private instruction
> to work independently
> to be disciplined privately?

14. Can children space themselves as they need or desire?
15. Do the relative amounts of space allocated to various activities reflect their importance in the program?
16. Does the environment provide feedback (mirrors for grooming and posture; handwriting samples)?

C. *Objectives*
17. Are opportunities for incidental learning included?
18. Are criterion measures realistic for individual children?

D. *Teaching Methods*
19. Does the teacher use a variety of teaching methods?
20. Does the teacher model behaviors s/he wishes the children to learn?

### Assessment—Part One

**Assessment Checklist** continued

|  | Yes | No | Undecided |
|---|---|---|---|
| 21. Is peer-tutoring used to maximize learning? | | | |

*E. Behavior Management*

22. Can the teacher list consequences that are successful with individual students?
23. Are consequences delivered consistently?
24. Are consequences delivered quickly?
25. Are consequation techniques determined experimentally for individual children?
26. Is an attempt made to move children from contrived to natural consequation techniques?

*F. Evaluating Instruction*

27. Does the teacher evaluate the environment?
28. Is learner progress recorded regularly?
29. Do students participate in evaluation by observing and recording behaviors?
30. Are student's achievements communicated to parents?
31. Are student's achievements communicated to the students themselves?
32. Are achievements reported as soon as possible after their occurrences, not just at report periods?

*G. Materials*

33. Are materials useful for the particular needs of individual students?
34. Are materials relevant to curricular objectives?
35. Do materials use task-embedded reinforcers?
36. Are self-instructional materials used?
37. Is there variety in the materials used?
38. Are there adequate materials to engage all the children without disputes over property rights?

TOTALS:

The next two checklists are designed for recording observations of an individual student functioning in the classroom environment. Note that the form calls for observation of teacher style and methods as well as student responses.

In-class Observation*

PUPIL NAME _____ SCHOOL _____

I. A. Reason for referral:
   B. Needs as seen by classroom teacher:
II. A. Physical environment (include lighting, sound, color, number of students, seating, organization of classroom, daily schedule):
   B. Instructional materials available (include those student in using):
   C. Time and duration of observation and activities observed:
III. A. Management and instructional techniques of the teacher (use of positive or negative reinforcement. Note disruptive behavior and teacher-child interaction. Modality used by teacher in presenting material and type of follow-up, and so forth:
   B. Behavior in group situations (large, small):
   C. Coping level, reaction to stress, frustration:
   D. Behavior in structured vs. non-structured situations:
   E. Degree of self-direction, ability to organize work, degree of independent functioning; ability to complete assigned work at school and home and ability to attend to task:
   F. Interaction with peers:
   G. Academic functioning and skills in:
   Pre-academic:
   Reading:
   Written work:
   Math:
   Social studies:
   Motor—gross and fine:
   Learning style:
   Language:
   H. Areas of interest:
   I. Additional information

OBSERVER'S NAME _____
TITLE _____

*Developed by Santa Barbara County Comprehensive Plan for Special Education, Santa Barbara County Schools, Santa Barbara, California, 1975.

## Classroom Observation*

| Student's Name | Teacher's Name |
|---|---|
| School | Grade |

*Developed by Santa Monica Unified School District, Department of Special Services, Santa Monica, California, 1975.

# Assessment—Part One

**Classroom Observation** continued

Time of Day          Length of Observation (Minutes)

Classroom Setting: (Approximate number of students, room arrangement, and so on)

Specific Activity (Reading, Math, etc.—Size of group, etc.)

Observations of student interactions with peers as they affect functioning in the regular program.

Additional Comments:

_____ _____ In the judgment of the classroom teacher, was the student's behavior during the observed period of time "typical" of his usual school performance?
Yes    No

Signature of the Observer
(Resource Specialist, Program Specialist, Psychologist)

Date

    Rather than relying solely on published checklists, teachers or resource persons can design their own. Teacher-designed checklists are particularly relevant when the purpose is to assess the extent to which teaching has been effective (evaluation). Instructional objectives, or terminal behaviors, stated earlier for the student can simply be expressed as checklist items; for example, "Counts by 10's to 100" or "uses adverbs correctly." Cartwright and Cartwright (1974) suggest that teachers through experience in working with students, can add checklist items that allow variations from the expected behavior to be noted. In this way, the diagnostic value of the checklist is increased. These authors point out that the checklist is used most efficiently when the items are listed by the teacher in the order in which s/he expects the behaviors to occur. Dates when the behavior are noted can also be placed beside the checklist items.

A useful technique for observing several students simultaneously is the Participation Chart. The names of the students are listed in a column and space is provided beside each name to record the sequence and frequency of each person's participation in group activities or discussions. The number of times each student participates is totalled and can then be compared with the others in the group. A teacher who is concerned that the same few students always dominate group discussions might use the Participation Chart approach to test out his/her hunch. Figure 4 is a sample chart showing hypothetical data on verbal interactions and was adapted from Almy (1959, p. 30).

**Figure 4** *Sample Participation Chart*

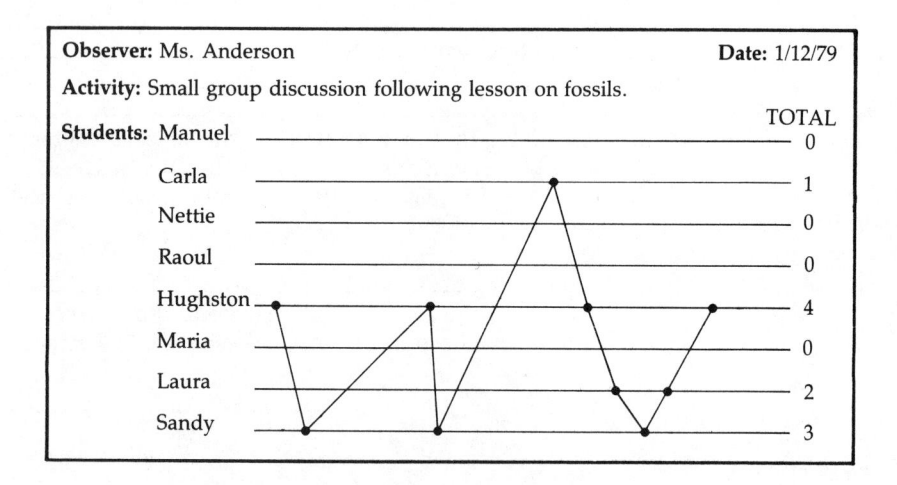

| Observer: Ms. Anderson | Date: 1/12/79 |
|---|---|
| Activity: Small group discussion following lesson on fossils. | |

| Students | TOTAL |
|---|---|
| Manuel | 0 |
| Carla | 1 |
| Nettie | 0 |
| Raoul | 0 |
| Hughston | 4 |
| Maria | 0 |
| Laura | 2 |
| Sandy | 3 |

Both Almy (1959) and Cartwright and Cartwright (1974) provide additional discussion and illustration of the use of Participation Charts.

## Choosing a Method

Selection of one particular observation method over another depends largely on the target behavior itself and the instructional decision to be made. Hall, Hawkins, and Axelrod (1975) suggest some considerations in choosing a specific observation method:

- the duration of the behavior being studied
- how obvious the behavior is
- the number of behaviors being recorded
- the amount of behavioral change expected
- the degree of precision desired in measurement
- the amount of time and attention which can be devoted to recording the behavior. (p. 199)

In addition, examine whether the method focuses on positive as well as negative behaviors (many checklists do not), and whether data summaries, collected via the method being considered, are easily read by classroom teachers.

## Limitations of Observation

1. *Observer bias*. The personal element in observation can never be completely removed; the way we see others grows out of our own experiences with people, and we do not see precisely the same things as the person next to us does.
2. *Halo effect*. This refers to the tendency to give a higher or lower rating to a behavior than it deserves as a result of a generally favorable or unfavorable impression already held by the observer toward the observed. We tend to rate children we like more generously—those who bother us, more severely.
3. *Logical error*. The observer makes an assumption about the relationship of two characteristics given knowledge of one characteristic, for example, a child with articulation difficulties is presumed to have language comprehension lag.
4. *Limits of human memory*.
5. *Unreliability of observation data*. The data may not be truly representative of the student's typical functioning; this problem is often the result of making too few observations (the child may have been at a low ebb) and of arriving at conclusions too soon without considering the observation data in context. In addition, the observer is limited in the amount of time s/he can spend observing a single student or group.

## Tips for Improving Observation

1. *Don't rely on memory*—make a record while the observation is being conducted.

2. *Record details objectively, accurately,* and as completely as possible without evaluating (unless using a predetermined rating system). Learn to sort out your feelings from the facts.
3. Where possible, *use several ratings,* taken by a number of different observers.
4. *Be aware* of the influence of "halo" effect and logical error and consciously monitor observation behavior to eliminate these biases.
5. *Operationally define behaviors* to be observed so that there is ready agreement between two observers as to what constitutes an instance of $X$ behavior.
6. *Design or select* recording instruments that focus on positive as well as negative behavior.
7. *Gather information over an adequate period of time* and a variety of situations to insure that a reliable, valid, and sufficient sampling of behavior is obtained prior to drawing conclusions.
8. *Look for patterns of behavior* that can be substantiated through other means of assessment.
9. Where possible, *have others observe the same behavior* and compare findings. Outside observers often pick up data that the teacher does not see because s/he is too close to the situation.
10. *Be as unobtrusive as possible* during the observation period to minimize the effect of the observer on the observed.
11. *Observe* during times when learners are working independently.
12. *Make use of time* when learners are being supervised by others, such as at recess or during team-teaching.
13. *Make prearranged schedules* for observation.
14. *Develop coding or shorthand systems* for recording information.
15. *Become selective in observations* and focus on behaviors which tend to be representative of behavior patterns.
16. *Decide* if another assessment procedure would yield the same information and be less time-consuming.
17. *Regard observation data as hypotheses* to be tested, not conclusive evidence about the child.
18. *Observe the child performing a particular task;* your job of

drawing an inference is enhanced by the circumscribed nature of the task and the anticipated type of response (Meyen, 1972, p. 155).

19. *Observe the child within the curricular areas of the mainstream,* for "The assumption is that performance on mainstream curriculum tasks . . . is criterion performance and the handicapped child's failure to function typically on these tasks leads to his being considered a problem" (Deno & Gross, 1972, p. 118).

## Outcomes of Observation

The use of systematic observation methods allows us to gather firsthand evidence on which to base educational decisions—decisions about further assessment, learner objectives, teaching procedures, instructional materials, behavior management, and classroom environment. Observation of baseline behavior and of environmental variables can suggest hypotheses to be tested in the instructional phase.

Observation techniques permit us to study some very critical kinds of learning that do not result in a permanent product, such as cooperating with members of a group, or doing daily chores. Through observation we can evaluate the extent to which such learned behaviors are transferred into everyday living. Problem behaviors can be detected much earlier by the teacher who uses a standard format for recording observation data, and thus can gather information on the student's behavior patterns.

Observation is an efficient tool to evaluate learner achievement of stated objectives. Daily or weekly observation records may reveal small gains or improvements that would otherwise go unnoticed.

Depending upon your purpose, and the behaviors being studied, the rigorous application of observation methods may produce an almost sufficient data base for beginning to plan instruction. This is often true for affective, social, and management behaviors. For information processing and academic skill problems, the observational data will frequently point to specific areas which require more precise measurement or testing. The opposite is also true; formal assessment may be followed by "in situ" observation. Through observation of the student's behavior at school, you may decide that it is essential to gather information from the home, perhaps through interviewing.

## INTERVIEWING*

> If you give a child a hammer, things to be pounded become the most important things around. (Willems & Rausch, 1969, p. 45, on the "Law of the Hammer")

The "Law of the Hammer" dictates that our information is often limited by our choice of assessment tools. Systematic observation of behavior in the classroom, as noted earlier, may only be useful in the case of frequently occurring behavior problems. This is especially true where the method of observation is cumbersome and must be done by someone other than the classroom teacher. Consequently, exclusive reliance on systematic observation could cause us to focus too intently on common problems such as task-related classroom behavior, talk-outs, noncompliance with classroom rules, and so on, and to ignore assessment of problems such as fighting with peers, lying, stealing, temper tantrums, and poor achievement. Systematic observation might also miss outside environmental events influencing student behavior: lack of breakfast before school, domination by an older sibling outside of school, illness, teacher-pupil interaction when the observer is not present, or major contingencies affecting student behavior of which the observer is unaware.

The "Law of the Hammer" implies that exclusive reliance on any single method of data collection is likely to bias the diagnostician. As will be shown later in the section on testing, reliance upon psychometric testing of cognitive processes has provided a limited scope for the remediation of academic problems.

## Types and Uses of Interviewing

The interview offers some major advantages as an informal method of data collection. While various precautions must be exercised in its use, the resource teacher would be foolish to avoid interviewing school staff and the student him/herself as the initial assessment strategy, and indeed should conduct further interviews when systematic observation and psychometric testing have proven fruitless. The major advantage of the interview is its efficiency and almost unlimited scope. The types of information appropriately gathered by interview include:

- assessment of teacher concerns about student behavior;
- description of classroom rules and performance objectives (teacher expectations);

---

*The entire section on interviewing was developed and written by Dr. Karl Skindrud, School of Educationa, California State College, Dominguez Hills, Carson, California, 1976.

- estimation of low base rate behavior problems not accessible to one-hour classroom observations;
- assessment of parent concerns regarding student behaviors in the home and classroom;
- description of home management and tutoring procedures (parent expectations);
- description of provision for biological, developmental, and social needs in the home (sleep, diet, peer relations, for example);
- obtaining a history of early development (birth injuries, trauma, serious illnesses, attention, family constellation, and so on);
- assessment of student motivational variables (such as interests, reinforcers, fears, expectations, cooperation, and so on);
- negotiation of work contracts;
- persuasion of the teachers, parents, or the student of the importance and/or possibility for improvement in student behavior, performance, and so on;
- informal evaluation of attempts to remediate behavior problems or performance;
- assessment of attitudes.

Approaches to interviewing vary from open to structured. The *open* interview has the advantage of allowing the informant to immediately share any major concerns about the student. Rather than seeking specific information, the interviewer uses the basic interviewing skills of attending, asking open-ended questions, paraphrasing and encouraging further conversation, reflection of feeling, and summarization.

Eventually, the interviewer will want to move into a *structured* format and begin probing for specific information so that the information gathered is not entirely biased by the informant's perceptions. The outline below has been suggested by Kanfer and Saslow (1968) for the comprehensive assessment of all possible environmental and developmental determinants naturally related to problem behaviors. Their outline has been adapted to the school situation by the present author:

1. *Analysis of the problem situation.* What are the behavioral excesses, deficits, and assets of the student as seen by the teacher? by his parents? by him/herself?

2. *Clarification of the problem situation.* Who objects to the problem behaviors? Who tends to support them? What events led to the crisis resulting in referral? What consequences does the problem have for the student? for the teacher? for peers? parents? siblings? What would be the benefits of removal of the problem for the student and others? Does the problem behavior occur in the classroom? on the playground? to and from school? at home? Does the problem only occur in reading, or math? during seatwork or group activities? with one teacher or all teachers?

3. *Motivational analysis.* How does the student rank various incentives in their importance to him/her? Which of the following reinforcing events is most effective in initiating or maintaining his/her behavior: adult approval, peer approval, choice of free activities following seatwork, group participation, competition, tangible reinforcers, independent projects, avoidance of teacher disapproval, peer disapproval, aversive consequences? Under what specific conditions do these motivational variables appear effective? Do they require parent approval or cooperation? Who or what has the most effective and widespread control of the student's current behavior? Can the student relate reinforcement contingencies to his/her own behavior, or does s/he fail to perceive the influences controlling his/her behavior? Which motivational variables and events are most accessible for utilization in the school?

4. *Developmental analysis.* What are the student's current biological limitations (physical defects, sensory limitations, results of serious illnesses)? What is the student's response to them? What is the student's relevant developmental history? How will these biological conditions limit response to remediation? What are the characteristic features of the student's present sociocultural milieu (ethnic and socioeconomic affiliation)? Are his/her attitudes congruent with his/her milieu? Have there been changes in this milieu that are pertinent to current behavior? What are the most recent major changes in the student's behavior? Are any of these changes correlated with recent major changes in the student's developmental history or sociocultural milieu? Can the problem behaviors be traced to a model in the student's social environment from whom s/he has learned these behaviors?

5. *Analysis of environmental contingencies maintaining problem behaviors.* What conditions, persons, instructional settings or

strategies, reinforcers, or contingencies tend to change his/her behavior? Can these conditions be maximized without deleterious effects to the student? Are there situations where the student manifests appropriate self-management of problem behaviors? How does s/he achieve such control—by manipulation of self or others? Are more severe problem behaviors subject to acceptable aversive consequences by others? Is there a correspondence between the student's verbalized self-control and observations by others? Is teacher and/or self-monitoring necessary to increase self-awareness or acquire additional information?

Other structured formats are available for the collection of information on the classroom, learning and behavior problems, developmental histories, and so on. While the above format appears to comprehensively assess those critical environmental and developmental variables most functionally related to learning and behavior problems, any one area could deserve more in-depth probing. Often a school nurse has forms available for obtaining detailed information on the early developmental histories of children. Such medically-related information may be best obtained by her, unless she is unavailable. A general strategy is to look for immediate environmental causes. If adequate attempts to improve the environmental management of the problem behaviors are unsuccessful, then interdisciplinary assessment may be necessary to determine significant developmental deviations impairing progress.

## Limitations of Interviewing

The major limitation of the interview as a data collection technique is its retrospective and interpretive nature. You are relying on the informant's memory of past events with all its susceptibility to selective recall. Recent research has determined that retrospective global judgments are more susceptible to bias than discrete behavioral observations (O'Leary, Kent, & Kanowitz, 1975).

Checking the information sought by interviews with several informants familiar with the problem situation may increase reliability. Interviews with the teacher, parent, and *student* are minimally required in any attempt to remediate serious learning or behavior problems.

## Tips for Improving Interviews

Interviewing teachers, parents, and students who have learning and/or behavior problems at school is a useful method of data collection. However, as is often the case in working with individuals where there is a problem, the information provided may be consciously or unconsciously biased by the informant. How the resource teacher initiates and conducts the interview can significantly improve or interfere with the communication process.

Adopting a habitual role of "fact-finder" (seeking information and ignoring feelings), "fix-it specialist" (solving the problem for another), "advisor" (telling another what to do), "judge" (evaluating others' feelings), and "questioner" (always seeking more information) can turn off others to openly sharing the information they have. Seeking complete information from others in a problem situation is more productive where the interviewer recognizes the other person's strengths as well as weaknesses, presents himself/herself as having experienced similar problems and recognizes the other person's feelings (often expressed nonverbally). It may also be helpful to recognize how others tend to see you as an interviewer. Ms. Nice Guy (always friendly, but unassertive); Ms. Tough Guy (aggressive and domineering); or Ms. Logical (objective, but lacking awareness of feelings). Self-awareness of one's own behavior patterns in interpersonal situations allows one to deal more effectively with others in an interview situation (Tubesing and Tubesing, 1973). Some tips on improving communication in the interview situation follow:

1. *Listen attentively to the informant.* Communicate this attentiveness through a relaxed posture, use of varied eye contact, and verbal responses, which indicate an attempt to understand the informant.

2. *Ask open-ended questions initially.* For example: "What is your major concern about Sally?" "What do you feel could be done to improve the situation?" "What has been done to deal with the problem?" You will obtain more information of potential usefulness through open invitations to talk (although more time may be required) than through the use of close-ended questions such as, "Is Billy a problem in math?" "Does he have difficulty relating to his peers during recess?" "Have the parents been cooperative during conferences?" Such specific questions can be directed to the teacher (parents, or student) *after* you have heard their interpretation of the problem.

A typical problem with closed questions is that the interviewer leads the client to topics of interest to the interviewer only. Too often an interviewer projects his own theoretical orientation onto the information he is trying to gather. Often if the interviewer relies on closed questions to structure the interview, s/he is forced to concentrate so hard on thinking up the next question that s/he fails to listen and attend to the informant.

3. *Recognize and use nonverbal communication.* Learn to "read" body language as clues to another's true feelings about the problem situation. The voice: its loudness, tone, rate of speed, firmness, and phrasing. The face; its tenseness, eye contact, responsiveness, and willingness to smile. Body posture: orientation to the interviewer, amount of tension (clenched fist, sweaty palms, and so on). The language pattern: the nature of the topics discussed, outside information, personal feelings, beliefs a person holds very important, or perceptions.

    The nonverbal cues, together with what is *not* said, may communicate more than a person's words taken alone. Often a teacher is really saying she's "had it" with a certain problem student, but she's unwilling to admit defeat and does not say it. Recognizing her true feelings may open the door to cooperative efforts in solving the problem.

4. *Paraphrase and summarize the informant's message.* If not done to excess, this conveys interest, crystallizes the message, and checks the interviewer's perception of the informant's intended communication. Paraphrasing is a restatement of the informant's communication in order to test your understanding of his/her comment. It is a statement in your own words of what the informant's comment conveyed to you. For example, *Teacher:* "I've got 35 students and they each have their own problems. Parents are coming in and asking me to give their child special attention. The administrator wants this, the reading specialist that, the social worker something else. They never offer to help with any of my problems." *Interviewer:* "You feel that everyone is making demands on you without being of assistance."

5. *Recognize different levels of communication and their effects* (Tubesing & Tubesing, 1973). Advice, interpretation, support, probing, and paraphrasing each elicit different responses in the informant. What may be appropriate at one point may be inappropriate at another. *Paraphrasing* is the least restrictive and encourages the informant to give his/her view of the problem. *Probing* gets information but limits areas about which the informant can talk. *Support* ("All people feel that way at

times") tends to shift the focus from the feelings of the informant to those of the interviewer. *Interpretation* gives information but intellectualizes the conversation (moves away from the feeling level) and closes off further communication. It may be clear to the teacher that "interpretation" and "support" are attempts by a busy resource person to dodge helping the teacher with a pressing problem. *Advice* sets one person above another and may put the informant on the defensive.

## Outcomes

The proposed framework for interviewing the teacher, the parent, other professionals, or the student, permits us to determine possible environmental or developmental causes for the problem behaviors. The interviewer may see correlations among changes in the environment, the onset of developmental problems, student attitudes, and the occurrence of the problem behaviors. Environmental events that covary with the problem behaviors suggest possible avenues for appropriate intervention. Does the teacher always counsel the student following temper outbursts? What preceded the temper outbursts—no breakfast, lack of sleep, teasing by a dominant sibling? Has the student recently been promoted from a slow class where s/he was a "star" to a competitive class where s/he "feels like a nobody?" Would reducing task difficulty, increasing teacher attention, or improving home cooperation be sufficient to reduce problem behavior?

These are all hypotheses that will need to be explored further and checked against assessment information gathered from other sources. Some of these hypotheses will need to be tested out in the instructional setting itself, and refined as feedback is received from the teacher, parents, and the student. Only such continuous evaluation—often by the informal interview of these significant individuals—will permit the ultimate resolution of the problem.

## SCHOOL RECORDS

An obvious and important data base for the assessment process is school records or "cum" folders—when they are available. Depending on the completeness of the student's file, valuable information may be found here that will give some historical perspective on the student's current problem, as well as guidelines for further assessment. Look for anecdotal comments on skills taught, methods and materials used. There may also be specific information on skill levels attained by the student in criterion-referenced skills sequences. In addition, you may discover random pieces of information that need to be followed up, such as the child's referral to a community mental health agency. Was the referral completed? What were the outcomes? To obtain such data in the assessment phase may save valuable time.

It is useful to prepare a *brief* chronological summary of the student's educational history, including test scores, achievement status, and pertinent comments, all of which will provide the assessment team with a framework for viewing the student's current functioning.

Affleck, Lowenbraun, and Archer (1980) offer an important word of caution regarding the use of school records:

> Child performance is greatly affected by teacher expectations. You should guard against forming any negative impressions from the child's records that might interfere with working with the child. Additionally, you should remember that the information might better reflect what the child has been exposed to instead of what skills have been mastered. (p. 62)

# TESTING

## Process Testing

Testing is characterized frequently as a formal assessment method; observing and interviewing are usually considered to be informal methods. There are two general types of tests—process tests that are norm-referenced, and skill tests, many of which are criterion-referenced.

The tools used in process testing are "formal," in that they are standardized tests, administered by specially trained persons, in other than classroom settings (Hammill, 1971). Tests here include the well known Stanford-Binet, Wechsler Intelligence Scales, Illinois Test of Psycholinguistic Abilities, and the Frostig Developmental Test of Visual Perception. These tests, among others, are used to measure underlying processes such as intelligence, language, and perceptual abilities. Their value is in their objectivity, known reliabilities, validities, and national reputations (Hammill and Bartel, 1978).

When used by well-trained professionals, formal tests of process variables can identify personality dynamics related to the child's presenting problem, as well as problem-solving strengths and weaknesses (Stellern & Vasa, 1973). In addition, ability tests can serve to confirm or rule out the presence of mental deficiency, point out general areas of academic failure, and demonstrate modality strengths and weaknesses. Hamill (1971) cautions, however, that

> at worst, the formal evaluation is instructionally useless and will (1) demonstrate the obvious, namely, dwell at length on what is already vividly apparent to the teacher, (2) stress excessively etiological factors, such as brain dysfunction, which are of no value to the teacher, or (3) dwell at length on the interpretation of minimal and dubious evidence. (p. 343)

In addition to the problems that Hamill has identified, there are other serious issues surrounding the use of tests; some of them are discussed below.

*Many standardized ability tests are discriminatory.* There is considerable evidence to demonstrate the fact that a disproportionately large number of students from minority groups have been placed in special education programs as a result of their performance on standardized tests of mental ability normed on the Anglo population (Mercer, 1975). Thus, many tests in common use are inherently biased in favor of the white, English-speaking, middle class majority. The issue extends beyond the confines of the school; in fact, "the matter of test bias and the relevancy and use of test results has become a central concern of the movement for civil rights and for equal opportunity regardless of race, language, or national origin" (Laosa, 1976, p. 10). Potential sources of bias in tests include item or content bias, language bias, and examiner bias. Test items are biased if they do not assess students through relevant, familiar content. Most intelligence and achievement tests require receptive and expressive language abilities; other tests rely on language to transmit information from the examiner to the child. Language bias is present if the student being tested does not speak/understand English adequately. Examiners may introduce bias during or after the administration of a test. Bersoff and Ysseldyke (1977) cite studies illustrating that "given identical objective test data, educational personnel reach different kinds of identification and placement decisions as a function of the race, sex, socio-economic status, and physical attractiveness of the child" (p. 86).

In summary, the major criticisms of standardized tests are that tests

1. do not reflect linguistic or cognitive styles, values, experiences of minorities, and therefore are biased and unfair;

2. may be used to segregate students into homogeneous groups that limit opportunity;
3. are sometimes administered incompetently with the result that scores do not reflect student's real ability;
4. may lead to self-fulfilling prophecy (low test scores mean low achievement);
5. may rigidly shape school curricula and restrict change;
6. do not provide information relevant to instructional planning;
7. are limited in scope of behaviors assessed;
8. promote notion of innate, fixed abilities;
9. may represent in some instances an invasion of privacy (adapted from Laosa, 1976, pp. 10–11).

*Teachers need to be able to determine the special educational needs of students.* The probability of assessment information being translated into instructional action is increased when the teacher is enabled to participate in a meaningful way in the assessment. For the mildly handicapped student, we need measurement tools that can be used by the teacher, in the classroom settting. Tools must measure the discrepancy between the child's level of essential skills and the minimum level required to participate in mainstream education. Analysis of student performance on a quantitative, normative instrument is not sufficient to establish realistic goals, objectives, and an individualized prescriptive program. Formal assessment data must be combined with data on how the student interacts with the total learning environment if we are to have a sound basis for educational programming.

*There is a growing body of evidence that questions the remediation of auditory-perceptual, psycholinguistic, or visual-motor processes.* Such remediation is typically planned on the basis of ability test scores. The contention that process remediation is a prerequisite for academic achievement cannot be supported empirically (Cohen, 1969; Hammill, Goodman, & Wiederholt, 1974; Hammill & Larsen, 1974 a, b; Ysseldyke, 1973). Ability training for the purpose of facilitating academic achievement appears, at best, to be in a highly experimental stage and not appropriate for widespread adoption by the public schools.

## Skill Testing

The testing of specific skills is generally designated, along with observation and task analysis, as an "informal" assessment method, although standardized tests for academic areas may be included. Informal assessment is, according to Hammill and Bartel (1978, p. 7), "undertaken by an educationally oriented person, usually an educational diagnostician or teacher," in the classroom, for the purpose of determining very specific "instructional or behavioral needs." These needs then define the student's program. The rationale for skill testing is that we can measure performance directly, without inferring process or ability strengths and weaknesses. We can thereby determine the student's position on various skill continua and gain information about what instruction the student needs in order to progress to the next skill level. Instructional programs then can be designed to teach directly specific component skills (for example, naming letters) and their integration (for example, spelling words), as opposed to training general underlying abilities such as perception. Both diagnostic tests and criterion referenced measures are asepcts of, or approaches to, skill testing. Specific diagnostic tests and criterion referenced tests will be described in a later section that deals with assessing various academic behaviors. Criterion referenced measurement is discussed below.

**Criterion-Referenced Measurement (CRM)**

CRM is a method for testing skill development and student progress which is based on the principles of task analysis. Task analysis refers to the identification of major, sequential steps through which the learner must progress in order to get from his/her present, observed level to the desired terminal behavior. Terminal behaviors are *benchmarks* or *universals,* such as "demonstrates self-care skills," or "demonstrates ability to use checking and savings accounts," both of which might be goals for students at a particular age or grade level. Terminal behaviors are frequently attained by the student through accomplishing a number of specific instructional objectives. Task analysis is the process of breaking each of the objectives leading to the terminal behavior into component parts and sequencing the parts into a series of steps, or tasks, to be presented to the student. If the desired terminal behavior is "reads at grade level," we must consider all of the skills that the student must possess in order to be able to do this. Such skills are sometimes called "en route" or "enabling objectives," and in this example might include identifying basic sight vocabulary and using word attack skills effectively. We then need to look closely at what underlying skills are implied in these behaviors—recognizing and naming letters of the alphabet, for example. When we have identified all the skills, we list them sequentially. We then have a checklist of skills which we can use to assess where the student is in terms of being able to read at grade level—what skills are already in the student's repertoire.

Instruction begins at the student's present level in the skill hierarchy and proceeds step-wise until each major objective involved in reading at grade level is met. To summarize, task analysis enables us to identify a specific set of skills that should be assessed prior to

instructional planning, and, thus, what tasks are appropriate for the student. Task analysis is used frequently, and often intuitively, by competent teachers.

Criterion-Referenced Measurement or Testing is simply a more formalized use of task analysis. CRM is any test that is purposely designed to provide measures that can be interpreted in terms of specified performance standards. Criterion-referenced testing requires a clearly defined and delimited domain of learning tasks and thus requires breaking down the curriculum into manageable units and sequences. The mastery of one set or subset of behaviors is prerequisite in order to progress to the next unit of instruction. Results of the criterion-referenced test can be used to gear the instructional sequence to the individual student's rate and style of learning, individual goals, and so forth. Use of criterion-referenced tests allows for recycling or follow-up instruction on missed or failed items.

Information from criterion-referenced tests can also assist the teacher in evaluating the effectiveness of the "match" between the student, the method, the material, the environment, so that any or all can be modified to insure success for the student. In addition, the teacher can evaluate the learning sequence itself. Because the test items on a CRM instrument are directly related to the objectives of instruction, if the student does not pass the test, the blame probably rests in the instruction itself.

Criterion-referenced measurement is part of the movement in education toward instructionally relevant testing for assessment, placement, and evaluation. In using CRM we are asking the question "What can the student do?" not "How does s/he compare with others?" "The meaningfulness of an individual score is not dependent on comparison with others" (Popham & Husek, 1969, p. 1), as it is with norm-referenced tests. Let's look at some examples:

> Steve, in looking over his test results found that . . . with his raw score of 92 . . . he ranked at the 79th percentile rank and at the seventh stanine. His raw score had been compared with those scores obtained by his classmates. (Smith, 1973, p. 2)

> Mary's score is second from the top.
> Danny's score is lowest in the class.
> David's score is average.

These statements are examples of the use of traditional norm-referenced tests. The progress of these students has been assessed in relation to the performance of the others in their class by using the same instrument. The students are aware of how they rank with their classmates, or with the reference group on whom the test was standardized, but they have no feedback on the extent to which they met, or failed to meet, the objectives of instruction. Now, contrast the preceding statements with the following:

> Ted can add all combinations of single digit whole numbers from 1 to 9 without error.
> Helen can spell 90% of the words from the unit word list.
> Betty can type 40 words per minute with no more than 2 errors.

These statements are examples of the use of a criterion-referenced test. The student's performance on specific skills is described in behavioral terms without reference to the performance of other members of the class. Also, the criterion, or level of satisfactory performance, is built in: 100%, 90%, 40 wpm, and no errors. The following chart summarizes a few of the critical differences between norm-referenced and criterion-referenced testing.

## Comparison of Norm-Referenced Testing and CRM

| *Norm-referenced* | *Criterion-referenced* |
|---|---|
| Reference points are average, relative points. | Referenced points are fixed at specified, cut-off points. |
| Evaluates individual performance in comparison to a group of persons. | Evaluates individual performance in relation to a fixed standard. |
| Are used to evaluate a student as "below grade level," "at grade level," or "above grade level." | Not concerned with grade level descriptions. |
| Fails to indicate which individuals have mastered the spectrum of instructional objectives. | Identifies individuals who have mastered the spectrum of instructional objectives. |
| Generally poor aids in planning instruction. | Geared to provide information to be used in planning instruction. |
| Is vague in relation to the instructional content. | Is content-specific. |
| Is more summative than formative. | Is more formative than summative. |
| Does not operationally define mastery and/or success. | Operationally defines mastery and/or success. |
| Applies poorly to the individualization of instruction. | Applies directly to the individualization of instruction. |
| Is not concerned with task analysis. | Depends upon task analysis. |
| Does not lend itself to applied behavioral analysis. | Lends itself to applied behavioral analysis. |
| Standardized tests are classical examples. | Does not tend to be standardized. |
| Tests not sensitive to the effects of instruction. | Tests very sensitive to the effects of instruction. |
| Tests have a low degree of overlap with actual objectives of instruction. | Tests are directly referenced to the objectives of instruction. |
| Test items evaluated in reference to persons. | Test items evaluated in reference to instructional objectives. |
| Tests results interpreted in reference to a person's position in relation to the scores of others. | Tests results interpreted in reference to a person's position in relation to the curriculum. (Housden & LeGear, 1974, pp. 191–192) |

The issue is not that one approach is good and the other bad; it is that one should understand and know how and when to use each. A major problem to date has been the lack of information on just what norm-referenced tests are designed to sample, as well as improper interpretations being made from the resulting data. We must remember that we cannot speak with precise certainty about norm-referenced data—this is a big danger. It is important to examine your purpose in testing and to understand which type of test is most appropriate to accomplish a particular purpose. If your purpose in testing is to select the top few students, and identify the average, or to survey the relative attainment of students in terms of generally accepted skills and knowledge outcomes, use a norm-referenced test. If your purpose is to assess what *specific content* and *objectives* have been *attained* and to *determine progress* students have made on sequential units of curricula, use CRM. Sample test materials are discussed in the next section of this chapter. In certain areas, criterion-referenced measurement may be irrelevant because no meaningful criterion applies—this is the case in a social studies curriculum, for example.

Criterion-referenced testing is important to any subject where future academic success is dependent upon cumulative information or skills. It is most important and relevant in the more structured subjects such as reading and math. There are certain tasks that, by their very nature, must be performed at a specifiable, high level in every situation, such as landing an airliner, compounding a prescription, and obeying safety signs. In these situations we do not care how one compares with others but how well he or she performs according to a set standard. Here criterion-referenced measurement is a necessity.

To sum up, then, the three major uses of CRM are for *placement*, *assessment* and *evaluation and instructional planning:*

*Placement:* a criterion-referenced test may be used as a pretest; use it to assess students' mastery for placement at appropriate instructional levels and/or placement in learning groups.

*Assessment:* criterion-referenced testing can be used to target behaviors that need to be shaped through instruction. Criterion-referenced testing can help identify specific skill deficiencies for remediation. Through CRM, a teacher can obtain samples of learning outcomes and identify and analyze common errors as instruction proceeds.

*Evaluation and instructional planning:* analysis of criterion-referenced test items aid in evaluating the effectiveness of instruction.

Errors, or the failure to achieve objectives, may indicate that the instruction was inadequate or that the objectives were beyond the reach of the learners. This information should be used to revise procedures, methods, materials, or the objectives themselves, to order to insure learner success in the future.

Bloom (1971, pp. 91–92) provides additional comparative information on diagnostic, formative, and summative evaluation. In the following chapter a sampling of procedures and instruments to assess a student's present performance levels in various skill areas is provided, along with a process approach to planning the assessment.

## Study Questions and Activities

1. Traditional psychometric approaches to assessment in special education have often been criticized for lacking relevance to the classroom (instructional planning). In what ways will the move to informal, educationally oriented assessment make instructional planning more effective? More efficient?

2. Indicate which observation recording procedure (a. anecdotal, b. event, c. duration, d. time-sampling, e. placheck) would be most appropriate for collecting data in each of the following school situations:

__ The principal has asked for a description of all "incidents" created by Billy on the playground during the coming week.

__ What percent of the nursery school class make use of the sand table during free activity time daily?

__ The teacher can only record Sandra's behavior during one minute every half hour during the day.

__ Rodger's mother wishes to know how many "cuss words" the teacher has observed him using during a typical school day.

__ The teacher wishes to lengthen the amount of time Shy Sally and Withdrawn Willy engage in social interaction with their peers.

3. Mrs. Hammond, a new resource teacher, decided to obtain independent classroom observations of Howard Hazzard, a third grader reported to have behavior problems. Mrs. Hammond observed Howard during his reading circle and the aide observed him during his math seat work. When the aide and

Mrs. Hammond compared their observations, they were surprised to find no behavior problems observed during reading and a multitude of problems during math. Mrs. Hammond and the aide had both used identical recording systems (event recording) and both observed exactly one hour. Give at least two possible explanations for their disagreement. How could Mrs. Hammond and her aide resolve this disagreement?

4. Visit a classroom (nursery or elementary preferably) of a cooperating teacher and ask permission to observe (or interview the teacher regarding) the most hyperactive pupils in the room. If observed, the pupils should be seen during at least two different periods of the day. Conduct an informal behavior analysis to determine the environmental correlates of the behavior problems. This can be done by listing in columns side-by-side (see the "is-plan" format used by Precision Teachers): (1) the behaviors of greatest concern to the teacher; (2) the setting(s) in which these problem behaviors occur; (3) the teaching methods, materials, and instructions presented the pupil during the high problem periods; (4) the consequences provided the pupil (by teachers and/or peers) for appropriate and inappropriate behaviors during the high problem periods. On the basis of the correlations between problem behaviors and environmental variables observed, generate hypotheses regarding possible environmental causes (e.g., teaching methods, expectations, instructions, consequences, feedback, peer attention, etc.) Suggest possible strategies for remediating the problem behaviors on the basis of the hypotheses generated.

5. Given the following list of referral problems, describe at least two informal techniques for assessing baseline behaviors or entry skills for each of the following referral problems (all from different 6th-grade boys):

   a. "Does not understand instructions or appropriately follow directions (English spoken at home)."

   b. "Neither his classmates nor I can understand his speech when reciting in class (English spoken at home)."

   c. "Lacks motivation to complete assignments. Never turns in work on time. Always doing other things (talking, reading comics, etc.)."

   d. "Reads like molasses. I hate to call on him to read because it takes him five minutes per paragraph. It's embarrassing."

e. "He complains that his math assignments are too difficult. He works at grade level in social studies and reading."
f. "Poor peer relations. I am unaware of any friends and do not know how to group him for class projects or field trips."
g. "Never raises his hand or waits his turn. Blurts out, interrupts, and disrupts class discussions interminably. Gets in fights for 'taking cuts' in lunch line."
h. "Can read aloud, but does not understand what he has read. Recites some facts, but these are often unrelated to the story read."
i. "Recently moved here from Mexico. He does not follow directions, nor express himself in class. If he does not improve, he should be considered for the EMR class."

# References

Affleck, J. Q., Lowenbraun, S., & Archer, A. *Teaching the mildly handicapped in the regular classroom* (2nd ed.). Columbus, Ohio: Charles E. Merrill, 1980.

Almy, M. *Ways of studying children: A manual for teachers.* New York: Teachers College Press, Columbia University, 1959.

Bersoff, D. N. & Ysseldyke, J. E. Non-discriminatory assessment: The law, litigation, and implications for the assessment of learning disabled children. In S. Jacob (Ed.) *The law: assessment and placement of special education students.* Lansing, Mich.: Michigan Department of Education, 1977.

Bloom, B. S., Hastings, J. T., & Madaus, G. F. *Handbook on formative and summative evaluation of student learning.* New York: McGraw-Hill, 1971.

Cartwright, C. A., & Cartwright, G. P. *Developing observation skills.* New York: McGraw-Hill, 1974.

Cohen, S. A. Studies in visual perception and reading in disadvantaged children. *Journal of Learning Disabilities*, 1969, 2 (10), 498–507.

Deno, S., & Gross, J. The Seward-University project: A cooperative effort to improve school services and university training. In E. N. Deno (Ed.), *Instructional alternatives for exceptional children.* Arlington, Va.: The Council for Exceptional Children, 1972.

Hall, R. V. *Behavior modification: The measurement of behavior.* Lawrence, Kan.: H and H Enterprises, 1971.

Hall, R. V., Hawkins, R. P., & Axelrod, S. Measuring and recording student behavior: A behavior analysis approach. In R. A. Weinberg & F. H.

Wood (Eds.), *Observation of pupils and teachers in mainstream and special education settings: Alternative strategies.* Minneapolis, Minn.: University of Minnesota Press, 1975.

Hammill, D. Evaluating children for instructional purposes. *Academic Therapy Quarterly,* 1971, *6* (4), 341–353.

Hammill, D. D., & Bartel, N. R. (Eds.). *Teaching children with learning and behavior problems* (2nd ed.). Boston: Allyn and Bacon, 1978.

Hammill, D., Goodman, L., & Wiederholt, J. L. Visual-motor processes: Can we train them? *The Reading Teacher,* 1974, *27* (5), 469–477.

Hammill, D. D., & Larsen, S. C. The relationship of selected auditory perceptual skills and reading ability. *Journal of Learning Disabilities,* 1974, *7* (7) 429–435. (a)

Hammill, D. D., & Larsen, S. C. The effectiveness of psycholinguistic training. *Exceptional Children,* 1974, *7,* 429–435. (b)

Harms, T. Evaluating settings for learning. In B. C. Mills & R. A. Mills (Eds.), *Designing instructional strategies for young children.* Dubuque, Iowa: William C. Brown, 1972.

Housden, J. L., & LeGear, L. An emerging model: Criterion-referenced evaluation. In William Georgiades & D. C. Clark (Eds.), *Models for individualized instruction.* New York: MSS Information Corporation, 1974.

Kanfer, F. H., & Phillips, J. S. *Learning foundations of behavior therapy.* New York: Wiley, 1970.

Kanfer, F. H., & Saslow, G. Behavioral diagnosis. In C. M. Franks (Ed.), *The behavior therapies: Appraisal and status.* New York: McGraw-Hill, 1969.

Laosa, L. M. Historical antecedents and current issues in assessment of children's abilities. In T. Oakland (Ed.), *With bias toward none.* Lexington, Kentucky: Coordinating Office for Regional Resource Centers, 1976.

Mercer, J. R. Psychological assessment and the rights of children. In N. Hobbs (Ed.), *Issues in the classification of children.* (Vol. I), San Francisco: Jossey Bass, 1975.

Meyen, E. L. *Developing units of instruction for the mentally retarded and other children with learning problems.* Dubuque, Iowa: William C. Brown, 1972.

O'Leary, K. D., Kent, R. N., & Kanowitz, J. Shaping data collection congruent with experimental hypothesis. *Journal of Applied Behavior Analysis,* 1975, *8* (1), 43–52.

Phillips, J. S., & Ray, R. S. Basic interviewing skills manual. Unpublished manuscript, 1972.

Popham, W. J., & Husek, T. R. Implications of criterion referenced measurement. *Journal of Educational Measurement.* 1969, *6* (1), 1–9.

Risley, T. R. Spontaneous language in the preschool environment. In J.

Stanley (Ed.), *Research on curriculums for preschools.* Baltimore: Johns Hopkins, 1971.

Sabatino, D. Resource rooms: The renaissance in special education. *Journal of Special Education,* 1972, *6* (4), 335–347. (a)

Sabatino, D. School psychology—Special education: To acknowledge a relationship. *Journal of School Psychology,* 1972, *10* (2), 99–105. (b)

Semmel, M. I. Application of systematic classroom observation to the study and modification of pupil-teacher interactions in special education. In R. A. Weinberg & F. H. Wood (Eds.), *Observation of pupils and teachers in mainstream and special education settings: alternative strategies.* Minneapolis, Minn.: University of Minnesota Press, 1975.

Smith, C. W. *Criterion-referenced assessment.* The Hague, Netherlands. A Paper Presented at the International Symposium on Educational Testing, July 1973.

Smith, R. M., Neisworth, J. T., & Greer, J. G. *Evaluating educational environments.* Columbus, Ohio: Charles E. Merrill, 1978.

Thorndike, R. L., & Hagen, E. *Measurement and evaluation in psychology and education.* New York: Wiley, 1955.

Tubesing, D. A., & Tubesing, N. L. *Tune in: Empathy training workshop.* Milwaukee, Wisc.: Listening Group, 1973.

United States Office of Education, Title 45 of the Code of Federal Regulations, Implementation of Part B of the Education of the Handicapped Act, 1977.

United States Public Law P. L. 94–142. *The Education for All Handicapped Children Act,* 1975.

Willems, E. P. & Rausch, H. L. (Eds.). *Naturalistic viewpoints in psychological research.* New York: Holt, Rinehart and Winston, 1969.

Ysseldyke, J. Diagnostic-prescriptive teaching: The search for aptitude-treatment interactions. In L. Mann & D. A. Sabatino (Eds.), *The first review of special education.* Philadelphia, Pa.: Journal of Special Education Press, 1973.

# Resources

## Observation

Allen, K. E. et al. Early warning: Observation as a tool for recognizing potential handicaps in young children. *Educational Horizons,* 1971–72, *50* (2), 43–55.

Boehm, A. E., & Weinberg, R. A. *The classroom observer: A guide for developing observational skills.* New York: Teachers College Press, Columbia University, 1975.

Simon, A., & Boyer, E. G. (Eds.). *Mirrors for behavior: An anthology of classroom observation instruments.* Philadelphia, Pa.: Research for Better Schools, 1970.

## Interviewing

*Psychosituational interview.* Edwardsville, Ill.: Southern Illinois University, 1974. This is one in a series of 38 Microteaching Modules; it is a half-inch videotape (15 minutes) with a manual. The module is designed to train teachers in how to conduct a parent interview. Direct inquiries to Emmet G. Beetner, Special Education Microteaching Clinic, Southern Illinois University, Edwardsville, Ill. 62025.

## Precision Teaching

Haughton, E. Great gains from small starts. *Teaching Exceptional Children.* 1971, 3 (3), 141–146.

Kunzelmann, H. P. (Ed.), Cohen, M. A., Hulten, W. J., Martin, C. L., & Mingo, A. R. *Precision teaching: An initial training sequence.* Seattle, Wash.: Special Child Publications, 1970.

Starlin, C. Peers and precision. *Teaching Exceptional Children,* 1971, 3 (3), 129–139.

White, O. R., & Haring, N. G. *Exceptional teaching for exceptional children: A multimedia training package.* Columbus, Ohio: Charles E. Merrill, 1980.

# 5

# Assessment—Part Two

Assessments of mildly or moderately handicapped students conducted by school assessment teams typically involve the areas of academic, affective, language, sensorimotor, and social functioning and, for secondary students, career and vocational aptitude. In this chapter we present specific comments regarding assessment in these and other behavioral areas, as well as some representative tests and techniques. The major intent is to provide ideas and suggestions and to promote the use of educationally relevant assessment tools. The information presented is offered in this spirit. It should not be interpreted as exhaustive, final, or sufficient; nor, should the tests mentioned be construed as comprising a standard battery. We regard the consistent use of a standard battery as inefficient and sometimes unprofessional. We urge, instead, that assessment be relevant to the student in question and based on the requirements of the situation. The essence of competence as an educational diagnostician is the ability to select and/or devise one's own assessment procedures to determine the unique educational needs of students.

## Assessing Academic Skills

In assessing the academic skills of mildly or moderately handicapped students, it is important to consider the curriculum of the mainstream education program. If the student is to succeed in a regular class, s/he must acquire the basic skills appropriate for his or her grade placement. We need to know what those skills are, how to determine the extent to which the student mastered them, and how those skills are taught in the regular class. We must avoid concluding that, because a child has been referred for further assessment, s/he cannot learn and make academic progress in the regular classroom. Some suggestions for assessing reading and math competencies are listed below. Many of these suggestions are drawn from the works of Hammill and Bartel (1978), Smith (1969), and Affleck, Lowenbraun and Archer (1980), whose books are highly recommended as handbooks for resource teachers. Representative criterion-referenced materials are listed at the end of this chapter, along with other assessment resources.

### 1.0 Reading

Standardized tests can provide estimates of a child's reading ability but typically they yield little or no information on a child's reading process. Often the teacher will need to construct skill-specific tests, or probes, to determine what instruction the student needs. Boyd (1975), Brabner (1969), and Affleck, Lowenbraun and Archer (1980) offer extensive summaries of *informal* devices that can be used to determine level of instruction and specific reading difficulties. Only a sampling of these techniques is presented here. The reader is advised to consult primary sources.

1.1 *Checklists:* These can be teacher-constructed to reflect common reading problems such as "adds words," "omits words," or "makes guesses." The checklist can be designed to cover general reading problems as well as those related to oral reading and to comprehension. Boyd (1975) suggests that the teacher keep such a record on each student.

1.2 *Word Recognition Tests:* One example is the *San Diego Quick Assessment* (LaPray and Ross, 1969). A graded word list is constructed using words from basal readers and the Thorndike Word List. LaPray and Ross include lists up to the eleventh grade. The graded word list allows the teacher to determine reading level and to identify word analysis errors. Classroom teachers can also construct their own word recognition tests, based on the students' reading material (see Boyd, 1975, pp. 23–24).

1.3 *Comprehension Checks:* Boyd (1975, pp 24–26) gives detailed instructions for designing informal tests of comprehension skills. Brabner (1969) defines hearing comprehension as the "highest level at which a child can understand what is read to him" (pp. 73–74), stating that at least 70% should be comprehended. Informal assessment involves selecting paragraphs from basal readers and carefully constructing questions on the content. Silent reading comprehension level should also be checked; the 70% score also applies here. Brabner (1969) recommends a test involving sentence absurdities which has been found very useful with socially disadvantaged children and young adults:

> *Basic Test of Reading Comprehension*
> by S. A. Cohen & R. D. Cloward
> Mobilization for Youth, Inc.
> 214 E. Second Street
> New York, NY 10009

1.4 *Informal Reading Inventory:* This is a diagnostic reading test based on a series of graded books or other types of reading materials, such as newspapers. The inventory can be used to detect reading difficulties and also to select appropriate reading materials for students.

1.5 *Checks for Verbal Concept Formation and Vocabulary:* Brabner suggests using subtests of standardized reading tests and asking the student questions on word meaning. "Book analysis" is another technique in which the teacher analyzes the vocabulary from the basal reader into lists of nouns, verbs, and so on, then finds a picture that corresponds to the word. The child reads the word and selects the correct pictorial representation (Brabner, 1969, pp. 75–76).

1.6 *Standardized Tests:* Both group and individual tests are available; some tests are primarily achievement measures, while others are diagnostic tools. Group standardized reading tests should be considered as screening instruments, rather than assessment devices. Boyd (1975, p. 29) includes a highly useful comparative summary (originally compiled by Farr and Anastasiow, 1969) of the more common reading tests. Ward, Cartwright, Cartwright, Campbell & Spinazola (1973) summarize a comprehensive approach to assessing reading performance.

> Evaluation of a learner's progress in reading needs to include criterion-referenced tests on his reading skills, some more general testing of his comprehension and application of reading (perhaps by teacher-pupil conferences), and teacher observation of his atti-

tude toward reading to detect evidence of both independence and enjoyment in reading.   (p. 349)

In their book, *Teaching Children with Learning and Behavior Problems,* Hammill and Bartel include chapters on the two additional academic areas of spelling and writing.

## 2.0 Arithmetic

Spencer and Smith (1969) cite two areas of potential weakness in arithmetic: "(1) those skills that are necessary for an adequate understanding of quantity, including the development of a minimum level of skill in computation; and (2) the application of quantitative concepts and computational skills in the solution of arithmetic reasoning problems" (p. 153). These authors list some simple techniques that classroom teachers may use to study the arithmetic performance of individual students. Included are:

2.1 *Observation:* List specific arithmetic operations where students are weak and systematically collect data on individuals (for example, reverses digits; omits a column; fails to borrow). A diagnostic chart developed by Buswell and John (1925) is a useful resource; this chart is included in the Spencer and Smith chapter cited above (pp. 168–69).

2.2 *Examining Written Assignments:* Checking written work can provide valuable progress information. Spencer and Smith (1969, p. 157) suggest that a student whose error rate is greather than 10% should receive a more detailed assessment. Systematic procedures for analyzing students' written work are described in detail by White and Haring (1980).

2.3 *Oral Questioning:* Return to a level where the child has been successful and proceed to where the difficulty arises by asking the student to explain his/her reasoning methods aloud. This approach should be used with great care so as not to precipitate an emotional outburst from a child who is confused and upset about arithmetic performance. The teacher can also question the child about his/her feelings regarding arithmetic thereby discovering motivational or attitudinal problems.

Bartel (1978) lists both general and specific factors that may be involved in arithmetic difficulty. General factors include ineffective instruction, poor reading and/or memory ability, and problems in abstract thinking. Specific factors are disabilities that show up only in certain situations, such as failure to learn to tell time. Bartel points out that, compared to reading, few formal or informal assessment techniques have been developed for arithmetic skills. Both Bartel

(1978) and Spencer and Smith (1969) present summaries of the more widely used formal achievement and diagnostic tests in arithmetic, including the California, Stanford, and SRA Achievement Tests. Additional informal techniques described by Bartel (1978) are:

2.4 *Analysis of Survey Test Performance:* While the diagnostic value of standardized achievement tests is limited, their value can be increased when the teacher analyzes the types of errors the students make, for example, computation versus reasoning errors.

2.5 *Teacher-Made Tests and Records:* Teachers can create short written tests designed to measure specific skills and facts that have been taught. Again, through error analysis, the teacher can identify more precisely the student's problem and therefore can design remediation. Teacher-constructed check sheets listing basic math skills can be used as an ongoing progress summary on the student. Excellent examples of teacher-made tests and inventories can be found in Affleck, Lowenbraun and Archer (1980) and in White and Haring (1980), along with guidelines on how to construct skill tests.

## Assessing Language Skills

A comprehensive language assessment should examine the student's functioning in the major language components of morphology, syntax, and semantics, as well as short-term and long-term memory skills. We also need to compare the student's performance across the various communication skill areas: reading, writing, listening, and speaking. It is also important to contrast language skills displayed at school with those evidenced by the child in the home, or community environment. Informal techniques for language assessment, as noted by Bartel (1978), include:

1. *Vocabulary Assessment:* By using objects or pictures the teacher attempts to elicit the correct verbal response from the child.
2. *Articulation Assessment:* Errors can be noted during vocabulary testing and remedial practice provided on-the-spot.
3. *Comprehension Assessment:* Comprehension can be checked, by reading a short paragraph to the student and then asking questions. With younger children, the teacher can give short verbal commands to perform certain behaviors, such as "Put the doll in the bed," "Put the pencil on the table," and so on.
4. *Syntax Assessment:* The teacher can keep records of deviations in verb tense, use of plural, possessive, and contractions, use of the negative, passive tense, the imperative, and so forth.

For more complete descriptions of these assessment procedures the reader should consult Bartel (1978).

Formal approaches to language assessment are discussed in a comprehensive volume by Wiig and Semel (1980):

*Assessment of Children's Language Comprehension* (ACLC, Foster, Giddan, & Stark, 1972)

*Carrow Elicited Language Inventory* (CELI, Carrow, 1974)

*Clinical Evaluation of Language Functions* (CELF, Semel & Wiig, 1980)

*Illinois Test of Psycholinguistic Abilities* (ITPA, Kirk, McCarthy, & Kirk, 1968)

*Northwestern Syntax Screening Test* (NSST), Lee, 1971)

*Peabody Picture Vocabulary Test* (PPVT, Dunn, 1965)

*Test of Auditory Comprehension of Language* (TACL, Carrow, 1973)

*Test of Linguistic Development* (TOLD, Newcomer & Hammill, 1977)

Great caution must be exercised when such tests

> are given to children who come to the testing situation from diverse ethnic and cultural groups, having a wide variety of values, traditions, and rules of speaking. All of these factors definitely influence and cause linguistic interferences throughout the testing process. When tests are administered to children having 'different' though 'equal' cultural and linguistic experiences than are required to pass the test, then there is great potential for test discrimination to occur. (Liles, 1979, p. 2)

Liles (1979) goes on to suggest that, "We can attempt to modify and adapt existing devices so that there is no confusion between linguistic diversities and linguistic deficiencies" (p. 4). Resources to assess bilingual and limited-English-speaking students are included at the end of this chapter.

## Assessing Perceptual-Motor Functioning

Included in this area are educational techniques to assess visual and auditory perception and gross motor skills. Medical evaluation is necessary to determine problems in sensory processing (vision, hearing). While there are a number of formal perceptual-motor tests available, including the Frostig, Bender, and the Memory for Designs Test (Graham & Kendall, 1960), these are, in the opinion of

Hammill (1975), more appropriate for screening groups of children than for studying individual performance. For a review of formal tests in this area the reader should consult Hammill (1975).

Both Smith (1969) and Hammill (1975) offer several informal procedures, useful to teachers and resource persons, based on interpreting the child's actual performance in teacher-directed activities. Many of the tasks used in perceptual *training* programs are themselves appropriate as assessment tasks. Subtests from formal assessment instruments can also be used diagnostically. Again, experience with children and a sound knowledge of developmental norms are necessary. Teacher observation is a primary source of information on the child's perceptual-motor functioning.

Smith (1969) suggests some behaviors to watch for as we observe an individual student.

1. how s/he holds a pencil—draws, writes
2. how well s/he can copy or trace
3. techniques used to form numerals and letters
4. consistent pattern of reversals
5. moving about without tripping and bumping into things
6. identifying and separating foreground objects from background
7. discrimination of size, shape, and color

In attempting to isolate the perceptual-motor difficulty, the assessment activity chosen should emphasize only one process at a time (Smith, 1969).

Hammill (1975) lists some steps the teacher can follow to determine the presence of auditory perception problems. These include:

1. repeating an auditory test or subtest (for example, memory for digits);
2. using reinforcers for correct responses to see if performance improves; and
3. checking to see if the problem involves symbolic, auditory memory skills, such as recalling words, phrases, following directions.

As mentioned earlier, there is a growing controversy over the use and value of perceptual training programs. Larsen and Hammill (1975) reviewed over 60 correlational studies that focused on the relationship of visual perception and academic performance. These researchers reported that the relationship between these variables is not great enough to be of use to teachers and that reading improvement cannot be expected as a result of perceptual-motor training. Hammill (1975) takes a strong stand on this issue, stating that, "In general, perceptual-motor training is viewed as more acceptable for preschool than for kindergarten or school-aged children, and is never recommended as a substitute for teaching language, reading or arithmetic skills" (p. 230). This statement has definite implications for the extent to which assessment should focus on perceptual-motor behaviors.

## Assessing Vocational and Career Needs*

In discussing career and vocational education, Kokaska points out that

> career education is a larger concept, directed at the total person. It includes vocational training and certainly contributes to the student's understanding of the array of occupations and the specific requirements of any one work role. (1979, p. 2)

Brolin and Kokaska (1979) have identified 22 major competencies that are essential to an individual's economic, social, and personal fulfillment. These competencies, listed below, are grouped into three skill areas: daily living, personal/social, and occupational guidance and preparation. Each of the competencies may be further broken down into 102 subcompetencies, with corresponding instructional objectives, each of which offers a basis for a comprehensive assessment of student needs over the school-aged years.

### Career Education Curriculum Competencies

**A. Daily Living Skills**

1. Managing family finances
2. Selecting, managing, and maintaining a home
3. Caring for personal needs
4. Raising children, living in families
5. Buying and preparing food
6. Buying and caring for clothing
7. Engaging in civic activities
8. Using recreation and leisure
9. Getting around the community, achieving mobility

---

*Portions of this section were researched and written by Linda Polin, now at the Center for the Study of Evaluation, University of California, Los Angeles.

### B. Personal-Social Skills

10. Achieving self-awareness
11. Acquiring self-confidence
12. Achieving socially responsible behavior
13. Maintaining good interpersonal skills
14. Achieving independence
15. Achieving problem-solving skills
16. Communicating adequately with others

### C. Occupational Guidance and Preparation

17. Knowing and exploring occupational possibilities
18. Selecting and planning occupational choices
19. Exhibiting appropriate work habits and behaviors
20. Exhibiting sufficient physical-manual skills
21. Obtaining a specific occupational skill
22. Seeking, securing, and maintaining employment (Kokaska, 1979, p. 14).

Most instruments that assess vocational and career needs are based on the goals of the program for which the particular assessment is being done. There appears to be great commonality among the goals of vocational and career programs established by the various state and local education agencies across the country. The following are examples:

1. employability,
   economic self-sufficiency,
   family living,
   personal habits, and
   communication ability (from Halpern, Raffeld, Irwin, & Fink, 1975a).

2. awareness of vocational education in context of personal capabilities;
   interests;
   positive self-concept, motivation;
   positive attitude toward work world;
   increased understanding or relationship of the U.S. economic system and work to one's own economic situation;
   achievement of necessary consumer awareness; and
   increased responsibility (from California State Department of Education, 1974).

3. self-awareness, self-worth;
confidence, increased self-concept;
greater understanding of interpersonal relationships;
discovering, developing, clarifying values system;
decision-making competency;
positive attitude toward world of work;
awareness of job trends likely in future; and
appreciation of leisure time, cultivation of hobbies, recreation activities (from Lewis, Simpson, & Miles, 1974).

Representative approaches to assessing vocational and career education needs are briefly described below. It is essential to remember that the problems of test bias discussed earlier also apply to career and vocational assessment. Fair (1980) cautions:

> The applicability of standard vocational instruments for handicapped members of minority groups should be questioned. The use of a single instrument to determine the vocational interest or attitudes of handicapped members of minority groups is not acceptable. Comprehensive vocational assessment is even more important with these students.   (p. 10)

1. *Rehabilitation Research and Training Center, University of Oregon, Eugene.* This center developed *The Social and Prevocational Information Battery* (Halpern et al., 1975b), which consists of nine tests measuring social, prevocational abilities in terms of the five long-range goals cited on p. 141. This battery was created from secondary curricula for educable mentally retarded students and was standardized against that population. An outstanding feature of these tests is their attempt to facilitate valid responses from handicapped students by avoiding reliance upon written presentation and response modes. Almost all of the items in the nine tests are exclusively oral in presentation, and often the response mode is simply placing a mark beside a pictorial representation, or indicating whether an item is true or false. Each test requires approximately 15 to 30 minutes to administer, is simple to score, and may be administered to a small group.

2. *Rocky Mountain Educational Laboratory* (1969) developed a pupil test battery for the social-affective area which includes an adaptation of an existing scale which they renamed *Opinions About Work*. The second test in this battery is the *Manpower Attitudes* test, developed by the Center for Economic Educa-

tion, College of Business Administration, Ohio State University. Both tests use a Likert-type scale for responses. Note that these tests were *not* developed for use with handicapped students. Both would likely require further adaptation in readability, and perhaps intellectual levels, before they would be appropriate for mildly or moderately handicapped students. The final test in this battery is called *Work Cases* and was developed from responses received from 50 large firms or corporations. The test consists of 10 case problems that involve values-related decisions.

3. *Yonkers Career Education Project* uses a diagnostic battery as the initial step in their program (LeVoci, n.d.). In addition to two standardized tests that measure academic achievement and assess relationships at home, at school, and with peers, the battery includes an adaptation of a vocational interest scale. Renamed *Occupational Awareness*, this test is used to determine the student's general level of understanding about job tasks, titles, and environments. The last test in this battery is the *Occupational Preference* test, described as a timed drawing experience in which the student draws eight occupations s/he would possibly want to pursue, and a ninth picture—his or her preferred choice. Student responses to both of these instruments are assessed verbally via student-teacher discussion. In addition to the formal assessment described above, the Yonkers model utilizes a "Recommendation Sheet" as the next step in assessment toward planning. The educational planning team reviews the results of the battery and provides further recommendations or other assessment information related to program goals. The recommendation sheet stays with the student, providing a cumulative record of data from the battery and other (e.g., observational) assessments. The educational planning team then completes a Prescriptive Instructional Activities form where student progress on specific activities is continuously recorded.

The basic appeal of the Yonkers Career Education Project model is its openness to input and feedback related to short-term goals. Also, the diagnostic assessment battery does not rely exclusively on written presentation and response modes, and it allows for direct teacher input during prescription and planning.

The above noted program goals and test batteries offer assessment ideas for the affective and social awareness domain of vocational and career education. Readily assessable skills and achievement aptitudes areas of vocational and career education have a wealth of instruments; so only two will be mentioned below.

The *Differential Aptitudes Tests* (1966 forms L and M) consist of the following tests: verbal reasoning, numerical ability, abstract reasoning, clerical speed and accuracy, mechanical reasoning, space relations, and language usage.

*The Ohio Trade and Industrial Education Services* program (1972) includes achievement tests in 12 job areas (for example, carpentry, cosmetology, and dental assisting). Note that these tests were not designed specifically for exceptional students, and may require adaptation. Other excellent sources of information on skill and achievement assessment instruments in the area of vocational education include:

1. *Michigan Career Education Resources,*
   Michigan State University, Erickson Hall,
   East Lansing, Michigan 48824.
   Materials in this collection include prevocational skills assessment for special education students.

2. *National Center for Research in Vocational Education,*
   Ohio State University,
   1960 Kenny Road,
   Columbus, Ohio 43210.
   This center disseminates a variety of materials and products related to various aspects of vocational and career education, some of which focus on the needs of handicapped students.

3. *Project FIVE H (Formula for Improving Vocational Education for the Handicapped)*—a joint venture of the California State Department of Education, Chancellor's Office of the California Community Colleges, and University of California, Los Angeles (Extension). The second phase of the project, FIVE H II, resulted in two products that contain components on vocational assessment. For further information, contact:
   J. Lyman Goldsmith, Director,
   Room 617, UCLA Extension Administration Building,
   10995 Le Conte Avenue,
   Los Angeles, CA 90024

4. *Project SERVE*
   Descriptive information about assessment and instructional methods used in this high school and post-high school vocational program for special needs students may be obtained by writing to:

Charles Wrobel, Director of Student Personnel and Special Services,
Project SERVE,
3300 Century Avenue W.,
White Bear Lake, Minnesota 55110

## Assessing Reward Preferences

Motivation is an important but often neglected type of student entry behavior. A child's willingness to perform a given task is related to variables such as fear of failure and interest in the task. Interest can often be stimulated by providing appropriate and meaningful reinforcement. Cartwright and Cartwright (1970) have developed a technique called *Modified Reward Preference Assessment.* Five reward categories are used: (a) adult approval, (b) competition, (c) consumables, (d) peer approval, and (e) independence. The teacher lists four appropriate sample rewards in each category and develops sets of test cards; each card depicts sample rewards from two different categories (for example, Adult Approval/Independence: "Teacher gives you an A"/"Free time in the classroom.") The cards then are presented systematically to each student. The child makes one choice per card and the choices are tallied for each reward category. The category with the highest number of choices is then assumed to be the most preferred. Validity of the results can be tested in the classroom by providing various forms of the preferred type of reward for acceptable performance. Stellern and Vasa (1973) use a *Reinforcement Inventory* (pp. 187–88) to help identify what the learner regards as rewarding and aversive (unpleasant). The inventory contains questions such as "What do you like to read?" and "I will do almost anything to avoid. . . ." Dunn and Dunn (1975) present an extensive *Learning Style Questionnaire* (pp. 95–110) that includes 22 items related to what motivates the student. The information gained from the student can then be used to increase the success of planned intervention strategies. Less formalized approaches to determine what students find rewarding or reinforcing are discussed in the context of a total contingency management system by Langstaff and Volkmor (1975).

## Assessing Social and Affective Behavior

In this area we are concerned with the student's ability to relate to other persons, to display a positive view of him/herself, and to profit from life experiences. Ward et al. (1973) point out that the two major sources for self-concept development are the student's direct experience with success and failure, and the feedback s/he receives from other people regarding personal strengths and weaknesses. For the mainstreamed mildly handicapped student, the development and protection of a positive self-view is of heightened importance and it is the responsibility of educators to assist the students in developing behaviors that will result in the attainment of peer assimilation and acceptance so that the social milieu of the regular class will be beneficial rather than damaging to the self-concept (Kaufman, Gotlieb, Agard, & Kukic, 1975). Sociometric techniques are often a helpful starting point.

Generally, teachers and resource teachers are not qualified to administer or interpret personality tests or tests of social development. For this reason, this section will present only informal approaches. Situational observation and interviewing are the two main techniques that can assist the teacher to identify social-emotional problems. Actually, observation has some distinct advantages over interviewing and other self-report techniques in this behavioral realm since it is not so dependent upon the child's trust in the teacher (interviewer). Lister (1969, p. 181) offers a number of situations in which the student can be observed which will provide a picture of his/her personal and social effectiveness.

1. informal discussion periods
2. self-directed activities
3. discussion of controversial issues
4. informal social activities outside the classroom
5. role-playing and drama
6. creative art activities
7. on the playground

Lister (1969) cites several behaviors, including dishonesty, withdrawal, fatigue, and over-identification with adults, which he describes as "external symptoms represent(ing) the coping efforts of children who view themselves as inadequate to meet the challenges and opportunities of their daily lives" (p. 184). Assessment techniques presented by Lister (1969) include the following:

1. *Expressive Methods,* such as drama, role-playing, or art productions, can provide clues as to how the student views him/herself and others. These approaches are extremely open to the problems of personal bias on the part of the teacher and must be used with utmost caution. Selective data-gathering

to support our own beliefs about a child's problems must be avoided. In addition, many of the expressive techniques are quite powerful and should not be attempted by the inexperienced.

2. *Self-Report Techniques* include interviews, open-ended questions, questionnaire checklists, autobiographies, and diaries. Many of these methods are discussed thoroughly in a book on values by Raths, Harmin, and Simon (1978). Respect for the student's privacy is critical here.

3. *Leaderless Groups* in which students discuss a topic and report on the group consensus, or work out assigned problems, provide a vehicle for the study of leadership and cooperation.

In summary, the assessment process, as it relates to the social, personal, and affective behavior of mildly handicapped students, should focus on identifying those behaviors that enable the student to function effectively and joyfully with normal agemates—behaviors that can be nurtured and strengthened in the classroom milieu by caring teachers. Clinical evaluations of personality dynamics should be left to other competent specialists such as school psychologists and therapists who should be consulted immediately when significantly deviant emotional or social behaviors are noted. The essence here, as in all assessment, is to find out what students need educationally. As David Nyberg writes in his powerful book, *Tough and Tender Learning*:

> Feeling good about yourself is necessary for doing most things well . . ., and it is certainly necessary for sensing any joy in being conscious. It would therefore seem to me that all the motivation junk that teachers are supposed to learn and use on students means nothing more than learning how to notice what kids are telling you they need in order to feel good about themselves so they can get on with whatever mysteries are calling them. (1971, p. 32)

## PLANNING ASSESSMENT—A SYSTEMS APPROACH

As implied earlier, process testing and skill testing are based on two very different theoretical models—the ability training model and the task analysis model (Ysseldyke & Salvia, 1974). Although we are emphasizing skill testing in this chapter, there is a place in the assessment phase for process testing as well. Our intent is to present an argument for a *systems* approach, which allows the learning process itself—not psychometric tools—to be the initial, and indeed primary, vehicle for assessment of the mildly or moderately handicapped.

A system approach to educational assessment is based on three basic assumptions:*

1. In studying student behavior, we cannot ignore the values, customs, beliefs, and languages that are part of the student's experiential background. Assessment data must be collected so that the identification of learner differences is related to environmental demands at home and at school, rather than solely to conditions within the learner.
2. Assessment is an individualized process, focusing only on those areas where there are questions about the student's performance. A basic assessment battery, administered to every student who is referred, is not appropriate.
3. Parents are included as knowledgeable partners in the assessment process; their involvement and informed consent are not invited as a courtesy, but extended as a legal right.

A systems, or sequential, approach to assessment involves four phases. Data from one phase are used to make decisions about information needed in the next phase. Initial assessment ends when sufficient data on the learner's instructional needs have been gathered to make sound placement and programming recommendations.

*Phase I:* School Variables
- Educational History/School Records
- Classroom/School Functioning (peer, teacher interaction, classroom management, teaching/learning style)
- Health/Medical History
- Language Use/Dominance

*Phase II:* Skill Variables
- Language Development/Proficiency
- Basic Skills (self-help; reading, math, and so forth)
- Social/Affective Functioning
- Vocational/Career Interests and Skills
- Motor Skills

---

*Discussion of these assumptions and the four phases of assessment are based on a paper, "An Ecological Approach to Assessment," by Andrea Carroll, Gabriele Gurski, and Keren McIntyre included in Pasanella, A. L., *Module III—Assessment*, a training program developed for the California State Department of Education, 1978.

*Phase III:* Adaptive Behavior/Medical Variables
- Home/Community Role Functioning
- Medical Assessment
- Developmental History

*Phase IV:* Ability Variables
- Sensorimotor Functioning
- Cognitive/Intellectual Functioning
- Psycholinguistic Abilities
- Psychological Adjustment

For many students who are referred from the regular classroom, it will be appropriate to begin with Phase I assessment: situational and variables and health factors that may have impact on student performance. The implication of the systems approach is that we should only proceed to Phase IV assessment when we have ruled out the possibility that the student's learning problems in school are due to such factors as inappropriate instructional methods, poor hearing, conflict between expectations of the home and the school, and so on. Also inherent in this approach is the notion that assessment should begin with informal techniques and proceed, if necessary, to the use of formal or standardized assessment devices.

# An Assessment Plan

Based on the questions raised by the Referral Analysis (see Chapter 3), the assessment team, or a subgroup of its members, meet to plan how any needed assessment will be conducted. An Assessment Plan is a written statement of *why* the assessment is to done, *what* assessment instruments and techniques are proposed; and *who* (classroom teacher, psychologist, and so forth) will conduct the assessment. As the plan is developed, decisions are made as to whether to begin with observation or interviews, and whether certain tests should be administered. A sample format for an Assessment Plan appears as Figure 5. When completed, the plan is presented to the student's parents with a request for their consent to the proposed assessment. For non-English-speaking parents, or parents who do not use a written language, all of the information on the form must be translated into their home language and/or communicated to them in such a way that their informed consent may be obtained. At this time parents would also be notified of their rights and of procedures to appeal any recommendations with which they disagree that result from the assessment.

**Figure 5**

Proposed Assessment Plan for _____

_____ has been referred for individual assessment. The purpose of this assessment is to: _____

_____. Assessment is planned as indicated below.

_____
Date

| | School Variables | ✓ | Assessment instruments/ techniques | Person responsible | Completion date |
|---|---|---|---|---|---|
| I | School Variables | | | | |
| | 1. Educational history | | | | |
| | 2. Classroom functioning | | | | |
| | 3. Health/Medical history | | | | |
| | 4. Language use/Dominance | | | | |
| II | Skill Variables | | | | |
| | 7. Language development/ proficiency | | | | |
| | 8. Basic skills (reading, math, and so forth) | | | | |
| | 9. Social/Affective | | | | |
| | 10. Vocational/Career | | | | |
| | 11. Motor | | | | |
| III | Adaptive Behavior/ Medical Variables | | | | |
| | 12. Home/Community role functioning | | | | |
| | 13. Medical Assessment | | | | |
| | 14. Developmental history | | | | |
| IV | Ability Variables | | | | |
| | 15. Sensorimotor | | | | |
| | 16. Cognitive/Intellectual | | | | |
| | 17. Psycholinguistic | | | | |
| | 18. Psychological Adjustment | | | | |

ASSESSMENT CANNOT BEGIN UNTIL A COPY OF THIS FORM HAS BEEN SIGNED AND RETURNED.

I hereby give my permission for the assessment described above to be made. I understand that the results will be kept confidential and that I will be invited to a meeting to discuss the results.

_____          _____
Signature of Parent/Guardian                              Date

## Considerations in Providing Nondiscriminatory Assessment

Rhetoric dealing with the issue of bias in assessment frequently focuses specifically on the assessment instruments themselves. Indeed, in Chapter 4, we pointed out some of the problems inherent in the use of standardized tests. Our position is, however, that merely using different tests, or using existing tests in a different manner, is a limited response to the mandate to provide a fair assessment of learning needs. Nondiscriminatory assessment is an exceedingly complex area, and one deserving of much more indepth discussion than can be provided in this text. There are no simple answers or easy solutions to the reduction or elimination of bias in assessment. Here are some important points to consider as we strive to protect the rights of children.

1. Assessment must be viewed within the context of the educational decision-making process presented in Chapter 2. In this context it is an ongoing activity intimately related to instruction and not merely a one-time measure of student performance or abilities. We need to guard against the introduction of bias at each step in the process.

2. We must be conscious of our own beliefs, values, attitudes and of how they influence the assessment procedures we select, the way we use them, and how we interpret their results.

3. We must have a positive regard for cultural and linguistic differences and assume the responsibility for studying how these differences may effect both school and test performance. We need to be able to distinguish between behaviors that are deviant and those that are developmentally appropriate given a particular child's social, cultural, or language background. To do this we must study the "interaction between the behavior of an individual and the various environmental contexts in which that behavior occurs" (Thurman, 1977, p. 329).

4. We need to gather and use *all* the relevant data from *all* available sources as bases for making decisions about a student's school placement or instructional program.

5. The whole decision-making process, from screening to review of the IEP, should be designed to ensure fair treatment of *all* students. Efforts to provide nondiscriminatory assessments are not to be limited to the special characteristics of children for minority groups.

Essentially we support Tucker's (1977) view that:

- There is no magical test, or test battery, that is nonbiased or culturally fair.
- We cannot waste any more time looking for such tests.
- We do *not* need to totally abandon the use of standardized tests.
- We *do* need to learn to use more appropriately the assessment resources currently available to gather information about the motivations, aspirations, values, learning styles of the children and families we serve.

A view of assessment as only one step in a multi-step educational decision-making process and the use of a systems approach based on a sound understanding of the strengths and weaknesses of various assessment procedures is currently our best safeguard.

## REPORTING ASSESSMENT OUTCOMES

The assessment phase culminates with a report on the outcomes. The assessment report should provide data in answer to two questions:

- Does a handicapping condition exist?
- Does the child require special education and/or related services to meet his/her unique educational needs? (National Association of State Directors of Special Education, 1978. p. 5)

Even when the answer to one or both questions is "No," a report should be prepared, discussed with the student's parents, and forwarded to the person who first referred the student. When both of the above questions can be answered "Yes," the assessment report will become the data base for the design of the student's IEP.

The types of information the IEP team will need from the assessment report are:

1. *a statement of present levels of performance,* written in behavioral as well as in clinical terms;
2. the *implications* of such levels of eligibility and programming;
3. *recommendations* for goals/objectives and for special techniques;
4. *supporting data* including:

    (a) *test results:* The tests administered for placement should be specified, and their conclusions should be clear. The techniques used to obtain programming assessment data should present information in appropriate instructional areas, such as the various aspects of reading (comprehensive, word attack and so on). If instruction is needed in physical areas, the report of a specialist might be needed to describe what these areas are, what to do, and where to begin.

(b) descriptions of any *conditions that may have affected the validity of the tests used*, including any obvious disabilities and situational variables. (National Association of State Directors of Special Education, 1978, p. 6)

If the assessment report is to be relevant to instructional planning, the student's educational needs must be clearly defined. In order to make a precise determination of student needs, it will be necessary to analyze, summarize, and compare all the various pieces of information gathered through assessment. It requires a great deal of practice to effectively use assessment data to develop sound instructional recommendations. Cross-validating data across and within tests and comparing it with observation and interview information is a necessary step when a variety of assessment techniques have been used. Needs statements should be supported by at least two sources of evidence.

Sabatino (1972) suggests that a learning profile be prepared for each student that includes: a diagnostic summary, a graphic picture of academic achievement, and a statement on the student's preferred reinforcers. *An Individual Student Profile Form*, used by the South Carolina Region V Resource Room Project (1975), summarizes weaknesses and strengths and specifies the student's best sensory mode. (See p. 154.)

Various formats can be used to state, summarize, and prioritize student needs. Regardless of format, arranging need statements in priority order is critical for instructional planning and teaching. Care should be taken to express the assessment findings in a way that they will not be detrimental to the child's progress after she/he returns to the regular program. This is best accomplished through emphasizing the student's positive aspects as well as areas where change or improvement are needed.

In summary, the best guideline for determining student needs is the discrepancy between his/her level and manner of functioning and the instructional processes of the regular classroom.

*Individual Profile Form\**

INDIVIDUAL PROFILE FOR Jimmy (Case Study #1)

  I. *Weaknesses*
    1. Language—can't find right words for definitions (expressive)
    2. Would rather give up than struggle for word attack skills
    3.
    4.

  II. *Strengths*
    1. Arithmetic
    2. Factual information
    3. Good understanding of directions and explanations
    4. Sports—is a good team member

  III. *Best Sensory Mode*
    Assumption: Visual, Kinesthetic
    *Best Reinforcer*
    Sport related activities

  IV. *Academic Performance (current)*
    Reading 1.9  Spelling 1.7  Math 6.1

  V. *Areas of Needed Remediation (i.e., beginning blends digraph; carrying with 2 place addends)*
    1. Verify vowel sound understanding
    2. Sound blending
    3. Syllabication rules—for sophisticated sound blending (5th grader needs to feel this blending is not "baby junk.")
    4.

  VI. *Materials Recommended for Specific Remediation*
    1. Conquests—(1 to 1, then present on cassette)
    2. *Linguistic Reader*
    3. Language Master for reinforcing activity
    4. Graflex for reinforcing activity

  VII. *Anticipated Area of Highest Achievement*
    Reading. Spelling level will always be lower than reading.

  VIII. *Recommendations to Classroom Teacher*
    Continue to support and praise his math achievement, schedule resource room so it does not interfere.

  IX. *Method for Evaluation*
    Oral review and test.

---

\*South Carolina Region V Educational Services Center, *The Resource Room: An Access to Excellence*, 1975, p. 27.

## Study Questions and Activities

1. How does a systems approach to assessment of the mildly handicapped differ from traditional approaches to assessment in special education? What additional variables are assessed in the former (especially where classroom observation is emphasized) that are often overlooked in the latter?

2. Review the issue of process versus skill testing presented in Chapter 4. How does a systems approach to assessment resolve this issue?

3. Brainstorm the minimal survival skills (preacademic, academic, and social) for succeeding in an elementary or secondary school (can orally read class texts at 80 words correct per minute, can answer literal, interpretive and critical comprehension questions on material read, can work cooperatively with classmates on class projects, completes written assignments accurately and on time; can assert own rights, and so forth). Divide into teams of two or three and task analyze each terminal objective into subskills. Use the hierarchy of subskills generated to develop a placement test or rating scale to assess informally a pupil's baseline for the purpose of planning remediation and evaluating pupil progress.

## References

Affleck, J. Q., Lowenbraun, S., & Archer, A. *Teaching the mildly handicapped in the regular classroom* (2nd ed.). Columbus, Ohio: Charles E. Merrill, 1980.

Bartel, N. Assessing and remediating problems in language development. In D. D. Hammill & N. R. Bartel (Eds.), *Teaching children with learning and behavior problems.* Boston: Allyn and Bacon, 1978.

Bartel, N. R. Problems in arithmetic achievement. In D. D. Hammill & N. R. Bartel (Eds.), *Teaching children with learning and behavior problems.* Boston: Allyn and Bacon, 1978.

Bender, L. *The Bender Visual Motor Gestalt Test for Children.* Los Angeles: Western Psychological Services, 1962.

Bennett, G. K., Seashore, H. G., & Wesman, A. G. *The differential aptitude tests.* New York: The Psychological Corporation, 1966.

Boyd, J. E. Teaching children with reading problems. In D. D. Hammill & N. R. Bartel (Eds.), *Teaching children with learning and behavior problems.* Boston: Allyn and Bacon, 1975.

Brabner, G. Reading skills. In R. M. Smith (Ed.), *Teacher diagnosis of educational difficulties.* Columbus, Ohio: Charles E. Merrill, 1969.

Brolin, D. E. & Kokaska, C. J. *Career education for handicapped children and youth.* Columbus, Ohio: Charles E. Merrill, 1979.

Buswell, G. T., & John, L. *Diagnostic chart for fundamental processes in arithmetic.* Indianapolis, Ind.: Bobbs-Merrill, 1925.

California State Department of Education. *Career education: A position paper on career development and preparation in California.* Sacramento, Ca.: Author, 1974.

Carrow, E. *Test of auditory comprehension of language.* Austin, Texas: Urban Research Group, 1973.

Carrow, E. *Carrow elicited language inventory.* Austin, Texas: Learning Concepts, 1974.

Cartwright, C. A., & Cartwright, G. P. Determining the motivational systems of individual children. *Teaching Exceptional Children,* 1970, 2 (6), 143–149.

Dunn, L. M. *Peabody Picture Vocabulary Test.* Circle Pines, Minn.: American Guidance Service, 1965.

Dunn, R. & Dunn, K. *Educator's self-teaching guide to individualizing instructional programs.* West Nyack, N. Y.: Parker Publishing Co., 1975.

Fair, G. W. Career education and minority handicapped students, *Career Development for Exceptional Students,* 1980, 3 (1), 3–11.

Farr, R., & Anastasiow, N. *Tests of reading readiness and achievements: A review and evaluation.* Newark, Dela.: International Reading Association, 1969.

Foster, C. R., Giddan, J. J., & Stark, J. ACLC: *Assessment of children's language comprehension.* Palo Alto, Calif.: Consulting Psychologists Press, 1972.

Frostig, M., Maslow, P., Lefever, D. W., & Whittlesey, J. R. B. *The Marianne Frostig Developmental Test of Visual Perception.* Palo Alto, Calif.: Consulting Psychologists Press, 1964.

Graham, F. K., & Kendall, B. S. Memory for designs test: revised general manual. *Perceptual and Motor Skills,* 1960, 11 (2), 147–190.

Halpern, A. S., Raffeld, P., Irwin, L., & Fink, R. Measuring social and prevocational awareness in mildly retarded adolescents. *American Journal of Mental Deficiency,* 1975, 80 (1), 81–89. (a)

Halpern, A. S., Raffeld, P., Irwin, L., & Fink R. *The Social and Prevocational Information Battery.* Rehabilitation Research and Training Center in Mental Retardation, Eugene, Oregon: University of Oregon Press, 1975. (b)

Hammill, D. D. Assessing and training perceptual-motor processes. In D.

D. Hammill & N. R. Bartel (Eds.), *Teaching children with learning and behavior problems*. Boston: Allyn and Bacon, 1975.

Hammill, D. D., & Bartel, N. R. (Eds.). *Teaching children with learning and behavior problems* (2nd ed.). Boston: Allyn and Bacon, 1978.

Kaufman, M. J., Gottlieb, J., Agard, J. A., & Kukic, M. B. Mainstreaming: Toward an explication of the construct. *Focus on Exceptional Children*, 1975, *7* (3), 1–12.

Kirk, S. A., McCarthy, J. J., & Kirk, W. *Illinois Test of Psycholinguistic Abilities*. Urbana, Ill.: University of Illinois Press, 1968.

Kokaska, C. J. What is career education? *Exceptional Teacher*, 1979, *1* (5), 1, 2, 14, 15.

Langstaff, A. L., & Volkmor, C. B. *Contingency management*. Columbus, Ohio: Charles E. Merrill, 1975.

LaPray, M., & Ross, R. The graded word list: Quick gauge of reading ability. *Journal of Reading*, 1969, *12* (4), 305–307.

Larsen, S., & Hammill, D. D. The relationship of selected visual perceptual skills to academic abilities. *Journal of Special Education*. 1975, *9* (3), 281–291.

Lee, L. L. *Northwestern Syntax Screening Test*. Evanston, Ill.: Northwestern University Press, 1971.

LeVoci, J. P. Career education: Implication for special education. Career Education Monograph Series, n.d. (4) Yonkers, N.Y.: Yonkers Career Education Model Projection.

Lewis, J., Simpson, D., & Miles, D. *Student needs assessment guide* (A Component of the Community Experience Based Career Exploratory Program for Vale Middle School and a Sixco Project). Vale, Ore.: School District 15, and Salem, Ore.: Oregon State Department of Education, Division of Community Colleges and Career Education, 1974.

Liles, R. D. Strategies for non-biased assessment of diverse linguistic behaviors. (Mimeo) Paper prepared for California State Department of Education, Sacramento, 1979.

Lister, J. L. Personal-emotional-social skills. In R. M. Smith (Ed.), *Teacher diagnosis of educational difficulties*. Columbus, Ohio: Charles E. Merrill, 1969.

Los Angeles Unified School District, Special Education Division, *System FORE—An Approach to individualizing instruction*. Los Angeles, 1972.

National Association of State Directors of Special Education. *Writing individualized assessment reports in special education: A resource manual*. Washington, D. C., 1978.

Newcomer, P. L. & Hammill, D. D., *Test of Language Development*. Austin, Texas: Empiric Press, 1977.

Nyberg, D. *Tough and tender learning.* Palo Alto, Calif.: National Press, 1971.

Pasanella, A. L. *Module III: Assessment.* Sacramento, Calif.: California State Department of Education, 1978.

Raths, L. E., Harmin, M., & Simon, S. B. *Values and teaching: Working with values in the classroom.* (2nd Ed.) Columbus, Ohio: Charles E. Merrill, 1978.

Rocky Mountain Education Laboratories. Image of the world of work (Volume II). *Development of Instruments and Evaluation.* Greeley, Colo.: Author, 1969.

Semel, E. M. & Wiig, E. H. *Clinical evaluation of language functions.* Columbus, Ohio: Charles E. Merrill, 1980.

Smith, R. M. Perceptual-motor skills. In R. M. Smith (Ed.), *Teacher diagnosis of educational difficulties.* Columbus, Ohio: Charles E. Merrill, 1969.

Smith, R. M. (Ed.). *Teacher diagnosis of educational difficulties.* Columbus, Ohio: Charles E. Merrill, 1969.

South Carolina Region V Educational Services Center. *The resource room: An access to excellence.* Lancaster, S. C.: Author, 1975.

Spencer, E. F., & Smith, R. M. Arithmetic skills. In R. M. Smith (Ed.), *Teacher diagnosis of educational difficulties.* Columbus, Ohio: Charles E. Merrill, 1969.

Stellern, J., & Vasa, S. F. *A primer of diagnostic-prescriptive teaching and programming.* Laramie, Wyo.: Center for Research, Service and Publication, College of Education, University of Wyoming, 1973.

Thurman, S. K. Congruence of behavioral ecologies: A model for special education programming. *Journal of Special Education, 1977, 11* (3), 329–333.

Tucker, J. A. Operationalizing the diagnostic-intervention process. In T. Oakland (Ed.), *Psychological and educational assessment of minority children.* N.Y.: Bruner/Mazel, 1977.

Ward, M. E., Cartwright, G. P., Cartwright, C. A., Campbell, J., & Spinazola, C. *Diagnostic teaching of preschool and primary children.* The Pennsylvania State University: Computer Assisted Instruction Laboratory, College of Education, 1973.

White, O. R. & Haring, N. G. *Exceptional teaching: A multimedia training package.* Columbus, Ohio: Charles E. Merrill, 1980.

Wiig, E. H., & Semel, E. M. *Language assessment and intervention for the learning disabled.* Columbus, Ohio: Charles E. Merrill, 1980.

Ysseldyke, J. E., & Salvia, J. Diagnostic-prescriptive teaching: Two models. *Exceptional Children, 1974, 41* (3), 181–185.

# Resources

Babikan, E., & Buchanan, A. *Developing a system of criterion referenced assessment: Reteaching cycles in textbook supported mathematics instruction.* Los Angeles: Southwest Regional Laboratory. The system described in this paper may be applied to any math text. Describes how to establish desired instructional outcomes and create criterion exercises.

Baxter, I., Barber, L., & Thurber, G. *Development and implementation of secondary special education programs.* Lansing, Mich.: Michigan State Department of Education, 1975.

Clymer, T. (Ed.). *Reading 360.* Boston: Ginn and Company, 1969. Criterion-referenced reading assessment and materials for elementary through junior high school levels.

Connolly, A. J., Natchman, W., & Pritchett, E. M. *Key Math: Diagnostic Arithmetic Test.* Circle Pines, Minn.: American Guidance Services, 1971. A criterion-referenced test providing four levels of diagnostic information for students in grades kindergarten through nine.

*Diagnosis: Level A.* Chicago: Science Research Associates, 1973. This package contains 34 criterion-referenced tests of reading skills (grades 1–4). Also included are: *Survey Test; Prescription Guide; Class Progress Wall Chart;* and *Teacher's Handbook.*

Gooden, B. L. *Career development guides: Special education.* Jefferson City, Mo.: Missouri State Department of Education, Research Coordinating Unit, and Montgomery County K–2 Public Schools, n.d.

Howell, K. W., Kaplan, J. S., & O'Connell, C. Y. *Evaluating exceptional children: A task analysis approach.* Columbus, Ohio: Charles E. Merrill, 1979.

*Individual Pupil Monitoring System.* Boston: Houghton-Mifflin. A series of criterion-referenced tests to measure pupil performance on specific math objectives. Objectives are cross-referenced to the most widely used mathematics programs (elementary).

*Language Arts Skill Center.* New York: Random House. A Criterion-referenced system for assessing and remediating vocabulary, spelling and punctuation skills at the regular junior high school level.

Mann, P. H., & Suiter, P. *Handbook in diagnostic teaching: A learning disabilities approach.* Boston: Allyn and Bacon, 1974. A practical handbook for teachers, containing techniques and ideas for assessing learning skills and for individualizing instruction. Directions on how to develop assessment inventories and criterion-referenced tests are given. Spelling and reading inventories are provided.

Mercer, J. R. et al. *System of multi-pluralistic assessment* (SOMPA). New York: Psychological Cooperation, 1977–78. A culturally specific assessment model consisting of a structured family interview, an adaptive behavior inventory, a health history inventory, and pluralistic norms for use with the WISC–R.

Meyers, E.S., Ball, H. H., & Crutchfield, M. *The kindergarten teacher's handbook.* Los Angeles: Gramercy, 1974. This book contains informal assessment procedures to be used by the kindergarten teacher in cooperation with the school psychologist. Techniques for planning individualized instruction are discussed; also included are charts and record forms.

Ohio State Center for Vocational and Technical Education. Ohio State University, 1900 Kenny Rd., Columbus, Ohio: Thelma Turner, Publications Department, (614) 486–3655.

Pletcher, B. *A guide to assessment instruments for limited English speaking students.* New York: Santillana Publishing Co., 1978.

*Santa Clara Inventory of Developmental Tasks.* Huntington Beach, Calif.: Richard L. Zweig Associates, 1974. An indexed notebook of assessment tasks and materials for children from birth through seven years.

Saville-Troike, M. *Bilingual children: A resource document.* Arlington, Va: The Center for Applied Linguistics, 1973.

Shepard, L. Norm-referenced vs. criterion-referenced tests. *Educational Horizons*, 1979, *58* (1), 26–32.

Silverman, R. and Russell, R. *Oral language tests for bilingual students: An evaluation of language dominance and proficiency instruments.* Portland, OR: Northwest Regional Educational Laboratory, 1977.

Stephens, T. M., Hartman, A. C., & Lucas, V. H. *Teaching children basic skills: A curriculum handbook.* Columbus, Ohio: Charles E. Merrill, 1978.

# 6

# Designing the IEP

> The movement toward the individualization of instruction, involving the participation of the child and the parent, as well as all relevant educational professionals, is a trend gaining ever wider support in educational, parental, and political groups throughout the nation. (Report of the U.S. House of Representatives, 1975, p. 13)

Individualizing programs to accommodate individual differences in children has been an objective of the American educational system for years. P.L. 94–142 mandates provision of an individualized education program (IEP) for all handicapped students. This mandate for the handicapped could well serve as the impetus toward providing a quality education for *all* children.

*The IEP defined.* For the past five years, school personnel across the nation have been developing procedures and forms necessary to comply with the IEP mandate. At the same time, educators have been concerned with interpreting the law and its regulations. What is the real meaning and intent of the law? The IEP is defined in P.L. 94–142 as:

> a written statement for each handicapped child developed in any meeting by a representative of the local education agency or an

intermediate educational unit who shall be qualified to provide, or supervise the provision of, specifically designed instruction to meet the unique needs of handicapped children, the teacher, the parents or guardian of such child, and whenever appropriate, such child, which statement shall include (A) a statement of the present levels of educational performance of such child, (B) a statement of annual goals, including short-term instructional objectives, (C) a statement of the specific educational related services to be provided to the child, and the extent to which the child will be able to participate in regular educational programs, (D) the projected date for initiation and anticipated duration of such services; and (E) appropriate objective criteria and evaluation procedures and schedules for determining, on at least an annual basis, whether instructional objectives are being achieved. (Refer to Section 4(a) (19) of the Act.)

Ballard and Zettel (1977) elaborate on the meaning of the term *Individualized Education Program:*

- *individualized* means that the IEP must be addressed to the educational needs of a single child rather than a class or group of children;
- *education* means that the IEP is limited to those elements of the child's education that are more specifically special education and related services as defined by P.L. 94–142; and
- *program* means that the IEP is a statement of what will actually be provided to the child, as distinct from a plan that provides guidelines from which a program must subsequently be developed (p. 181).

There are two main parts to the IEP provision: first, the IEP *meeting* at which parents and school personnel jointly make decisions about a handicapped child's program, and secondly, the IEP *document* itself which is a record of the decisions reached at the meeting.

The actual writing of the IEP is only one step in the total Instructional Programming Process. It is the step in which professionals and parents come together to discuss, plan and document decisions based on the outcomes of the Identification, Referral and Assessment phases of the process. The purpose of this chapter is to provide information on the purpose, benefits, and required components of the IEP, and how it is written. We will also discuss some of the current issues related to "best practices"—taking the IEP mandate beyond paper compliance and toward quality of instruction.

# PURPOSE AND INTENT OF THE IEP

### What an IEP Is

1. The IEP is *an extension of procedural protections*—a safeguard for the child and his or her parents. Through the IEP, we recognize that the child should be treated as an individual with individual needs. The IEP is a technique for sharing decision-making powers among school personnel and parents.
2. The IEP is *a management tool*—a blueprint for instructional planning. It enables the school and parents to identify the student's strengths and needs and to focus on remediating those need areas. The IEP also enables the school and parents to measure and monitor student progress.
3. The IEP is a *compliance/monitoring document*. The IEP is a device to promote accountability on the part of the school and the parents and to assure that the child is receiving an appropriate education.
4. The IEP is *a communication vehicle*. The IEP helps make certain that all participants know and understand what the child's needs are, what will be provided, and what the expected results may be. It is a means of communication among planners, implementors and evaluators.
5. The IEP is *a sound educational practice*. Educators should be able to articulate what *every* child needs and what will be done to help him get there.

### What an IEP is Not

1. The IEP is *not a lesson plan*. It is a blueprint for an educational program that leads to more detailed planning on a day-to-day or week-to-week basis. It is a state or local option whether or not to require more detailed planning in the form of Individualized Implementation Plans (see Chapter 7).
2. The IEP is *not a contract*. Teachers do not get fired because a child does not meet the goals and objectives specified in the IEP. However, teachers and other educators must be able to demonstrate that they made a "good faith" effort to implement the student's IEP as written and/or attempted to revise the IEP if it was not working.

# THE IEP TEAM

Developing and writing the IEP is intended to be a *shared* responsibility. Teachers do not write it alone. The team approach to IEP development involves coordination, communication and cooperation of all those who have a part to play in planning and implementing a successful program for the child. The law requires the following participants at an IEP meeting:

- a representative of the local education agency, other than the child's teacher, who is qualified to provide or supervise the provision of special education.
- the child's teacher.
- one or both of the child's parents.
- the child, where appropriate.
- other individuals at the discretion of the parent or agency (Section 121a344 P.L. 94–142 Rules and Regulations).

## Representative of the Local Education Agency

This person is most often the school principal, a supervisor, or other representative of the school district. The critical element here is that this person must have *authority* to commit agency resources required to implement the IEP.

## The Child's Teacher

This is interpreted to be the teacher who knows the child best or the teacher who is currently working with the student. The classroom teacher knows the learning environment, how the child is functioning in the classroom, and has ideas on the methods and techniques required to meet the student's needs. The classroom teacher can also serve as a valuable communication link with and for the parents, for s/he is more likely to know the child's parents.

## The Parents

Of all the team members, parents know the child best. They have a great deal of information to contribute about the child's behavior, likes and dislikes, and interests outside of school. They are also an important link with the child's past educational history.

## The Child

Students are too often left out or denied an opportunity to be involved in their program development. The law includes the child, *where appropriate,* and leaves the determination as to when it is

# Designing the IEP

appropriate up to state and local agencies. Students, especially at the upper age levels, should provide input related to how they learn best, their own interests, and their goals for the future. Survey information collected by the Bureau for Education of the Handicapped (1979) indicated that almost 25% of students between ages 16–21, and 13% of students between 13–15 years of age, attended their IEP meetings.

### Other Individuals

The other persons who attend the meeting should be dictated by the *unique* needs of the child. The counselor, social worker, speech therapist, or resource teacher are examples of other school personnel who might attend. Others could also include an ally or support person of the parents' choice: friend, another teacher, or a parent advocate. In order to facilitate the decision-making process and in the interest of time and cost effectiveness, it is important to keep participants limited to those who have a direct part to play in the meeting. It has been reported that some IEP meetings have involved as many as 28 people!

When the student is being evaluated for the *first time,* a member of the evaluation team or someone knowledgeable about previous evaluation procedures used with the student *and* the results must participate in the IEP meeting. The team approach to planning offers the opportunity to:

1. share responsibilities.
2. utilize a broader information base.
3. conform to due process requirements.
4. cross-validate hypotheses.
5. involve persons with a wide variety of skills and competencies.

See chapter 2 for more detail on the team approach to planning.

## IEP COMPONENTS

There are seven required parts or components of an IEP. These are:

1. Present performance levels.
2. Annual goals.
3. Short-term objectives and appropriate criteria.
4. Specific special education and related services.

5. Projected dates for initiation and anticipated duration of services.
6. Extent of participation in regular education.
7. Evaluation procedures and schedule for an annual review of the IEP.

## Present Levels of Performance

The student's present levels of performance are derived from the results of the assessment. The goal of the assessment process is to identify learning needs and potential intervention techniques (See Chapters 4 and 5 for a detailed discussion of the assessment process and specific techniques). Following the assessment phase and the analysis of the data collected, the team should be ready to make statements about what the student *can* and *cannot* do. Present levels of functioning are not lists of test scores. They are statements that tell what the student *can* and *cannot do* in areas such as academic achievement, self-help skills, social adaptation, prevocational and vocational skills, or psychomotor skills. Present levels of performance focus on what the child can do *now* (specific skill levels) and what s/he needs to learn next. The following statements are examples of present performance levels.

- "Can drink from a cup"
- "Cannot match shapes"
- "Can solve subtraction problems with minuends of 5 or less"
- "Cannot fill out a job application form"
- "Can follow 1 word commands"
- "Can accept a task but cannot follow it to completion"
- "Can read a fourth grade reader with 90% accuracy"
- "Recognizes numbers to 100"
- "Makes random marks on paper"

The Bureau for Education of the Handicapped (1979) suggested some points to keep in mind when developing statements of the child's present levels of educational performance.

1. They should be written in clear, understandable language so that all participants at the meeting can interpret them.
2. They should be essentially able to stand on their own.
3. They should be based on the child's evaluation results.

# Designing the IEP

4. They should cover all special education and related services needs.
5. They should relate directly to the other components of the IEP, for example, annual goals, short-term objectives, special education, and related services.

## Annual Goals

Goals are global aim statements that describe what the student needs to learn over a *year's time*. The primary purpose of stating goals is to provide direction as to the emphases, activities, and outcomes of the learner's educational program. Goals may be developed in any of the areas specified under present levels of performance. Examples of goal statements might look like the following:

- Increase verbal communication.
- Improve self-help skills.
- Learn basic word attack skills.
- Improve spelling skills.
- Increase reading comprehension skills.

Since a number of goals could be identified for an individual student, it is important to prioritize them so that instruction can be focused on areas of primary concern—this will prevent the teacher and student from becoming overwhelmed and frustrated. The National Association of State Directors of Special Education (1976) suggests some guidelines for prioritizing goals.

1. What are the parents' primary concerns? Is there some skill the parents would really like their child to learn above all others?
2. What are the teacher's primary concerns? Is there a priority area or skill that would enable the student to function more successfully?
3. What are the developmental sequences of skills to be taught? Can one pinpoint gaps in this student's learning that should be attended to immediately?
4. What behaviors are most readily changed?
5. Are there critical areas of need that, if not attended to, would involve risk to the child and/or others?

Another point to consider when prioritizing goals is the child's age and time s/he has left in school. Goals for a 10th grade student who cannot read may focus on vocational preparation as opposed to reading per se.

In summary, annual goals describe what the student needs to learn and provide focus for instruction. Annual goals are based on identified learner needs, and, in turn, become the basis for short-term objectives.

## Short-term Objectives

Short-term objectives are outgrowths of the goal statements, and relate directly to each goal. Objectives are developed according to goal priority, and form the basis for the evaluation of student progress. The criteria specified within each objective enable us to determine when an educational target has been met and when to focus on new targets.

Objectives are written behaviorally, are time-referenced, and include a criteria for success and/or an evaluation process and technique. Objectives include four parts.

1. The date: projected date of accomplishment (*when*).
2. The terminal behavior: *what* the student will be able to do.
3. The conditions: *how* the student will perform the behavior and what materials the student will use.
4. The criteria: to what extent (a minimum standard of achievement).

Criteria are the minimal acceptable performance standards for the behavior. Criteria statements can focus on the number of behaviors, the time a behavior takes, the characteristics of the process of performing a behavior, and the characteristics of the product of a behavior. Objectives and criteria must be closely tied to the assessment results, the student's present performance level, and his/her past rate of learning. It is important to set *realistic* criteria or we may set ourselves up for automatic failure. If a student is currently reading at a rate of 5 words per minute, reading 100 words per minute may be very unrealistic. Criterion levels set at 100% accuracy may be difficult to attain (depending on the task), and in general, should be reserved for behaviors essential for safety such as crossing the street or tasks such as learning an address, phone number, or flying an airplane. Examples of criterion statements include the following:

- at least five times daily

# Designing the IEP

- with four out of five correct responses
- without assistance
- with 80% accuracy

Here is an example of an objective that contains all four of the above components—the date, the behavior, the conditions, and the criterion:

Date: By June, 1980

Terminal behavior: Writes answers to arithmetic problems

Conditions: Given an addition fact sheet sums 0–18

Criterion: At a rate of 60 digits per minute with two or less errors

There is a wealth of information available on how to write objectives, and some references on behavioral objectives are listed at the end of this chapter.

Below are some sample objectives taken from actual instructional plans written for individual students. Objectives are included for some of the specific areas listed under present performance levels.

---

*Reading*

(S) will be able to decode 80% of the words on a teacher-made list consisting of sight and phonic words found in a fourth grade reader after the year of instruction.

By June, 1980, (S) will be able to recognize, within two attempts, 85% of the words that have been taught to him through the Sullivan Programmed Reading Program.

*Written Language*

(S) will be able to reproduce drawing and cursive writing equal to his age-mates as measured by a teacher-made test at end of school year.

*Computational Skills*

(S) will write his times tables through 10 at 80% accuracy on teacher-made test by end of school year.

By June, 1980 (S) will count to 20 by rote with 100% accuracy.
(S) will balance 30 entries in a checkbook with 100% accuracy, by the end of November.

*Self Concept*

(S) will be able to go into a "K" or first grade class on a regular basis as a tutor and teacher helper 45 minutes a day.

*School Adjustment*

To establish a demeanor and attitude with peers that involves impulsive pushing, shoving, or hitting no more than 10 times a day or 30% of the time.

*Vocational and Career Development*

(S) will be able to define and list common labor union terminology with 80% accuracy. (S) will be able to describe one particular future job and how s/he would prepare for it (that is, education s/he thinks the job would require, special skills, and so forth, at the end of a semester of instruction).

---

There has been some confusion about the meaning of *"objectives"* intended by P.L. 94–142. The Bureau for Education of the Handicapped (1979) moved to clarify the intent of the law when they issued the statement that "short-term instructional objectives are simply outcomes or milestones for indicating progress toward meeting the annual goals" (p. 12). ". . . the 'short-term instructional objectives' in the IEP requirement are not intended to address the specifics that are traditionally found in daily, weekly, or monthly instructional plans." (p. 13).

## Specific Educational Services

The Individualized Education Program must include specific special education and related services necessary to enable the student to accomplish his or her annual goals and short-term objectives. These services must be documented without regard to the availability of those services. This means that the team should list not only those needed services available within the agency but *all* services needed to meet the child's educational needs. The rules and regulations for P.L. 94–142 list "related services" such as transportation, speech pathology, audiology, psychological services, physical and occupational therapy, recreation, counseling services, assessment and medical

# Designing the IEP

services for diagnostic purposes, school health services, social work service in schools, and parent counseling) (Section 121a.13, P.L. 94-142 Rules and Regulations). Related services, then, are those additional services a student needs in order to benefit from special educational instruction.

## Extent of Regular Classroom Participation

The amount of time the student will spend in the regular classroom must be noted on the IEP. This can range from zero, for a most severely handicapped student who needs a more restrictive setting, to 100% for the student whose needs can be met primarily in the regular classroom but who may also need the services of an itinerant teacher of the visually handicapped or perhaps some resource teacher support.

## Dates for Initiation and Duration of Services (Time Lines)

The date when each service will begin and the length of time that service will be given is required. It is also necessary to indicate how often the service will be rendered—for example, "speech therapy three times per week for 30 minutes." Commitment of services and resources must be clear to all team members.

## Evaluation Procedures and Review Date

There must be a means or a method for collecting progress data from implementors and for comparing this data to the criteria set in the short-term objective. Evaluation procedures tell *how* progress data will be collected—for example, via teacher-made tests, student work samples, observation checklists, or criterion-referenced tests. For a valid evaluation of progress, the procedures utilized should be the same as those used in the initial assessment. In other words, pre and post procedures should be the same. If the assessment results yield precise information on skill levels, and if more informal types of assessment are incorporated into assessment plans (such as observation, and criterion-referenced measures), then specifying evaluation procedures will not be too difficult, and the collection of progress data should be less time-consuming. Evaluation procedures for each short-term objective must be listed on the IEP.

The law requires that the IEP be reviewed and/or revised at least annually. A review of the student's IEP may be requested at any time by the child's teacher, parents, or other school personnel.

Other review points may occur if the child transfers into another district, county, or state, and also if there is a change in placement. Key questions for the annual review meeting revolve around the extent to which objectives have been met. If there has been insufficient progress toward meeting objectives, then the following questions must be asked.

> Was the assessment valid?
>
> Were the goals realistic?
>
> Were the criteria realistic? Could they be accomplished within a year's time?

Other important questions to consider during the review meeting center around the placement itself: Is the placement appropriate? Would another placement be more appropriate? The date for the ✓ Annual Review Meeting must be written on the IEP. More information on Evaluation is presented in Chapter 7.

## Persons Responsible

A list of IEP implementors is no longer a required component of an IEP. However, we believe it is good practice to name those professionals (and parents, too) who are responsible for delivery of services and the implementation and monitoring of objectives listed on the IEP.

Designating responsibility helps increase accountability, adds clarity, and serves to organize the review process. At the annual review, each responsible person can report on his/her area of responsibility.

## Justification of Placement

Formerly, the proposed Regulations for P.L. 94–142 required that the IEP team provide a statement justifying the placement selected for the student. The justification is no longer required by the final regulations (1977). However, some states still require that the team be able to articulate *why* they chose the particular placement. We believe it is good practice.

# THE PLACEMENT RECOMMENDATION

Since the setting in which the program is implemented will greatly influence the student's success or lack of success, the placement

# Designing the IEP

recommendation is a critical decision point in the IEP process. A student's placement is determined *after,* and *because of,* the IEP team meeting.

The concept of least restrictive environment was discussed in Chapter 1. Since the focus of this book is service delivery to those handicapped students who are able to spend most or all of their day in a regular classroom setting, the discussion here will focus on key considerations for selecting a regular classroom placement for a particular student.

The primary consideration for any potential placement centers around the student's needs. The pros and cons of each placement alternative must be examined in light of what the team knows about the student's present skills and learning needs. "What is an optimal educational environment for one student may be failure inducing for another, due not to the category of placement it represents, but to the interaction of the child and the physical and interpersonal milieu which it offers (Pasanella et al., 1977, p. 114)."

In their description of *temporal, instructional,* and *social integration,* Kaufman et al. (1975) made some important points that the team must consider when examining placement alternatives. The *instructional environment* of the student's potential placement must be examined carefully as to the extent the student will share in the instructional environment of the regular classroom.

1. The child's learning characteristics and educational needs must be compatible with the learning opportunities provided to non-handicapped peers in the regular classroom. (p. 6)

An educational plan for a student must be directed toward helping the child secure the information s/he needs to remain in the regular classroom. The curricular materials in use in the regular classroom must be considered when developing objectives and related teaching strategies for the child.

2. Compatibility must exist between a . . . child's learning characteristics and educational needs and the regular classroom teacher's ability and willingness to modify his instructional practices. (p. 6)

A comfortable match between the teacher's teaching style and the student's learning style is critical. If a child functions most successfully in a rather structured environment, then placement in an open classroom would not be appropriate. If a teacher's most comfortable teaching mode is the lecture, then the child who learns best visually or kinesthetically would not fit there.

Any program designed for an individual child must also involve the teacher in its formulation and must fit the teacher's *modus operandi* in order to be successfully implemented.

> 3. The special education services provided to a . . . child (such as resource room help) must be compatible with and supportive to the regular classroom teacher's instructional goals for the child. (p. 6)

The inability of special education and regular education to complement one another results in an ineffective, segmented program.

*Social integration* is the potential relationship between the handicapped student and his normal peers. The likelihood that s/he will be included in the ongoing social milieu of the peer group is another important consideration. What problems are likely to occur? What can be done to help insure that the student will be accepted? What steps can be taken to help change attitudes? More information and ideas on helping both teachers and normal students to understand and accept the handicapped may be found in Chapter 7.

## THE IEP FORM

There is no prescribed format or form for the IEP. The design of the IEP form is left to the individual states and/or local education agencies. The form adopted for local use to record team decisions must contain the minimum components specified in P.L. 94-142 as well as any additional components required by individual state legislation. Schipper and Wilson (1978) have concluded, after working with school districts across the nation, "that the form itself is an important factor in eliciting the type and quality of information which is appearing on IEPs. For example, if two lines are provided for 'statement of educational performance', IEP developers will tend to fill that space only. This follows the old adage, unfortunate in this case; that 'structure dictates function,' rather than the reverse" (p. 12). The IEP form should meet the requirements of the law and at the same time be specific and complete enough to guide implementation. Schipper and Wilson (1978) have often noted problems in the following elements on IEP forms:

- lack of assessment data.
- no mention of the percent of time the child will spend in regular education.
- lack of place for date the IEP was developed.

**Designing the IEP**

- no names or identification of persons who developed the IEP. (pp. 12–13)

Figure 6 is but one example of an IEP form; all of the required components are explained in the example.

## Some Common Concerns

*How long are IEPs?* There is no prescribed length for an IEP. The length depends on the child's needs and the number of goals, objectives and services specified to meet those needs. Some IEPs cover the child's total educational program; others cover only a portion of their program. In the case of a student who functions successfully in a regular classroom and requires speech therapy or the services of a resource teacher for the visually handicapped, the IEP would cover *only* the special education (speech or resource teacher) services.

*When is the IEP written?* The IEP is written during the IEP meeting and before placement. It is *not* appropriate to develop the IEP before the IEP meeting and then present the finished product to the parents for their approval.

Parents are to be active participants. They must not be coerced into approving a program that they have had no part in planning. It *is* appropriate for professional staff to organize their information ahead of time and come to the meeting with recommendations to contribute.

*When is the placement made?* Placement is made after the IEP is written. It is *not* appropriate to place the student in a classroom and then ask the teacher to write the IEP. The IEP must be written *before* placement in order to comply with P.L. 94–142. The placement decision is based upon the IEP. And remember, it is a placement *recommendation* not a *decision* until the parent approves.

*Must every academic area be included in an IEP?* No. Only those areas where the student has special needs and requires special education services to meet those needs.

## THE LETTER vs. THE SPIRIT OF THE LAW

It is relatively easy to meet the letter of the law by holding a meeting and filling out a piece of paper ("paper compliance"). But it is more difficult to move beyond mere paper compliance and toward capturing the real spirit of the law by achieving quality and excellence in

**Figure 6** *Example of an IEP Form*

| | Type of program/class | Special Education and related services | Start Date | Duration of Service |
|---|---|---|---|---|
| Student's Name | Placement Recommendation Time spent with non-handicapped pupils | Special services which will be provided (e.g., speech, auditory training) | When the services will begin | How long the services will be given |
| School | Percent of time in Regular Education | | | |
| Meeting Date | Justification for type of Placement (include other alternatives considered): Why this placement was selected | Type of PE | | |
| Committee Members _____ | | | | |
| Parent Signature of Approval | Placement Date | Career Ed | | |
| | Annual Goals | Short-Term Instructional Objectives for each Goal (include evaluation criteria) | Evaluation Procedures | Review Date |
| Present Levels of Performance | What skills or behaviors the teacher and student are aiming for, arranged in order of importance | The specific steps to be accomplished toward reaching each goal over the school year; statements telling how well the student is expected to perform. | The way the progress will be measured | When the team will review the student's IEP |
| Academic Statements of what the student can and cannot do; based on assessment information | | | | |
| Self-help | | | | |
| Social | | | | |
| Psychomotor | | | | |
| Prevocational/vocational | | | | |

the delivery of services to handicapped children. Some steps for schools to take in order to begin moving toward quality include:

1. Make certain that IEPs contain *all* the required components. Then add those elements that were written into the proposed regulations but eliminated from the final regulations. These elements are (a) suggestions about special media and materials that would be useful, (b) the type of physical education program to be provided, (c) the individuals responsible for implementing the plan, and (d) statements to justify the placement decision.
2. Attend to the teaching and implementation processes by combining both the total service approach (IEP) with an individualized implementation plan (IIP) for each short-term objective listed on the IEP. (See Chapter 7 for more detail on the Individualized Implementation Plan). Developing an implementation plan may require a second team meeting with plan implementors to determine the classroom activities.
3. Develop and use an IEP form that allows for a meaningful program—a form that allows for systematic, detailed planning. The spaces on "paper compliance" forms are often so small that one can't write more than one or two words. Paper compliance is a waste of time.

In a position statement on qualitative issues related to the IEP, Walker and Kukic (1979) suggested the following as best practice standards:

1. Insure that diagnostic information used to develop the IEP yields direct implications for teaching and programming efforts.
2. Insure that there is a logical, consistent relationship between annual goals and short-term objectives and the strategies used to achieve them.
3. Develop a comprehensive IIP for short-term objectives of the IEP.
4. Insure that short-term objectives are written in behavioral terms.
5. Consider multiple types and sources of evaluation in assessing the impact of IEPs, e.g., context, input, process and product evaluation.
6. Develop a defensible rationale for the placement decision reached in relation to each handicapped child to whom services are given.
7. Insure that the comprehensive plan of service is written in a way that it serves as a true guide to instruction   (pp. 5–6).

Realizing both the letter and the spirit of the law will require new ways of organizing time, people, resources, and a great deal of dedication and commitment. The benefits to all children—not just the handicapped—should be well worth it.

## Study Questions and Activities

1. How does the written instructional plan described in Chapter 6 differ from the traditional lesson plan often required of teachers?

2. Does the federal legislation (P.L. 94–142), which requires written instructional plans, guarantee individualized, effective, coordinated instruction for all handicapped pupils? How does the preparation and implementation of these written plans assure the achievement of any or all of these laudable goals?

3. Why is it wise to establish priorities for the achievement of objectives included in a written instructional plan?

4. Obtain examples of written instructional plans from cooperating resource and consulting teachers in a neighboring school district. Critique these plans according to the following criteria: (a) Are the pupil's problem areas listed (from referral information)? (b) Have appropriate techniques been used to assess baseline or entry skills in each of the problem areas? (c) Are learning strengths as well as weaknesses indicated or implied? (d) Are objectives related directly to the pupil's areas of need? (e) Are priorities for areas of greatest need indicated? (f) Is the responsibility for implementation clearly indicated (that is, is the resource teacher, regular teacher, parent, or principal indicated)? (g) Are appropriate procedures for evaluation of pupil progress planned? (h) Is space provided to indicate pupils' progress during evaluation? (i) Is there a clear correlation between referral problems, assessment techniques, written objectives, and evaluation techniques throughout the plan? If the planning format used is unsatisfactory relative to these criteria, develop your own format for writing IEPs—one that you feel is both workable and satisfactory.

5. Select approximately four compatible referral problems listed in Chapter 3, Activity 8, to describe Harold Hazzard, a mythical but typical sixth-grade referral to an elementary resource teacher. Write a complete, hypothetical IEP covering com-

munication, reading, computational skills, and school adjustment which meets the criteria in Activity 4. above. Review Harold's instructional plan to ensure that there is a clear correlation between referral problems, assessment techniques, written objective, learning alternatives, and evaluation techniques. (This exercise may be done individually or as a group project. Either present individual written plans to your classmates and/or instructor for review, or select four members of the class to role play an IEP team meeting to plan Harold's instruction for the school year. If you choose to role play, use the roles of principal, resource teacher, school nurse, and referring regular teacher. (See Chapter 2, Activity 5.)

## References

Ballard, J., & Zettel, J. Public Law 94–142 and Section 504: What they say about rights and protections. *Exceptional Children*, 1977, 44, 177–184.

Kaufman, M. J., Gottlieb, J., Agard, J. A., & Kubic, M. B. Mainstreaming: Toward an explication of the construct. *Focus on Exceptional Children*, 1975, 7 (3), 1–12.

National Association of State Directors of Special Education. *Functions of the placement committee in special education.* Washington, D.C.: Author, 1976.

National Association of State Directors of Special Education. *Summary of research findings on individualized education programs.* Washington, D.C.: Author, 1978.

Pasanella, A. L., Volkmor, C. B., Male, M., & Stem, M. *Individualized educational programming: Emphasizing IEPs for very young and severely handicapped learners.* Los Angeles: Foreworks, 1977.

Torres, S. (Ed.) *A primer on individualized education programs for handicapped children.* Reston, VA: The Foundation for Exceptional Children, 1977.

Schipper, W., & Wilson, W. *Implementation of individualized educational programming: A problem or an opportunity?* Washington, D.C.: National Association of State Directors of Special Education, 1978.

Turnbull, A. P., Strickland B., & Brantley, J. C. *Developing and implementing Individualized Education Programs.* Columbus, Ohio: Charles E. Merrill, 1978.

Turnbull, A., & Schulz, J. B. *Mainstreaming handicapped students: A guide for the classroom teacher.* Boston: Allyn & Bacon, 1979.

Turnbull, H. R., & Turnbull A. *Free appropriate public education: Law and implementation.* Denver: Love Publishing Company, 1978.

United States House of Representatives. *Report No. 94–332, Education of all handicapped children act of 1975,* June 26, 1975.

United States Office of Education, Bureau for Education of the Handicapped. *Individualized education programs: BEH policy paper* (draft), November 5, 1979.

*United States Office of Education,* Title 45 of the Code of Federal Regulations, Implementation of Part B of the Handicapped Act, 1977.

United States Public Law, P.L. 94–142, *Education for All Handicapped Act,* 1975.

Walker, H., & Kukic, S. *Guidelines for monitoring the IEP process for quality and compliance: A resource for Utah.* Salt Lake City: Southwest Regional Resource Center, 1979.

## Resources

The Foundation for Exceptional Children, *Individualized Education Programs.* Reston, VA: Council for Exceptional Children. Three sound filmstrips, each approximately 13 minutes: I, "Fulfilling the Promise," a basic explanation of IEP components; II, "The First Steps," assessment process and setting goals and objectives; III, "From Conference Room to Classroom," implementing the IEP.

National Association of State Directors of Special Education. *Guide for Trainers: A Resource for Workshops on Developing Individualized Education Programs.* 1201 Sixteenth Street N.W., Washington, D.C. 20036. A manual that provides a tested training process and materials to be used in training IEP teams. A slide/tape show entitled "IEP Man" is also available.

# 7

# Implementing the IEP

> The *development* of IEPs is only the first step in the process; the real test for improving the quality of education for handicapped students is *implementing* the IEP.   (Turnbull & Turnbull, 1978, p. 124)

Implementing IEPs for handicapped students will not always be easy. However, we believe that good teachers already have the necessary skills to teach those handicapped students who are most likely to be integrated into regular classes. We do not feel that teaching the mildly handicapped takes an entirely new set of skills; however, it does require the refining of existing skills and learning how to apply them more systematically and precisely. Implementing IEPs successfully requires ongoing support from special educators—the resource teacher, the curriculum specialist, consultants, and other special service personnel. The regular teacher should not have to go it alone.

We have organized the information in this chapter around the attitudes and skills that we feel are absolutely essential for teachers who will be implementing IEPs. Integrating handicapped students into regular classrooms demands that the receiving teacher have

1. *a positive, accepting attitude toward the handicapped.* We believe that teachers must deal first with their own values and atti-

tudes toward handicapped individuals. Teachers must also know how to prepare nonhandicapped students within the regular classroom to accept the handicapped student socially.

2. *an understanding of what it takes to operationalize an IEP into daily classroom activities.* We describe the components of an Individual Implementation Plan.

3. *a knowledge of the basic principles of learning and how to systematically apply appropriate instructional strategies and behavior management techniques.*

4. *an understanding of how to teach basic subjects and how to individualize their content.*

5. *skills to measure student progress on an ongoing basis in the classroom.*

In this chapter, we deal with each of the five areas listed above. We have encapsulated the best of the current information available and then refer the reader to more indepth resources.

## UNDERSTANDING THE HANDICAPPED: PLANNING FOR SOCIAL AND INSTRUCTIONAL INTEGRATION

> A difference is only a difference when it makes a difference. Handicapped children have far more similarities than differences with the non-handicapped. (Turnbull & Schulz, 1979, p. 48)

A first step in planning for integration of handicapped students into regular classrooms is the preparation of teachers and the nonhandicapped students. There are some teachers who will welcome handicapped students with open arms. There are others who probably should never be asked to work with handicapped students. To place a student in a classroom in which the teacher has a negative attitude would be placing that student in a *restrictive* environment. One cannot expect to change attitudinal barriers overnight.

A first step in dispelling common myths and misconceptions about the handicapped is to obtain information. Teachers should learn all they can about handicaps and handicapped individuals and then, in turn, provide accurate information to their students. A second step is to get to know and appreciate handicapped persons as individuals.

The mildly handicapped students who are most likely to be integrated into regular classrooms may have

1. hearing handicaps,
2. visual handicaps,
3. learning handicaps, or
4. physical handicaps.

In addition, some of the basic facts that every teacher should know about each type of disability are listed, along with some specifics for accommodating particular learners in the regular classroom. The information presented is intended as an introduction. The reader is urged to seek out additional information from the organizations and resources given at the end of this chapter.

# HEARING HANDICAPPED

### What Teachers Should Know

- Hearing impairment is a low-incidence handicap. It is estimated that 3 in 4,000 school-aged children are deaf and 1 in 200 is hard-of-hearing.
- Most deaf individuals have some residual hearing, and many can be taught to speak. With proper teaching and amplification, many hearing handicapped individuals can learn to use their residual hearing productively.
- Most deaf students will require intensive help from qualified specialists and may only be able to be partially integrated into the regular classroom.
- Some hard-of-hearing students will be able to function in the regular classroom full time without special help; others will require additional support.
- Reading is the most important and the most difficult task faced by hearing impaired students because reading is derived from spoken language.
- Many hearing impaired students tend to experience their world visually; thus, they miss many important cues. They need auditory training lessons designed to improve their listening abilities.

### About Hearing Aids

- Learn how a hearing aid functions and be familiar with its maintenance.
- Learn how to check the aid to be certain it is working.

- Keep an extra battery and cord at school.
- Learn how to eliminate squealing by adjusting the earmold and/or turning down the volume.
- Teach classmates how a hearing aid works and let them listen with it.
- Remember that the aid amplifies *all* sound—not just speech. It helps the student to keep peripheral noise levels down.
- It is the wearer, not the aid, who does most of the work in interpreting sounds and conversation.

## The Hearing Handicapped Student in the Regular Classroom

1. Find out about the student. Does s/he read lips? Can s/he hear when in close proximity to the speaker? Does s/he need an interpreter?
2. Experiment with seating positions. Get feedback on where the student hears or lipreads best.
3. Talk normally and at a moderate rate. Do not exaggerate mouth movements. Use complete sentences.
4. Face hearing impaired students to facilitate lipreading.
5. Avoid producing a glare by standing with your back to a window. The student may not be able to read your lips.
6. Don't expect the student to lipread beyond eight to ten feet.
7. Use natural gestures while talking but avoid excessive movement.
8. Use an overhead projector whenever possible so you can face the class—this facilitates lipreading.
9. When communicating, use as many cues as possible. Glance at, point at, or touch the objects or people that you are talking about.
10. If the student does not give you his or her attention when you call their name, gently touch their shoulder, arm, or hand.
11. Ask the student to explain things to you to demonstrate that s/he understands the directions, content, and so on.
12. Write assignments on the board.
13. Be sensitive to signs of fatigue. It is extremely tiring to lipread for long periods.

# Implementing the IEP

14. Use student volunteers to take notes for the hearing impaired student so s/he can concentrate on watching the teacher.
15. Use a "buddy system" to provide special help when needed.
16. Use an experience-based approach to learning and plenty of visual aids.
17. Try to be consistent in your use of terms and labels. For example, in arithmetic the terms "grouping," "renaming," and "carrying" all refer to the same concept.
18. During class discussions, write key words and phrases on the board or overhead.
19. Do not underestimate the student!
20. Find out more about the *hearing impaired*; contact these organizations.

Alexander Graham Bell Association for the Deaf, Inc.
3417 Volta Place, N.W.
Washington, D.C. 20007

American Speech and Hearing Association
9030 Old Georgetown Road
Washington, D.C. 20014

Media Services and Captioned Films
Branch, Bureau of Education for the Handicapped
Washington, D.C. 20202
(Free loan of captioned films to schools serving the hearing impaired. Catalogs are available.)

National Association of the Deaf
814 Thayer Avenue
Silver Spring, MD. 20910
(Information clearinghouse)

## VISUALLY HANDICAPPED

### Facts Teachers Should Know

- Visual impairment is a low-incidence handicap.
- Most visually handicapped students are low-vision or partially-sighted and usually learn to read print.
- Most blind children have so little sight that they must depend on learning through other senses. They learn to read by using braille.

- Many blind individuals can learn to function well in a regular classroom with help from resource teachers and orientation and mobility instructors.
- Most partially-sighted students can participate fully in the regular classroom setting.
- Visually handicapped students should be encouraged to use the vision they have. Eyes benefit from being used, and use will not cause the remaining vision to deteriorate.

## The Visually Handicapped Student in the Regular Classroom

1. Find out about your student from parents, former teachers, and the school nurse. Does s/he use special adaptive aids or need special equipment? Can s/he read print?
2. Use a vocabulary that is related to sight, such as the words "see" and "look." Visually handicapped persons use those words, too.
3. For partially-sighted students, avoid situations that produce a glare, such as standing with your back to a window.
4. For safety reasons, keep doors and cupboards either open or closed—not ajar.
5. Call the student by name when you are speaking to him.
6. Talk directly to the student. Look him in the face and remind classmates to do the same.
7. Don't be afraid to ask if the student seems to need assistance, but ask *before* you assist.
8. Some visually handicapped students develop unusual mannerisms. Gently remind them about more appropriate behaviors.
9. Orient the student to the classroom and its layout.
10. Practice walking with the student to the playground, the restroom, and the cafeteria.
11. Prepare classmates to act as guides.
12. Tell the student who you are when you approach him or her and tell them when you leave.
13. Discover whether or not the student can read regular print. If so, be sure that the print quality and illumination are good when s/he is reading.

# Implementing the IEP

14. Locate large-print materials for the student to use if necessary.
15. Provide a portable reading lamp, if necessary.
16. Seat the student near a window where there is good light.
17. Provide black felt tip pens to prepare written work.
18. Avoid using blue ink dittos; they may be difficult to read.
19. Be sure that optical aids and magnifying devices are used correctly.
20. Encourage the student to *use* any adaptive aids s/he needs and to explain their use to other classmates.
21. If appropriate, provide a bookstand to bring work closer to the student's eyes and reduce fatigue.
22. Give the student precise directions concerning the location of objects in the classroom and elsewhere.
23. Provide concrete learning experiences whenever possible.
24. Capitalize on the use of other sensory channels—auditory and kinesthetic.
25. Remember that visually handicapped students can also be *visual* learners.
26. Don't underestimate the student!
27. Consult the following resources and organizations for further information on materials for the visually handicapped.

*Aids for handicapped readers*, Library of Congress, 1972.

*Reading materials in large type*, Library of Congress, Division for the Blind and Physically Handicapped, 1975.

American Foundation for the Blind
15 West 16th Street
New York, New York 10011
(publishes braille, large-type, and recorded books)

National Federation of the Blind
218 Randolph Hotel Building
Fourth and Court Streets
Des Moines, Iowa 50309
(contact for addresses of state & local associations, agencies & resources)

American Printing House for the Blind
1839 Frankfort Avenue
Louisville, Kentucky 40206
(Catalogs of materials available)

# LEARNING HANDICAPPED

### Facts Teachers Should Know

- Most learning handicapped students grow up to develop normal social and communication skills and function well in society beyond school.
- Most learning handicapped students are not identified until second or third grade, when academic work becomes more difficult.
- Individuals with mild to moderate learning handicaps are most likely to be placed in a regular classroom.
- Some learning handicapped students can function fully in the regular classroom setting; others will require special resource support.
- Identifying the student's strengths and weaknesses, developing instructional strategies to meet his/her needs, and getting on with instruction is the key to success. It is a waste of time to argue about causes, labels, and handicapping conditions.
- Often, learning handicapped individuals take longer to learn things, have a shorter attention span, have difficulty recalling information, have trouble generalizing information, and/or have difficulty with abstractions.
- Learning handicapped students also have many strengths. Find out what their strengths are and build on them.
- Carefully plan instructional activities to maximize success and minimize failure. Use systematic instruction techniques.

## The Learning Handicapped Student in the Regular Classroom

1. Break objectives into small tasks that are manageable for the student.
2. Make certain that directions are clearly understood.
3. Reduce the length of assignments. Provide several shorter assignments on the same subject or concept and use a variety of materials.
4. Provide frequent opportunities for a change of pace for students with short attention spans. Allow these students to move, collect papers, replace equipment, and so forth.

**Implementing the IEP**

5. Specify and discuss class rules. Implement a behavior management system. Select appropriate rewards and be consistent about enforcing consequences.
6. Establish structure and routine. Allow the student to check off work completed.
7. Provide concrete, practical experiences. Allow many opportunities to practice new skills in a variety of ways.
8. Keep looking for the instructional technique(s) that best fits the child's learning style.
9. Help students increase short attention spans by creating a quiet place to work that is free from distractions.
10. Use a learning contract to help the student stick to tasks.
11. Use peer tutors.
12. Allow the handicapped student to tutor younger students.
13. Do not underestimate the student!
14. Seek further information from the following organizations:

Association for Children with Learning Disabilities
5225 Grace Street
Pittsburgh, PA 15236

National Association for Retarded Citizens
2709 Avenue E East
Arlington, TX 76011

## PHYSICALLY HANDICAPPED

### Facts Teachers Should Know

- There are 82,000 school-aged children with motor impairments; there are many more with health impairments.
- The term physically handicapped includes students with motor impairments such as injuries or diseases of the spine, muscles, bones and joints, as well as neurological impairments. It includes students with cerebral palsy, muscular dystrophy and spina bifida. It also includes students with health impairments such as epilepsy, asthma and cystic fibrosis, arthritis, or diabetes.
- A person may be severely crippled or otherwise immobilized and have a brilliant mind.
- Having a physical disability does not necessarily mean exclusion from physical activities.

- Many physically limited students are able to function in the regular classroom without special assistance or adaptations. Others will require part-time placement in a resource room, or the services of a physical or occupational therapist, for example. Some will require specialized equipment such as wheelchairs or walkers.

## The Physically Handicapped Student in the Regular Classroom

- Find out as much as you can about the child and his or her condition from the student, the parent, school nurse, doctor and previous teachers. Seek answers to the following questions, if appropriate.

### Communication Questions

1. In what ways, and with what clarity, can this child communicate: (a) Intelligible speech? (b) Gesture language? (c) Consistent body movement(s) or signals for yes or no? (d) Pointing at symbols on a communication board? (e) Handwriting? (f) Using electronic communication device?
2. Must this pupil be allowed extended time to respond?

### Written Expression Questions

1. How are the pupil's understanding and skill levels assessed?
2. Can the child write or type?
3. If the child cannot write, type, or talk, in what other ways can s/he respond?
4. How can the pupil mark answers and record ideas?

### Learning Questions

1. What adaptations are necessary to help the pupil manage classroom equipment and materials, for example, pencils, paper, books, and other materials?
2. What, if any, behavior management techniques are used?
3. How (or through what mode) does this student best learn each different kind of task (auditory, visual, and so on)?

# Implementing the IEP

4. What special procedures or materials help the child learn?
5. What are top priority objectives for learning?

*Mobility Questions*

1. What limitations, if any, are there on mobility?
2. How does the child move from place to place?
3. When, and how, should the pupil be physically assisted (lifting, transfers, pushing, in and out of walker, tied in wheelchair, and so forth)?

*Self-help Questions*

1. What physical self-help activities can the pupil do for himself or herself?
2. If s/he cannot complete some tasks or activities independently, what assistance does the pupil require?

*Questions about Accommodation for Physical Differences*

1. Are there any restrictions on physical activities?
2. How can games and activities be adapted so the disabled pupil can participate?
3. What physical positions and postures are to be encouraged? discouraged?
4. What special emergency procedures should be anticipated? (Bigge & Sirvis, 1978, p. 351)

- For an asthmatic, epileptic or diabetic student, find out what to do in an emergency (such as a seizure) or how to prevent an emergency (for example, snacks for diabetics).
- Familiarize classmates with the disability.
- Become familiar with the way specialized equipment such as wheelchairs work and be alert to signs indicating malfunction.
- Make sure the student has easy access to facilities and classroom materials: Ramps and handbars for students in wheelchairs, height of classroom materials and equipment adjusted appropriately. Make certain desks are comfortable and at the correct height.
- Be alert to signs of fatigue and provide rest periods. Reduce the length of assignments, if necessary.
- Use adaptive instructional aids such as small adjustable chalk-

boards, book holders, page turners, or typewriters as warranted by student needs.
- Let the student be as independent and as mobile as possible. Allow other students to be helpful but don't encourage dependence.
- If students have coordination problems, tape papers to desk, provide large pencils, or use the chalkboard.
- Give oral tests if writing is a problem. The student may respond orally to the teacher, a peer tutor, or to a tape recorder.
- Don't underestimate the student's capabilities!
- Seek more information by contacting the following organizations:

  Epilepsy Foundation of America
  1828 L Street, N.W.
  Washington, D.C. 20036

  Muscular Dystrophy Association of America, Inc.
  1790 Broadway
  New York, N.Y. 10019

  National Foundation March of Dimes
  Box 200
  White Plains, NY. 10602

  United Cerebral Palsy Association
  66 East 34th
  New York, NY. 10016

  National Easter Seal Society for Crippled Children and Adults
  800 Second Avenue
  New York, NY. 10016

## PREPARING CLASSMATES

Preparation of nonhandicapped classmates is important in order to facilitate full integration and acceptance of handicapped students into regular classrooms. We have discussed the concept of least restrictive environment in Chapters 1 and 6. A particular regular classroom can be socially and emotionally restrictive because of the attitude of the teacher and the other classmates toward the handicapped student. Remember that you, the teacher, constantly convey information to your students about your own attitudes—provide a model of acceptance for students to follow. Show by your behavior that the handicap makes no difference with respect to

# Implementing the IEP

friendship, academic status, or any other relationship. We present some initial ideas here for your consideration in preparing your students to understand and accept handicapped students. We urge you to seek out one of the resources listed for additional ideas.

## Tips for Promoting Social Integration

- Be open and honest with your students. Don't avoid answering questions.
- Discuss handicapping conditions with your class (see Resources).
- Invite guest speakers—parents of disabled children or disabled adults.
- Read books to your class about people with handicaps.
- Hold class discussions. Allow students to ask questions and explore feelings.
- Emphasize how much alike we are, rather than different we are.
- Take the mystery away from adaptive aids such as wheelchairs, braces, and hearing aids. Expose children to them and provide explanations of how they work.
- Try simulation exercises such as a blind walk or a soundless movie.
- Encourage a buddy system.
- Arrange for nonhandicapped students to work in self-contained classes for the handicapped as helpers or tutors.
- Look for ways to capitalize on the handicapped student's strengths and provide status and recognition through athletics, drama, the school newspaper, chorus, or as peer tutors.
- Locate and view media—filmstrips and films—on the handicapped.

## Media for Students

"Hello Everybody . . ." is a series of six filmstrips with audio cassettes (10 minutes each) portraying elementary through secondary students with various disabilities in a mainstream setting. Appropriate for use with students third grade through high school. Available from SFA, James Stanfield Film Associates, P.O. Box 1983, Santa Monica, CA 90406. Titles include:

Hearing and Speech Impairment (Danny)

Visual Impairment (Toni)

Orthopedic Handicaps (Jed)

Developmental Disabilities (Sheila)

Learning Disabilities (Matt)

Behavior Disorders (Laura, John, Ken)

"People You'd Like to Know" is a series of 10 color films (10 minutes each) portraying students 11–14 years of age, with various disabilities in a mainstream setting. Appropriate for use with students third grade through high school. Available from Encyclopedia Britannica Education Corporation, 425 North Michigan Avenue, Chicago, IL 60611. Selected titles include:

Mary (Hearing and Speech Impairment)

Harold (Visual Impairment)

John (Cystic Fibrosis)

Paige (Down's Syndrome)

Mark (Learning Disability)

"Like You, Like Me" is a series of 10 animated films portraying students with various disabilities in a mainstream setting, both in and out of school. Appropriate for use with students from preschool through primary. Available from Encyclopedia Britannica Educational Corporation, 425 North Michigan Avenue, Chicago, IL 60611. Selected titles include:

Let's Talk It Over (epilepsy)

Let Me Try (mental retardation)

Let's Be Friends (emotional disturbance)

Doing Things Together (prosthetic-hand)

Everyone Needs Some Help (hearing/speech impairment)

See What I Feel (visual impairment)

## THE INDIVIDUAL IMPLEMENTATION PLAN

The Individual Implementation Plan is an extension of the IEP designed by those persons (classroom teacher, resource specialist, and special services personnel) who are responsible for implementing the student's IEP. These persons have the responsibility to align ongoing classroom instruction with the goals and objectives stated on the IEP. The IEP has sometimes been called the *Total Service Plan* because it describes the overall combination of services, goals and

# Implementing the IEP

objectives for a student's yearly program. The *Individual Implementation Plan* is an outgrowth of the IEP—the lesson plan. The Individual Implementation Plan

1. describes what will happen in the classroom on a daily basis;
2. details specific instructional *events* which will occur during the teaching process; and
3. is developed for *each* annual goal and corresponding short-term objectives specified in the IEP.

These *lesson plans* are developed by (a) assessing the student's functioning levels even more precisely than in the assessment phase—particularly as they relate to skill sequences and curricula; (b) selecting, developing, and ordering learning tasks; (c) specifying appropriate instructional techniques; (d) identifying appropriate instructional materials/media/resources; and (e) deciding on systematic methods for evaluating instructional success (continuous progress checks). Individual Implementation Plans typically have four major components:

1. Learning steps or tasks.
2. Instructional strategies or techniques.
3. Materials and resources.
4. Measures of student progress.

Figure 7 is an example of an Individual Implementation Plan with each component described.

**Figure 7** *Implementation Plan*

Student's Name

| Sequence of Learning Steps for Short-term Objective # _____ | Person Responsible | Instructional Strategies/ Techniques | Materials/ Resources | Start Date | Measure of Student Progress | Date |
|---|---|---|---|---|---|---|
| (1) | (2) | (3) | (4) | (5) | (6) | (7) |

Based on the goals, objectives, and services specified in the IEP, implementors will:

1. Develop *learning steps* and tasks necessary to achieve each short-term objective.
2. Assign *responsibility* for implementing *each* objective.
3. Specify *strategies, methods, and techniques* for teaching each short-term objective.
4. List *materials* necessary to carry out strategies and techniques.
5. Enter the *date* the implementor begins instruction on each program goal.
6. Provide a statement of the *level of mastery* required for each instructional objective.
7. Enter the date mastery was achieved or *progress checked*.

## Developing Learning Steps and Tasks

The first step in developing the Individual Implementation Plan is to determine the child's exact skill level and, from there, develop the intermediate steps that will take the student from where he or she is *now* to mastery of the short-term objectives set by the IEP team. These *intermediate* steps are called *learning tasks*. Learning tasks detail the *plan of action* or sequence of approximations toward the short-term objectives—in other words, the objectives are task analyzed.

Task analysis is the process of isolating, describing, and sequencing all the essential subtasks which, when the child has mastered them, will enable him or her to perform the objective. Defined a little differently by Worell and Nelson (1974), a "task analysis consists of breaking down a task or skill into sequential component parts for teaching" (p. 120).

Though the words *task analysis* may carry a negative emotional loading, just like the term *behavioral objective,* the process is actually simple. It can be said to resemble a road map, a description of how to get from one place to another as efficiently as possible. Success is the key to task analysis; we aim at making learning as errorless as possible.

The number of components or subtasks included in a task analysis depends on the child and the nature of the task. It is only necessary to break the task down finely enough so that the child can succeed at each step. A task analysis results in an instructional sequence. Task analyses tell *what* to teach not *how* to teach. The focus is *only* on that skill that we are trying to teach. To perform a task analysis, begin with the instructional objective and consider all the things the learner will have to do before he/she can perform the task to the criteria and conditions stated in the objective. Break the objective down carefully into subskills by working through the task itself. It is often helpful to work backwards from the terminal behavior, identifying all prerequisite en route behaviors. Ask the question, "What skills must the child have in order to perform this task?" When identifying sequential components keep in mind that it is necessary to move from concrete to abstract and from simple to complex. The resulting substeps are then arranged in a logical order to sequence. The sequence does not have to be perfect; it can be rearranged during the teaching process if it is not correct. A sample task analysis is shown in Figure 8.

When all the subskills and steps are listed for a behavioral objective, an instructional sequence has been formulated. Siegel and Siegel (1975) outline some important points to keep in mind when writing instructional sequences. Some of these are:

1. Avoid extraneous material—stick to the specific objective.
2. Don't spend too much time teaching the prerequisite. If a specific objective has been set for a child, the assessment process should have determined s/he has the prerequisite skills.
3. Use what the child knows—and this includes the prerequisite—to help learn the new.
4. Assume motivation—often too much time is spent on developing activities to "motivate" instead of concentrating on the task at hand.
5. Identifying sequential components (task analysis), keep in mind moving from concrete to abstract, simple to complex, and so on.
6. Avoid scientific jargon—use language that communicates to all who are involved with the child.
7. Don't just present, teach—require the child to *do* something to show s/he is learning (pp. 16–19).

There are a wide variety of reading methods and approaches: Phonics methods, linguistic approaches, modified alphabets, language experience approach, multisensory approach, programmed reading, and individualized reading (in paperback books). Some of these methods move in and out of vogue, but it is necessary to be levels—often to the level of adult functioning. Skill sequences delineate key skills and subtasks to be learned and the order in which they may be taught. It is possible to utilize these sequences to develop tasks related to objectives on the IEP. However, we must approach them with caution. Existing skill sequences only provide a basic framework and should not be used in a "lockstep" fashion for

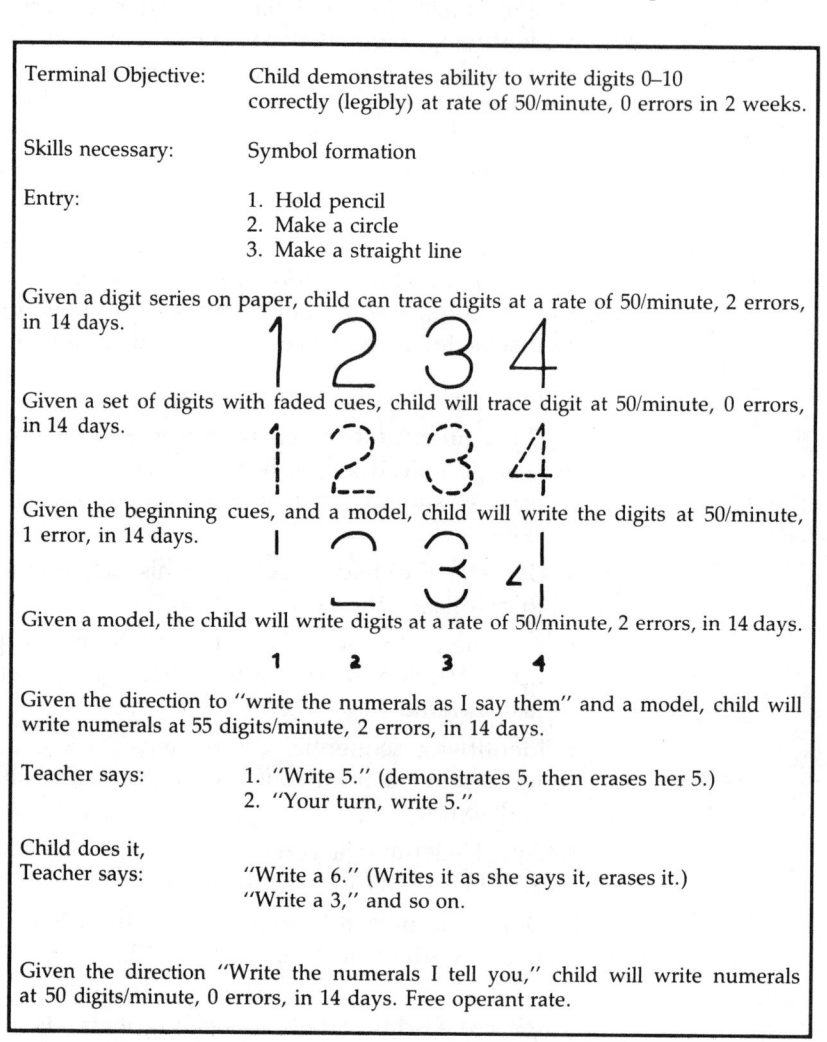

---

Terminal Objective: Child demonstrates ability to write digits 0–10 correctly (legibly) at rate of 50/minute, 0 errors in 2 weeks.

Skills necessary: Symbol formation

Entry:
1. Hold pencil
2. Make a circle
3. Make a straight line

Given a digit series on paper, child can trace digits at a rate of 50/minute, 2 errors, in 14 days.

1 2 3 4

Given a set of digits with faded cues, child will trace digit at 50/minute, 0 errors, in 14 days.

1 2 3 4

Given the beginning cues, and a model, child will write the digits at 50/minute, 1 error, in 14 days.

1 3 4

Given a model, the child will write digits at a rate of 50/minute, 2 errors, in 14 days.

1　2　3　4

Given the direction to "write the numerals as I say them" and a model, child will write numerals at 55 digits/minute, 2 errors, in 14 days.

Teacher says:
1. "Write 5." (demonstrates 5, then erases her 5.)
2. "Your turn, write 5."

Child does it,
Teacher says: "Write a 6." (Writes it as she says it, erases it.)
"Write a 3," and so on.

Given the direction "Write the numerals I tell you," child will write numerals at 50 digits/minute, 0 errors, in 14 days. Free operant rate.

---

**Figure 8** *Task Analysis: Writing numerals.**

*Towle, M. *Resource specialist training program, Volume V: Instructional strategies.* Eugene: University of Oregon, n.d.

every student. Any skill sequence must be reordered, added to, or deleted from, to make it appropriate for an individual child's ability and learning rate. Skill sequences then, are *never* finished products but are continually being revised and refined.

## Instructional Strategies and Techniques

> To individualize means to find the best match between the instructional strategy and the characteristics of the child. (Ward, Cartwright, Cartwright, Campbell, & Spinazola, 1973, p. 115)

Objectives and learning tasks tell us *what* to teach. Instructional strategies and techniques tell us *how* to teach. The assessment information should reveal child characteristics that have implications for planning methods and techniques. Some relevant child characteristics to consider are energy level, attention span, and sensory limitations, each of which may demand special materials or modes of instruction. With these special characteristics in mind, the next step in developing an implementation plan is to determine and describe the instructional methods and techniques that are most likely to promote learning success for the student. Worell and Nelson (1974) suggest three steps to develop intervention strategies and accomplish objectives:

1. specify materials and techniques
2. match these techniques to the learning needs of the child
3. design an appropriate behavioral management and/or motivational system.

Here are some suggestions for implementors when developing instructional strategies:

- Methods and techniques should be described in detail for both academic tasks and management of social behaviors.
- Activities should be specified for both the teacher and the student. Include activities the teacher performs as well as those the student performs. Three types of activities should be considered and incorporated: (a) presentation of lesson— mode of presentation (for example, tape, one-to-one with teacher or aide, worksheet or filmstrip, lecture), (b) practice for the student—a variety of ways to practice skills; (c) an evaluation procedure to determine success of strategies.
- Review instructional materials and make recommendations for several alternate materials that are matched to each task se-

quence. When choosing materials, consider the task and how it is taught as well as the child's characteristics and the type of materials, that is, concrete, pictorial, or abstract words and symbols. Include ideas for creating teacher-made materials. Where possible, indicate availability sources for instructional materials.

- Keep in mind the materials already in use in the regular classroom. Suggest adaptation and modifications of these materials.
- Suggest environmental conditions that would be optimal for the child, such as open vs. structured environment, group vs. tutorial instruction, and so forth.
- Determine through direct contact with the child and his/her previous teacher such things as reward preferences of the child and behavior management systems that have been successful. Some of this information is obtained during the assessment process.

Detailed information on instructional strategies and techniques is discussed later in this chapter under the heading "Some Principles of Good Instruction."

## Instructional Materials

When selecting materials for individual children, we must consider whether the material fits the objective we are working toward and whether the child has the prerequisite skills necessary to use the material. It has been suggested that materials fall into three categories of difficulty.

1. The *frustration level*—the child is making too many errors and therefore little or no progress toward mastery. If this is the case, we probably need to *slice back* or break down the existing task into smaller steps, or *step back* and use a different material altogether in order to get a prerequisite skill the child has not yet mastered.
2. The *instructional level*—the child can use the materials and is making some errors but also is making progress.
3. The *independent level*—the child can use the material with ease, with few errors, and is close to proficiency (White and Haring, 1976, pp. 181–182).

Use commercial skill sequences and materials whenever possible. Always examine the task sequence to determine if it moves from simple to complex, if it includes subtasks that lead to the terminal objective, and if it avoids "large jumps" from concept to concept. Some possibilities for alternative ways of learning a particular skill or task include utilizing

- the language master
- a tape recorder
- another student as a tutor
- a different book
- concrete materials
- a different response from the one called for originally, for example, tracing or matching before writing.

If adapting existing materials is not the answer, make your own sequences. It seems as though many teachers are always looking for the "magic" material or program—the one where it's all there for us and one that will fit every student. We must come to grips with the hard fact that there are no "magic" procedures; there is no all-encompassing material. In order to individualize and meet every student's educational needs, we will always have to make our own materials, and adapt or develop new skill sequences.

## Measures of Student Progress

The annual review of student progress by the IEP team, as required by P.L. 94–142, is one level of evaluation. Another level of evaluation is the continuous checking of progress in the classroom as the IEP is being implemented. The idea here is not to assess the student's ability for grading purposes, but to

- obtain information which is useful for modifying the instructional plan for continued success, and
- obtain feedback from the child.

As the IEP is being implemented in the classroom, we continually assess the student's performance, and in so doing, test the efficacy of the instructional plan itself. Gaps in instructional sequences may appear and are then modified and corrected, or instructional materials may be changed. The plan is updated as dictated by feedback from student performance. Methods for collecting student progress are discussed at the end of this chapter.

## SOME PRINCIPLES OF GOOD INSTRUCTION

At sometime in education courses, we all have been exposed to those principles, concepts, and techniques that come under the umbrella of "Good Teaching Practices." These are procedures such as direct instruction, motivational techniques, providing "follow-up" or appropriate practice, reinforcing appropriate behaviors and approximations, and sequencing tasks—easy tasks to more difficult ones. Teacher behavior is critical in the teaching/learning process. The ability to relate to students in a positive way comes up again and again in studies of effective teachers.

Studies conducted at the Exemplary Center for Reading Instruction in Salt Lake City, Utah, have identified some teacher behaviors that are important to, and correlate with, reading achievement of low ability students. The focus in these studies is on reading achievement, but it seems that some of the teacher behaviors that are effective in promoting gains in reading can also be generalized to other areas of instruction. According to the studies' results, the more effective teacher

1. deviates more from prescribed materials, such as basal textbooks, teacher's guides, and so on.
2. spends more time in direct instruction.
3. uses rewards such as social praise, and/or reward systems such as contingency management.
4. elicits oral responses from students. (It was found that use of oral group-responding techniques, where all children in a group respond in unison to every teacher stimulus, increases retention, comprehension, and accuracy in reading.)
5. moves from prompted to unprompted learning as she or he teaches.
6. teaches parents to teach their children.
7. expects high levels of mastery, with rate as a criterion. (This means the more effective teacher was more concerned with mastery of material than with number of books read or "covering" a predetermined amount of material. More time was spent on drill and review to insure mastery.)

"A certain mystique surrounding the education of mildly handicapped children has often convinced regular classroom teachers that teaching these children is substantially different from teaching most children in the regular classroom" (Affleck, Lowenbraun, & Archer, 1980, p. 23). True, there are some differences but more importantly, there are many similarities. Good teachers know how to assess, to group, and to instruct their students in the subject areas. Good teachers also know how to teach handicapped students. Many handicapped students have not learned from usual methods. Therefore, teachers need to be skillful, creative, and ingenious in planning instruction systematically so that their teaching makes a real difference. The following techniques may assist you to increase and refine the good teaching skills you already have and to make your teaching more precise and systematic.

## Systematic Instruction

Systematic Instruction, as defined by Haring (1978) is "an organized body of plans and procedures that leaves nothing to chance—a technology for teaching. Moreover, these plans and procedures are supported by data gathered on the child as he or she progresses through the prescribed program" (p. 21). Systematic Instruction depends on a thorough understanding of the phases of learning (acquisition, fluency, maintenance, generalization, and application) so that the teacher is able to match appropriate teaching procedures to the skill being learned. Systematic Instruction provides a hierarchy of procedures for skill acquisition including shaping, demonstration, modeling, and cueing. Systematic Instruction demands consistent application of appropriate behavior management principles and the implementation of a data collection and recording system to regularly monitor student progress.

## Stages of Learning

Affleck et al. (1980), Haring, (1978) and White and Haring (1980) outline the various stages of learning a new skill or concept. The first stage is *initial acquisition,* during which the child receives input on how to perform the behavior and gains some knowledge and minimal usage of the skill. Instructional procedures appropriate when a student is acquiring a skill are shaping, imitation, prompting, cueing, providing constant corrective feedback, and reinforcing even the slightest approximation of the desired behavior.

Next comes the *proficiency* stage, during which the child is improving fluency, accuracy, and rate of performance. When building proficiency in a certain skill, techniques include reinforcing correct responses, supervised practice and visual and verbal prompts.

The third stage is the *maintenance stage*. This stage occurs when the child has reached the level of proficiency desired and now engages in ongoing practice in order to maintain the skill. Practice, mixed practice, and fading are instructional techniques that are useful at this level.

Once the student has mastered a skill, s/he must be able to *generalize* the skill to other tasks and situations. Practice is recommended to enhance skill generalization.

Handicapped learners often have difficulty generalizing tasks from one situation to another. You may want to vary practice opportunities across instructional settings, at different times, and emphasize different components of the skill, in one-to-one or small peer groups, with different adults, or using different reinforcers and reinforcement schedules.

*Application* is the last learning phase. Application of a skill involves being able to enter into a novel situation, and perform that skill at appropriate times. Applying learned skills depends on ability to adapt and initiate appropriate responses without supervision or prompts.

"These phases—acquisition, fluency-building, maintenance, generalization, and application—become the basis for the teacher's plan to match the teaching procedure to the skill." (Haring, 1978, p. 22)

## Direct Teacher Activities/ Independent Practice Activities

Affleck et al. (1980) discuss two basic types of instructional activities that occur in classrooms: *direct teacher activities* and *independent practice activities*.

*Direct teacher activities.* These methods are used during the initial acquisition stage of learning. During this stage, the teacher must provide instructional input to students and explain or demonstrate a skill or concept. Techniques such as molding (actually guiding a child's response physically as in tracing letters of the alphabet), demonstrating, explaining, using audio-visual aids, and providing closely supervised practice are appropriate during direct-teacher instruction. These methods allow for immediate feedback to students to assist them in making correct responses initially and to prevent practicing errors. In their book *Teaching the Mildly Handicapped in the Regular Classroom,* the authors discuss in detail the following guidelines for providing instructional input and supervised practice during teacher-directed instruction.

1. Focus on skills at the level of initial acquisition.
2. Provide instructional input on how to perform the skill. (a)

Be sure the child is attentive. (b) Actively include the child in instruction. (c) Use visual stimuli in addition to verbal instruction. (d) Use consistent, simple vocabulary. (e) Present information in a logical, organized fashion. (f) Demonstrate the desired behavior.

3. Provide supervised practice of the new skills. (a) Provide prompts or partial prompts when needed. (b) Provide physical guidance when needed and appropriate. (c) Fade out use of cues and prompts. (d) Provide corrective feedback on performance (pp. 101–114).

*Independent-child activities.* Once the child has an initial understanding of the task, s/he needs practice and drill to increase proficiency. During this proficiency stage, the teacher can provide opportunities for practice which the child can do with a minimum of teacher direction. The teacher must plan for and utilize independent child activities in order to allow time to instruct other individual children.

Independent child activities can include using analogous tasks for drill, extended tasks, learning center activities, peer tutoring, aides, and parents. Activities at this level must still insure success, and feedback is still important for growth and reduction of errors. Feedback at this stage can involve use of self-correcting exercises, correction keys, peers checking each other, and written comments or smiling faces on teacher-corrected papers. Affleck et al. (1980) also provide some guidelines for independent child activities.

1. Focus on skills at the level of proficiency or maintenance.
2. Provide equivalent or analogous exercises for a specific objective.
3. Insure independence of task completion. (a) Use simple directions. (b) Use one task per page or assignment. (c) Use standard formats that the child can recognize. (d) Insure that the child knows the exact demands of the task and when she has completed the task. (e) Use responses that can later be corrected by the teacher.
4. Insure success on the child-directed tasks. (a) Use visual prompts. (b) Use verbal prompts.
5. Provide feedback on responses made (pp. 114–125).

Maintaining proficiency in a skill (maintenance stage) also involves the use of independent-type activities. Some skills (for example, math skills) are maintained through performance at higher levels, but some others are not. Spelling words, for example, often need much review and can be reviewed without the teacher's direct supervision. And don't forget the use of learning centers and games for review purposes.

## Teaching Procedures for Skill Acquisition

An effective teacher is aware that there are different ways of teaching a particular skill and therefore chooses the method most appropriate for the task and the individual student. Techniques for teaching a specific skill could include one or more of the following methods:

1. *Chaining*—a series of behaviors, performed in a given sequence, to bring about a single, complex behavior. Chaining can be *backward* or *forward*. In backward chaining the last step of the chain is taught first, then the next to the last step is taught, and so on. *Example*: "Pull shirt down three inches;" "Pull shirt down from armpits;" . . . "Put on shirt independently." In forward chaining, the first step in the chain is taught first, then the second step, and so on. *Example*: "Pull shoe laces tight;" "Pull shoe laces tight and cross the laces to opposite sides of the shoes;" . . . "tie shoe laces independently."

2. *Cueing or Prompting*—using a word, phrase, model, or signal of some kind, which has a high probability of triggering the desired response. *Example*: teacher provides the outline of alphabet letters for student to copy or, in counting, uses a verbal prompt ("seven") to help child recall the next number ("eight").

3. *Fading*—the student is gradually "weaned" from cues or prompts, since these will not typically be available in natural (non-instructional) situations. The aim is for the response to occur naturally.

4. *Shaping*—successive approximations to a correct response are reinforced; cueing and fading are frequently used to shape correct behaviors.

5. *Molding*—physically guiding a child's movements so that the child can experience how it *feels* to perform the task. This is a useful technique when the desired response is not present or when it occurs infrequently. (An example is to guide a child's hand as s/he prints a letter in their own name).

6. *Demonstration*—showing a child how to perform a task before s/he attempts it; the expectation is that the child will *imitate* the teacher's behavior. Demonstration should be combined with verbal cues ("Draw a circle").

7. *Modeling*—can mean providing the child with an example of the result of a *completed* task, for example, having the student assemble a place setting next to a preassembled place setting. This is a higher level instructional technique than molding or physical demonstration/modeling since it does not require or depend on teacher's presence. The teacher could be present, however, and combine the model with verbal cues, prompts, or signs, then fade these out.
8. *Practice*—requiring the child to repeat the same movement or response many times in succession (drill).
9. *Mixed Practice*—giving the child practice on a series of different tasks during a single instructional session. The purpose is to assist the child to learn to determine which movements or responses are required for which task (An example: Practice dressing skills involving tying, zipping, snapping).

**Learning Style/Teaching Style**

When designing instructional strategies, you will want to capitalize on the learning strengths of the student. Take into account your teaching style and how it matches the student's learning style. There are four important factors to consider in analyzing student learning styles and teacher teaching styles.

1. *Sensory channels.* Some students learn best through either visual, auditory, or manipulative types of activities, while other students have different preferences. The student's sensory preference for taking in information as well as his or her strongest method of response—verbal, written, or demonstration—must be considered. Individual teachers may find that they rely on teaching methods that use one sensory mode predominantly, and may want to vary their approach or use more of a multisensory approach to better accommodate individual learners.

2. *Human interaction.* Some children may prefer working alone while others do best in a group situation. Teachers should allow for children who need frequent or intermittent assistance and those who prefer to work without interruption. Grouping students will require attention to the above factors as well as attention to the size and composition of the group. Teachers may prefer to work in certain groups or with individuals, and this preference may interfere with maximum progress of students. If you seem to rely heavily on one type of setting for human interaction, you may want to try to vary your style for particular learners whose needs are different.

3. *Rate.* Some children are quick to grasp new skills and work rapidly. Other children work more slowly to learn new skills, to complete their work, or both. It may be necessary to vary the *amount* of work required or the *time* allowed for completion in order to match the student's learning rate.

4. *Structure.* Some students may need to know exactly what is expected of them; others may prefer more freedom and choice in their activities, to relate their work to current interests. Some teachers tend toward structuring learning experiences tightly and some prefer more spontaneous, child-determined activities. Try to incorporate options from which children can choose, instead of prescribing every classroom activity.

Just as each student has a particular *learning style,* teachers can examine their *teaching* characteristics for ways in which their style is complementary or conflicting with the needs of their students. The matching of teaching and learning styles can be an important factor contributing to student success.

**Arranging Space and Time**

The physical arrangement of a classroom communicates something to students. A well organized, attractive classroom, with separate areas for different learning activities encourages orderly behavior and involvement. We can't ignore the intensity and amount of learning that takes place outside of school. We can't ignore the influence of television or the extent to which children learn from and teach each other. The classroom environment must invite involvement and foster intellectual and emotional growth for every child within it. A classroom organized around learning centers provides instructional options to accommodate a variety of learning styles and preferences. Figure 9 shows a room environment organized around centers. The *Achievement Center* is where most direct teacher instruction takes place and new concepts can be presented to the total group. The purpose of the *Library or Reading Center* is to help students learn how to use books for enjoyment and for seeking information. It is stocked with recreational reading books including high interest low vocabulary books, newspapers, magazines, crossword puzzles, spelling and word games, and dictionaries and encyclopedias. The *Activity Games Center* may include math activities such as cuisenaire rods, playing cards, flash cards, rulers, tape measures and play money. The *Audio-Visual Center* features equipment and software to develop communication skills and reinforce and expand other classroom content. The Language Master, filmstrip projector, cassette recorder, recorder player and *earphones* are some items to be used here. There is space for conducting science and social studies projects. There are also individual study carrels where students may go to work alone if they desire. Many handicapped students need a well-organized, structured environment where behavioral expectations are clear. Many students also need learning options and, at times, a quiet place to work where distractions are minimized. Time must also be organized so that there is a fairly consistent routine and students know what is expected of them and when they must do it. Most teachers develop and publicize a daily schedule that divides the day into discrete time periods for each subject. Schedules are a good idea but keep in mind that a fixed and rigid schedule does not always meet the needs of individual children. We must work on ways of creating flexible scheduling so that routines are familiar and regular to children, but time periods are more flexible. Flexible scheduling allows children opportunities to work at their own rate and allows the teacher the opportunity to work with individuals and small groups.

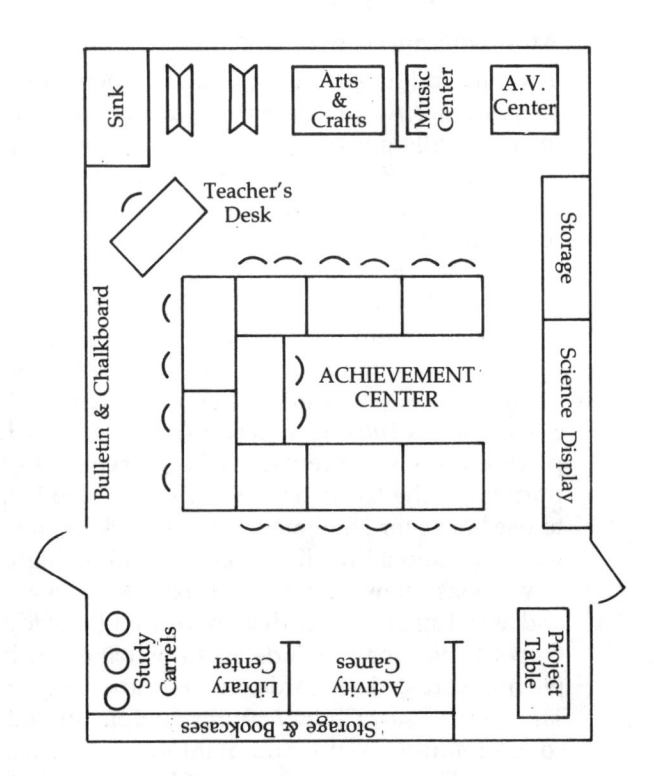

**Figure 9** *Room Arrangement*

# BEHAVIOR MANAGEMENT

Behavior management is one of the primary focal points for planning the integration of handicapped students into the regular classroom. Many procedures and techniques have been developed for changing behaviors in the classroom. Effective teachers are aware that unless a child's behavior is under control, learning cannot take place. They are aware that self-management and social skills are learned behaviors and can therefore be taught. Teachers of handicapped students must be familiar with reinforcement principles and how to systematically apply them to develop new behavior, strengthen new behavior, maintain new behavior, and modify inappropriate behavior. The first step a teacher can take is to establish clear rules and procedures for expected behavior in the classroom. Next, be aware of the basic procedures in changing behavior and how to apply them. And finally, learn how to reinforce appropriate behaviors and how to select appropriate reinforcers.

## Setting Classroom Rules and Procedures

Affleck et al. (1980) list four rules for stating classroom rules. Classroom rules should:

1. be few in number.
2. state what behavior is desired from students.
3. be simple and clearly stated.
4. be directly enforceable by the teacher (pp. 35–36).

Basic routine procedures for entering and leaving the classroom, storing personal belongings, restroom breaks and requesting help while working should also be clear, simple, and consistently enforced. Keep in mind that rules alone do little to influence behavior. They must be made important by providing reinforcement for behaving according to the rules.

## Basic Procedures for Changing Behavior

Volkmor, Langstaff, and Higgins (1974) summarized the basic steps toward changing student behavior.

1. *Observe the student in the classroom for a period of time in order to determine which behaviors should be changed.*
   The teacher observes that Rick's behavior seems disorganized. He wanders aimlessly around the classroom, never settling on a particular activity. As he moves around the room, he is often loud and noisy and disturbs other children. He refuses to cooperate in housekeeping chores.
2. *Pinpoint the behavior to be changed.*
   From the above description, the teacher could isolate several *specific* ways in which Rick's behavior should be changed; terminal goals for Rick would include:
   
   Able to use classroom time efficiently
   Able to make a choice of activity
   Being task-oriented
   Able to work independently
   
   For Rick, the teacher might decide that the critical behavior involves the *ability to make a choice of activity*.

3. *Describe the behavior in terms of what the student must be able to do.* The objective for Rick could be stated:
   When given a choice between using the ruler to measure five items in the room *or* using the scale to weigh five objects in the math center, Rick will *select* one of these activities and *go* to the appropriate area of the room within 10 seconds.
4. *Intervene.* An intervention is a planned strategy to change the behavior, either to increase it or to decrease it. (a) Discuss desired behavior (objective) with the child. (b) Provide opportunity, setting and materials for child to exhibit the behavior. (c) Provide immediate reinforcement for the desired behavior. (d) Provide frequent opportunities for the student to practice the new behavior.
5. *Evaluate.* Continue to observe the student to determine whether s/he has achieved the stated level of acceptable performance, and whether s/he maintains the behavior. (pp. 102–103)

## Reinforcing Acceptable Behavior

An essential part of the instructional planning process involves determining the child's reward preferences. Just what does this child prefer, both academically and recreationally? Important clues to the child's preferences and to what is most likely to work can be obtained during the assessment phase, from information on the classroom environment and observations of the child and teacher. This information then can be incorporated in the instructional plan.

Ward et al. (1974) suggest several consequences that can be tested as possible reinforcers.

1. *Attention and social reinforcers* may include praise, touch, and eye contact. Compliments, when genuinely merited, are often forgotten or left unsaid. Use them to reward learning instead of teaching or directing, as in, "That's a neat paper, if only you'd spelled those words right." A compliment is often a reinforcer.
2. *Food reinforcers* should be paired with social reinforcers and then gradually phased out.
3. *Knowledge of results* as a reinforcer means letting children know criteria against which they may evaluate their own learning, and teaching them to count and chart their own behavior. Then they can watch their own change and growth. (See the Precision Teaching entry in the resources section at the end of chapter.)

4. *Activities as reinforcers* might be the choice of a favorite activity for free time following performance of a specified task behavior. This option is also known as contingency contracting, which is discussed below.
5. *Token economies as reinforcers* involve the use of a token, point, or checkmark system as a reward for adequate performance of a specific task (pp. 122–124).

The types of reinforcers most likely to be useful in the regular classroom with normal and handicapped students alike include (a) *social reinforcement;* (b) *special privileges and activities;* (c) *progress charts, star charts, graphs,* and so forth; (d) *token economies; and* (e) *contracts.*

Sulzer and Mayer (1977); Volkmor, Langstaff, and Higgins (1974); Langstaff and Volkmor (1975); Turnbull and Schulz (1979); and Affleck et al. (1980); as well as others, provide detailed information on basic behavior management procedures and practical examples for immediate application in the classroom.

### Contingency Contracting

"Contingency contracting is a very effective technique for motivating students. Based on the work of Lloyd Homme (1971), contingency contracting is a method of behavior management which actively involves the child in the decision-making process. A mutual agreement between the child and the teacher is specified in advance. The basic premise of the contingency contracting system is the use of reinforcing events or activities (REs) to motivate task behavior and completion. It is an exchange of student work for a significant reward activity selected by the child. (Volkmor, Langstaff, and Higgins, p. 113)

Procedures for planning a contingency contracting program include:

1. setting up a reinforcement menu or list of available reward activities,
2. organizing the classroom into work or task areas and reward areas or centers,
3. developing a schedule for tasks and rewards,
4. preparing student tasks, and
5. explaining the system to the student. (For more information on Contingency Contracting see the Resources at the end of this chapter).

**Token Systems**

Tokens are objects or symbols such as checks, points, stars, and stamps which can be exchanged for other reinforcing items or privileges at a later time. The power of the token system is dependent on the reinforcing quality of the exchange reinforcers. Tokens are immediate symbolic rewards which the child can save and accumulate over a period of time. An advantage of the token system in the classroom is that it is relatively easy to design in such a way that all children can participate. (Volkmor, Langstaff, and Higgins, p. 125)

Tokens should be easy and quick to dispense to students and their value should be understood by all students. Token exchange for tangible reinforcers such as candy, toys, or trinkets should be withdrawn as soon as possible in favor of activity reinforcers.

There is a wealth of information available, in both print and nonprint media, on behavior management techniques and principles of reinforcement. A summary of some of the major procedures for classroom management was prepared by Volkmor, Langstaff, and Higgins (1974) and is reprinted below.

# Summary of Major Procedures for Classroom Management

1. Identify for yourself, and later with the child, the specific behavior to be changed.
2. List reinforcing events for individual students—or ask the child. Remember the classroom contains hundreds of events that are reinforcing to children. Anything that increases the frequency of desired behavior is a reinforcer.
3. Devise a strategy to promote the appearance of desired behavior; reinforce immediately.
4. Remember that new behaviors are not learned all at once; reinforce the child for approximations of terminal behavior (e.g., partially correct responses).
5. It is usually a good idea to start the response requirement at or slightly below the level at which the child is presently functioning. This procedure reduces the risk of the child being unsuccessful and not receiving a reward.
6. Design opportunities for the child to practice the new behavior.
7. Schedule rewards so that the child gradually learns to delay reinforcement.

# Implementing the IEP

8. Use reinforcing events (activities, privileges, free time) to reinforce desired responses. If concrete reinforcers or tokens are necessary, be sure they are accompanied by social reinforcement (smile, praise, or encouragement).
9. Be sure that behavioral contracts are clearly understood by the student—that he knows exactly what he must do in order to receive a specific reinforcement.
10. Focus on desired behavior and reinforce frequently. Desired behaviors are those which are incompatible with responses we want to eliminate.
11. Ignore inappropriate or undesired behavior unless someone is getting hurt.
12. The teacher's behavior (attention, scolding, gestures) may be reinforcing persistent undesired responses. Examine your own behavior to determine if you are inadvertently reinforcing inappropriate behaviors in children.
13. Provide opportunities for the child to display new behaviors in situations other than the one in which the behavior was originally learned, and reinforce him for doing so.
14. Remember that the use of punishment to manage behavior produces unwanted side effects such as escape, avoidance and negative feelings; therefore, use punishment only as a last resort.
15. If denial or isolation is used, be sure that the activities being denied or the environment from which the child is excluded is reinforcing to him in the first place. Otherwise, denial or "time out" will actually be positive reinforcers.
16. Always try to be fair and consistent; children will respect you for this (pp. 129–131).

## TEACHING SUBJECT MATTER AREAS

In this section we will discuss methods, techniques, approaches, and related materials that have been found useful for teaching the subject areas to handicapped children. We focus on Reading, Language, Math, and Social/Affective and Career/Vocational Education. There are several excellent texts that provide more comprehensive attention to teaching, subjects such as social studies, Science, Art, Music and Physical Education; these are listed in the bibliography for this chapter. Hammill and Bartel's *Teaching Children with Learning* and *Behavior Problems* and Turnbull and Schulz' *Mainstreaming handicapped Students: A Guide for the Classroom Teacher* are particularly good resources for all subject areas.

# Reading

Reading is the most basic skill; success in all academic areas depends on success in reading. Standardized group reading tests often do not give teachers all the information they need to know about every student. Students with poor reading skills will often require more intensive assessment.

An Informal Reading Inventory is one assessment device that can be used to determine a student's reading level. The informal reading inventory can be teacher constructed and teacher implemented. By trying the child in a particular reader and assessing word recognition and comprehension levels, the teacher can determine the appropriateness of reading material for instruction and for independent work. Two resources for more information on the Informal Reading Inventory and how to construct your own are:

Smith, P. B., & Bently, G. I. *Data bank guide, curriculum.* In *Teacher training program. Mainstreaming mildly handicapped students into the regular classroom.* Austin, Texas: Education Service Center Region XIII, 1975, pp. 55–61.

Guszak, F. J. *Reading checklist teacher's manual.* Austin, Texas: Teacher-Ade, 1974.

There are a wide variety of reading methods and approaches: Phonics methods, linguistic approaches, modified alphabets, language experience approach, multisensory approach, programmed reading, and individualized reading (in paperback books). Some of these methods move in and out of vogue, but it is necessary to be familiar with a wide variety of methods in order to be able to select the most appropriate method, or combination of methods, for a particular child.

*Basal reading series.* The most widely used reading approach involves use of the basal reading series. The series in use in the regular classroom must be considered when developing a reading plan for a child who is ready to be mainstreamed. The teachers' manuals are full of suggested methods and activities, often overlooked, which can be used to extend and intensify the regular reading program. Try to build some interesting remedial activities around the basal reading program already in use. Keep good records of specific skills that individual children have mastered and those on which they need help.

# Implementing the IEP

*Individualized reading.* This approach involves teaching word recognition and comprehension skills as each child needs them. The child reads materials of his or her own choice and at his or her own rate. The approach needs close monitoring by teachers and can be particularly relevant at the secondary level.

*Language experience approach.* This method is based on the experience and language of the child and incorporates writing, reading, speaking, and spelling. It may be used with both beginning readers and older students.

*Programmed reading.* (Sullivan et al.) Short and carefully sequenced learning units are presented while producing immediate feedback to the student's response.

*Fernald.* This method uses a multisensory approach that involves four modalities simultaneously—visual, auditory, kinesthetic, and tactile. It is a word-learning technique based on perception of the word as a whole and on child initiation of words to be learned.

*Gillingham phonics.* This is an "alphabetic system" that stresses auditory discrimination abilities, with supplementary emphasis on kinesthetic and tactile modalities. It provides a systematic approach to reading, spelling, and writing adapted to all levels through high school.

*Spalding phonics approach.* This is based on auditory phonograms representing basic sounds in the English language.

## Tips for Teaching Reading

- Use peer tutoring: Good readers help poor readers and poor readers help younger students.
- Try tape recording stories so the student can follow along visually while listening.
- Set up a reading learning center with a wide range of alternatives.
- Provide extra drill for students through the use of games such as word wheels, word bingo, Scrabble or Boggle.
- Encourage use of informal reading materials such as comics, newspapers, catalogues, and posters; let students bring in materials to read.
- Use the Language Master for auditory input to build sight vocabulary.
- Use kinesthetic methods such as sandpaper letters or tracing to provide tactile input.

## Language

The language arts includes oral and written communication, listening, and reading. The ability to communicate well is related to every school area and is critical in adult life. Listening skills are rarely trained formally although children are expected to listen for long periods of time. Our society is becoming oriented to listening and there is increased attention among educators to teaching listening skills in school. Teachers can train listening skills by using earphones, tapes, by reading stories aloud, and by supplying games and activities that focus on fine listening skills.

Speaking skills are strengthened by providing opportunities for students to observe and describe various situations and events both in and outside the classroom. These are environments in which children, if encouraged, can feel comfortable to express themselves. One of the most famous and widely-used materials designed to stimulate oral language development is the *Peabody Language Development Kit*.

Written expression is important. Consider the following tips when planning activities that involve writing.

- Encourage letter or note writing among students.
- Make a typewriter available.
- Let students dictate stories to each other.
- Have students keep diaries.
- Provide old magazines so that students can make scrapbooks and caption them.

## Math

Grade level scores in arithmetic do not give enough information to let teachers know exactly what skills have been mastered and what skills to teach next. Diagnostic tests tend to be more precise and specific; one such test is Key Math published by American Guidance Service, Inc. Teachers can also develop their own criterion-referenced tests in arithmetic to pinpoint student strengths and weaknesses. The following are some selected approaches that may be used, or adapted for use, with children who have difficulty in arithmetic.

*Structural arithmetic* (Stern, 1963). This approach utilizes concrete materials for self-discovery of number facts. It presents carefully sequenced experiments from simple number concepts to mastery of arithmetical computation and problem solving.

*Montessori materials.* These are designed to be self-teaching, concrete materials.

*Cuisenaire rods.* This program uses wooden rods of varying lengths and color. It is based on a definition of mathematics as a process of observation and a discovery of relationships.

*Programmed math* (Sullivan). The stress is on computational skills, while providing immediate feedback to the student. The child must already have a conceptual foundation in mathematics.

Consider the following suggestions when designing instructional activities for handicapped students in arithmetic.

- Shorten tasks and worksheets to accommodate short attention spans.
- Utilize concrete materials whenever possible.
- Provide feedback to students on the number of facts learned per day by using graphs or charts.
- Use calculators.
- Make certain students practice a skill to a specific *proficiency* level before going on to next concept.
- Help students generalize concepts to everyday life—use time, money, and measurement, as examples.

## Social/Affective

> How a child feels is more important than what he knows. (Ward et al., 1974, p. 391)

The amount and kind of learning that occurs is greatly influenced by the way a child feels about himself, his peers, and his classroom environment. The child with a positive self-concept generally has a fairly realistic opinion of his strengths and weaknesses, and is generally accepted by his peers. The child with a negative self-concept generally has an unrealistic opinion of his strengths and weaknesses because of his direct experiences with failure and the feedback he gets from those around him in relation to his strengths and weaknesses. Children with damaged self-concepts may or may not possess the skills or competence that they themselves are certain they do not have. A low self-concept is characterized by chronic self-criticism and low self-evaluation. Problems in self-concept are critical in the education of exceptional children. A child must feel good about him or herself in order to maximally profit from instruction.

The teacher is in a key position to influence the social-emotional behavior, feelings, and attitudes of the learner. The expressed attitude of teachers toward exceptional children can greatly affect acceptance of that exceptional child by his peers. Teachers can create an environmental climate that ensures that the learner will:

a. feel his ideas have personal value and significance;
b. become more honest and open (this is encouraged by a teacher who is real, open, and honest with his own feelings); and
c. know that the teacher is sensitively understanding.

Table 1 is taken from the CARE handbook, *Diagnostic Teaching of Pre-school and Primary Children* (p. 392), and outlines some ways the teacher can promote positive social-emotional development among students.

**Table 1** *Characteristics of the Teacher, Environment, and Learner Which Facilitate the Teaching-Learning Process\**

| TEACHER | ENVIRONMENT | LEARNER |
|---|---|---|
| 1. Makes the subject matter *relevant* to the learner. | Subject matter is *relevant* to the learner. | Perceives subject matter as *relevant to him*. |
| 2. Perceives children and environment as *nonthreatening* to self. | Is *nonthreatening* to the learner. | Perceives teacher, environment, and peers as *nonthreatening* to his self. |
| 3. Creates an environment which encourages the learner to be *active* and *doing* in the teaching-learning process. | Encourages learner to be *active* and *doing*. | Is *active* and *doing* in the teaching-learning process. |
| 4. Is *honest* and *open*. | Conducive to *honest* and *open* interaction. | Is *honest* and *open*. |
| 5. Interacts within the teaching-learning process both at the *intellectual* and *feeling* levels. | Encourages *intellectual* and *feeling* levels. | Interacts within the teaching-learning process both at the *intellectual* and *feeling* levels. |
| 6. Feels *accepted*, involved, comfortable, respected, and competent within the teaching-learning process. | Promotes *acceptance*. | Feels *accepted*, involved, comfortable, respected, and competent within the teaching-learning process. |

*Spinazola, C. Application of the diagnostic teaching model to social emotional development. In Ward et al. (1973), pp. 392–393.

# Implementing the IEP

**Table 1** continued

| | | |
|---|---|---|
| 7. Enters into *positive* and *cooperative* relationships with children. | Encourages *cooperative, positive* relationships. | Enters into *positive, cooperative* relationships with teacher and peers. |
| 8. *Evaluates* himself and his own work. | Encourages *self-evaluation*. | *Evaluates* himself and his work. |
| 9. Is accepting and *trusting* of children. | Creates atmosphere of *trust*. | |
| 10. Is *sensitively understanding* of children. | Encourages *sensitive understanding*. | |
| 11. Is *flexible*. | Promotes *flexibility*. | |
| 12. *Plans* activities with children. | Encourages planning of activities with children and teacher. | |
| 13. Accepts his own limitations. | | |

The characteristics of the learner, the teacher, and the environment are all related to each other, and they are all interacting with each other in the teaching-learning process.

---

Procedures widely promoted for improving self-concept include use of puppets, dramatic play, sociodrama, and role-playing. Worell and Nelson (1974) suggest the following techniques for use with children with low self-esteem:

Set beginning achievement goals low to insure success.

Reward early and often at first.

Reinforce successful trials after failure. Never leave a child until he has produced a response that is correct enough to earn reinforcement.

Avoid overpraise. Children with a history of failure are suspicious of social reinforcement and may not believe that your enthusiasm is real.

Try providing nonsocial reinforcement initially for a suspicious child; tokens or points may be less threatening than your early enthusiasm.

Focus on working hard and trying. Reward the child for "getting a good start," or "trying hard," or "not giving up."

Select specific products and provide reinforcement for observable achievement.

Consider using programmed materials at first so as to provide small steps and frequent reinforcement.

Encourage overlearning of material so that correct responses can be repeated a number of times. This will avert terminal errors and may prevent backsliding and discouragement. Have the child test himself out in a number of situations, including role play, self-rehearsal, etc. (p. 171)

There are more and more books and materials commercially available aimed at the area called *affective education*. The following list names a few.

Anderson, J. et al. *Focus on self-development.* Chicago: Science Research Associates, 1973. Three developmental programs—Awareness, Responding, and Involvement—focused on developing the child's understanding of self, others, and environment. Includes filmstrips, cassettes, photoboards, activity books, and manuals.

Bessell, H., & Palomares, U. *Human development program.* San Diego: Human Development Training Program, 1972. Curriculum of methods and materials designed to give students the opportunity to understand and deal with their attitudes, values, and emotions. (Magic circle technique).

Dinkmeyer, D. *Developing Understanding of Self and Others* (DUSO). Circle Pines, Minn.: American Guidance Association, 1970. Kits of activities and materials designed to facilitate the social and emotional development of children.

Glasser, W. *Schools without failure.* New York: Harper and Row, 1969.

## Vocational and Career Education

The area of career/vocational education ranges from career awareness activities beginning at the elementary level and continuing through the secondary level, to actual on-the-job work experience programs. There is a need for increased effort toward integrating career education into the regular curriculum, especially for the mildly handicapped at the secondary level. There is a need for more utilization of community resources (people and facilities), teacher awareness, and information of what is available in the field in order to strengthen the career education components of the school program.

Many states have curricula and guides already prepared and there are increasing numbers of media and materials on career and vocational education available on the commercial market. The following is a sampling of materials available commercially.

*Career Awareness Materials* (primary level). Individual activities including career identity cards and occupation match-up game. Developmental Learning Materials, Niles, Illinois.

*Why Work Series.* Designed for use with the Job Corps. Includes 21 graded reading selections, some cassettes, a teacher's manual, and an objective test for each selection. Behavioral Research Laboratory, Palo Alto, California.

# Implementing the IEP

*World of Work Kit and Human Relations Kit.* Stories about work situations and simulation exercises for developing work habits published by Webster-McGraw Hill.

*SRA Materials Grades K–12.* Some of the many titles available are:
*Work: Widening Occupational Roles Kit*
*Job Experience Kits*
*Occupational Awareness Kit* (Grades 8–12)
Science Research Associates, Chicago, Illinois.

Additional resources may be found in the resources section at the end of this chapter.

## EVALUATING STUDENT PROGRESS IN THE CLASSROOM

Educational evaluation is an ongoing monitoring of pupil progress. Methods of evaluating pupil progress are specified within the IEP so that teaching/learning procedures can be evaluated continuously. Precisely state criteria within each objective should communicate clearly to the user (teacher) so that s/he can readily determine when the child has mastered each objective. Instruction and evaluation are interrelated.

According to Ward et al. (1974, pp. 71–78), educational evaluation consists of four components.

1. *Establishing a criterion* which specifies the amount and type of pupil behavior required to satisfy the objective—a well stated, complete objective supplies this information.

2. *Selecting an evaluation procedure.* The procedure is specified in the objective as the *conditions under which the behavior will be demonstrated.*

3. *Collecting evaluative information or data.* The teacher collects this data during instruction and records it.

4. *Making decisions based on the data obtained.* Data are compared to the criterion stated within a short-term objective and the plan is updated or revised. The teacher must decide, based on an analysis of progress data when it might be necessary to call for a Review of the IEP—if the IEP is *not* working.

## Selecting an Evaluation Procedure

There are many ways to collect data on student progress. The procedure and method for collecting data is dependent on the type of objective. Some objectives may require that the child demonstrate a behavior and the teacher *observe* and record. Other objectives may be measured by use of a multiple choice or true/false *pre- and posttest*. Many criterion-referenced curriculum programs and materials are now available which include pre/posttests and progress checks. Other behaviors may be measured via *verbal explanations* or *written statements* by the student. *Graphs* or *charts* are ways to display evaluative data. Several types of measurement procedures are briefly described below.

1. *Checklists*: easy to use; require yes or no answers about a pupil's behavior; appropriate for "either/or" situations such as taking medicine, bringing lunch money, sight vocabulary words, naming colors, writing numerals, and so forth.

2. *Per cent*: number of times behavior occurs out of the total number of opportunities for it to occur; used when a child has many opportunities to respond; standardizes behavior counts from day to day (e.g., 5 out of 10 times yesterday = 50%, 10 out of 20 times today = 50%); used most frequently for preacademic and academic behaviors in basic subjects when the primary concern is accuracy.

3. *Frequency or rate*: tells both *whether* a child performed and *how often* the behavior occurred during a given interval; greatest sensitivity to behavior change; used for both academic and social behaviors when the concern is accuracy and speed. (See Precision Teaching section).

4. *Latency*: how much *time* elapses between the stimulus and response; used for such behaviors as following directions, initiating task when instructed, and so on.

5. *Duration*: length of time a behavior occurs once it has begun; start and stop times are usually recorded; used for behaviors such as wearing glasses, building endurance, attention to task.

6. *Trials to criterion*: set a desired performance level, such as four correct responses in succession and record the number of trials needed before criterion is reached; used for more primitive responses such as grasping, swallowing; easy to collect (Pasanella et al., 1977, p. 204).

Gentry and Haring (1976) list some important points to keep in mind when selecting progress measurement procedures so that they are useful to both the child and the teacher.

1. Measures should be taken directly on the task or the objective being taught.
2. Measures should provide information about intended or critical outcomes of learning tasks, for example, a *duration* measure

for "wearing a hearing aid," a *frequency* measure for a sorting task.
3. Measures should be sensitive to rapidly reflect change.
4. Measures should be taken frequently—daily if possible.
5. Measures must provide reliable results.
6. Measures must be practical and easily administered during the teaching/learning process.
7. Measures must be efficient and economical.

## Collecting Data

Data may be collected during the teaching process, while the student is practicing, during the student's free time, or in a formal test situation. Data may be collected daily, weekly, or monthly, depending on the objective. If the objective involves reading rates, data should be collected and charted or recorded daily. In any case, it is important that the evaluation techniques yield immediate information about learning performance.

Examples for scheduling data collecting to fit individual objectives are:

1. Percent correct on math *daily*
2. Number of new words mastered *weekly*
3. Evaluation of child's attitudes toward school *monthly*.

Self-charting or recording of data by the student simplifies the data collection task for the teacher and can serve to motivate the student. (See the following section on Precision Teaching).

## Making Decisions

Decisions are made after the data are collected. Once collected progress data are compared with the criterion stated within the objective. If performance is adequate, move to a new task or objective. If the student's performance does not meet criterion, we must ask *why*. Sometimes minor adjustments in instructional methods, procedures, or materials may be the answer. At other times, it may be necessary for the teacher to call for a review of the student's IEP. It is important that the teacher ask for a review immediately if ongoing classroom progress checks reveal a significant problem. It is a waste of time to wait for the year end scheduled review if the student is not making progress.

Implementing the instructional plan and evaluating student outcomes occur simultaneously. Through adequate evaluation and systematic checking of progress, we are continually reassessing student needs. Ongoing assessment in the classroom and good teaching go hand-in-hand.

## Precision Teaching

Precision Teaching is a method for evaluating student performance and recording student progress data. The procedure has merit in that it can be taught to an entire class of students and thus involves the student in recording his or her own performance rate and planning his or her own interventions. The system can also provide the teacher with continuous data, visually displayed, related to achievement of short-term objectives on the IEP. The following abbreviated description of the method is taken from Volkmor, Langstaff, and Higgins (1974, pp. 159–162). More resources on precision teaching are found at the end of this chapter. The method involves the following materials:

1. A simple chart (see Figure 10). (a) The horizontal lines indicate frequency or the number of times the pinpointed or targeted behavior occurs in a designated time interval. (b) The vertical lines indicate days of the week. (c) There is also space around the edges for noting the student's name, the amount of time during which the behavior is being observed and counted, and the behavior which is being counted. Each child may have his or her own chart or several charts, each for a different behavior.
2. A timing device: kitchen timer, clock with second hand, a stop watch.
3. A counting device: a golf stroke counter, knitting counter, or paper on which tally marks can be recorded.

The method involves the following steps:

1. *Pinpointing* the behavior to be counted. A pinpointed behavior is one that is *observable*—is seen or heard; *countable*—involves movement that has a beginning and an end; and *repeatable*—happens often enough to make it appropriate to count. (Painting a picture may happen only once a day—when it is done, it is done—so it is not an appropriate behavior to count.) Behaviors such as "words read aloud,"

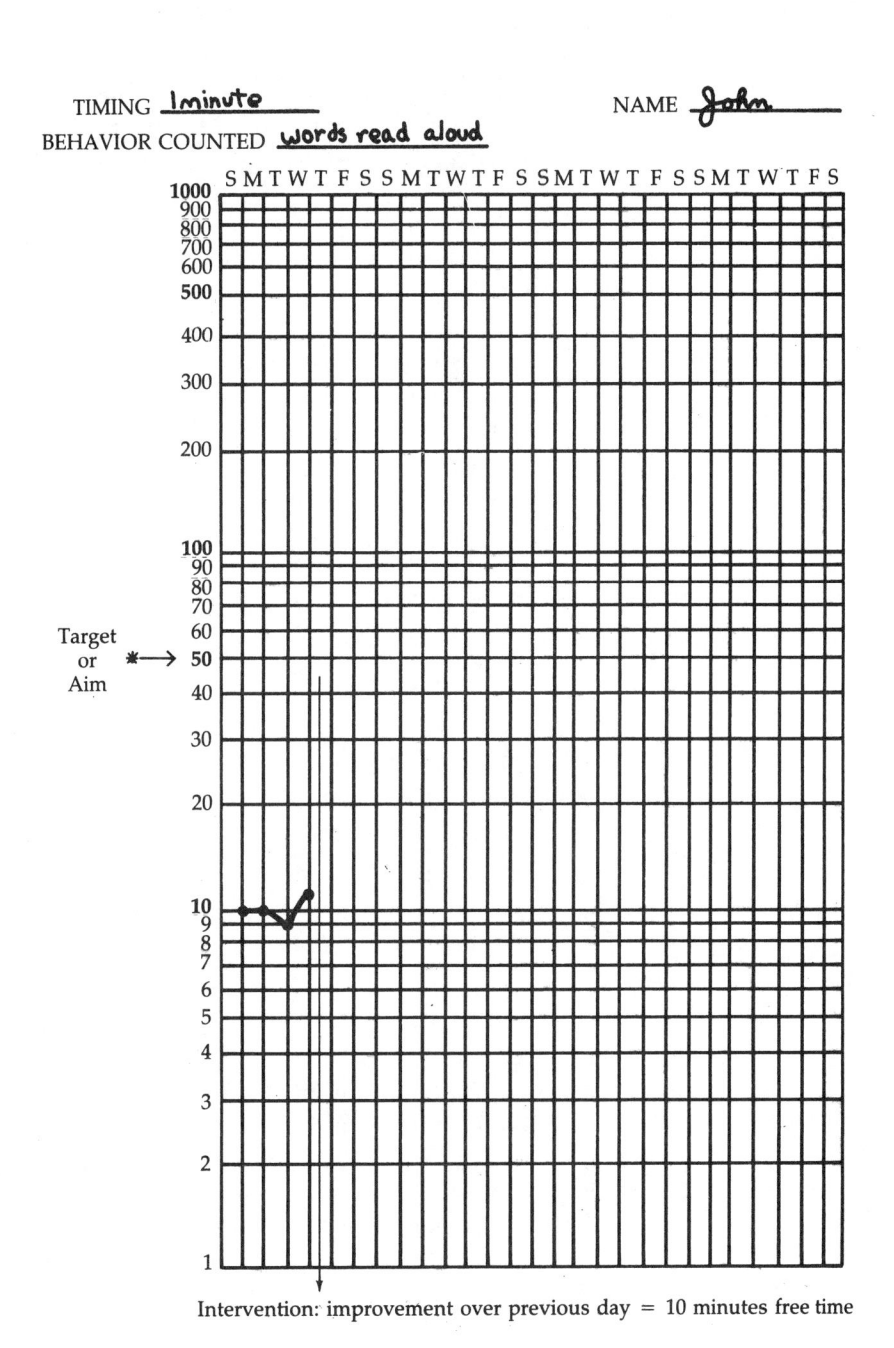

TIMING **1 minute**  NAME **John**
BEHAVIOR COUNTED **words read aloud**

Intervention: improvement over previous day = 10 minutes free time

**Figure 10**

"letters written," "math facts correct," and "saying thank you" are all examples that meet the three criteria above for as pinpointed behaviors and are appropriate to count.

2. *Observing and counting* the pinpointed behavior over a specified amount of time. Choose a time segment during which the behavior is likely to occur often enough to count. Common timings (or time samples) are 1 minute, 2 minutes, 5 minutes, or 10 minutes in duration.

> How many "words read aloud" in 1 minute.
> How many "letters written" in 2 minutes.
> How many "math facts correct" in 5 minutes.
> How many times child "says thank you" all day.

"Saying thank you" would be counted all day, as it is not likely to happen often enough in a 1 minute or 5 minute period to make it worth counting. Count the occurrence of the behavior over the chosen time segment. How many times did the behavior occur?

3. *Recording* the frequency of the pinpointed behavior on the chart.

> John read 10 words aloud in *1 minute* on Monday. (Place a dot where the Monday line intersects the 10 line—see sample chart.)
>
> John read 10 words in *1 minute* on Tuesday. (Place a dot where the Tuesday line intersects the 10 line.)
>
> John read nine words in *1 minute* on Wednesday. (Place a dot where the Wednesday line intersects the nine line.)
>
> John read 11 words in *1 minute* on Thursday.

Plot these rates on the chart and connect the dots.
When you have a sample of the rate of the pinpointed behavior over a few days, you are ready to decide whether it is necessary to intervene to modify the behavior by either increasing or decreasing it.

4. *Intervening* to either increase or decrease the behavior. It is important, at this point, to *involve* the child in setting goals for him- or herself and selecting reinforcing consequences. Plan the intervention with the child and *continue* to take the same daily time samples of the behavior until the goal or aim is reached.

> John, at this point, may set a target aim for himself of 50 *words* per minute. In order to reach this aim, he may

# Implementing the IEP

decide that he will try for 15 words per minute for the next few days. Together the teacher and John may decide that *if he improves* over the previous day's rate, he may engage in an activity of his choice for 10 minutes.

The visual representation of daily performance on a chart can be an important vehicle to motivate the child and involve him in planning his own program. It also provides the teacher with valuable information on student progress toward achieving the short-term objectives on the IEP.

## EVALUATING THE IEP

## The Annual Review

P.L. 94–142 requires that each IEP be reviewed at least annually to determine whether or not the annual goals and short-term objectives are being met. Key questions for the Annual Review meeting include:

- Is the child progressing as specified in the IEP objectives?
- Is the child approaching a point where she/he can exit to another placement?
- If the IEP does not seem to be appropriate, what adjustments seem to be necessary?

If it is determined that the goals and objectives have been met, a new IEP may be developed. If the student goals and objectives have not been met, the IEP is reexamined for appropriateness and deficiencies are targeted.

The checklist provided on the following pages is adapted from a technical assistance package for evaluating pupil progress developed by Joan Honeycutt (1980). This checklist is seen as a valuable aid to the IEP team during the required Annual Review. Use of the checklist can help *identify* deficiencies in the development and/or implementation of the IEP. Any deficiencies identified as having an impact on student performance must be analyzed in terms of the potential impact in the future. The team will then develop strategies to correct the deficiencies. For example, if it is determined that there was a gap in the initial assessment the team would recommend and plan to carry out additional assessment.

### Checklist for Determining Pupil Progress*

|  | YES | NO |
|---|---|---|
| 1. Were prior assessments adequate? | ___ | ___ |
|    a. Were present levels of performance determined and specified prior to IEP development? | ___ | ___ |
|    b. Were student learning styles identified and considered? | ___ | ___ |
|    c. Were student's strengths identified? | ___ | ___ |
|    d. Were student weaknesses identified? | ___ | ___ |
|    e. Was a current evaluation of student's overall development available and used by team in developing the IEP? | ___ | ___ |
|    f. Were assessments recent (completed within six weeks immediately preceding development of the IEP)? | ___ | ___ |
|    g. Were appropriate assessment techniques used? | ___ | ___ |
| 2. Were annual goals appropriate? | ___ | ___ |
|    a. Were the goals directly related to student's identified needs? | ___ | ___ |
|    b. Were special education goals more important to the student's long-range plan than the goals of the regular education programs he or she missed? | ___ | ___ |
|    c. Were the goals attainable in one year? | ___ | ___ |
|    d. Did the goals help the student to become less dependent upon special aids or special help? | ___ | ___ |
|    e. Did goals provide for maximum interaction with nonhandicapped pupils? | ___ | ___ |
| 3. Were the short-term objectives appropriate? | ___ | ___ |
|    a. Would achievement of each of the objectives lead to attainment of annual goals? | ___ | ___ |
|    b. Did the criteria relate to the type of behavior to be learned; were the criteria realistic; was the degree of mastery specified necessary before the student could move on to learning the next skill? | ___ | ___ |
|    c. Were the objectives in a logical sequence? If not, was there a reason for learning out of sequence? | ___ | ___ |
|    d. Were the objectives written in behavioral terms? Were behaviors to be learned clearly stated for implementors? | ___ | ___ |
|    e. Were the conditions under which the student was expected to perform specified in the objectives? | ___ | ___ |

*Adapted from Honeycutt, J. *The IEP team chairperson's travel guide for determining reasonable pupil progress.* Los Angeles, CA: California Regional Resource Center, 1980.

# Implementing the IEP

**Checklist for Determining Pupil Progress** continued

                                                                                                                         YES  NO

    f. Were the dates for accomplishing the objectives reasonable and realistic for this student?

4. Were the instructional strategies/activities appropriate?
   a. Are they age appropriate?
   b. Are they appropriate for this student's interest level?
   c. Was there adequate time allowed for this student to learn the prescribed skills?
   d. Are the strategies appropriate for the pupil's instructional level?
   e. Do strategies capitalize on the student's present skills, strengths, and past experience?
   f. Are the strategies and activities related to the short-term objectives?

5. Were the institutional resources adequate?
   a. Was there enough staff available to deliver the special education and related services specified in the IEP?
   b. Did persons responsible for implementing the IEP possess the necessary qualifications and experience?
   c. What inservice offerings were available to staff that would directly relate to the skills necessary to teach this pupil?
   d. Were there any problems in access, space, or other facility factors that had an effect on the implementation of the pupil's IEP?
   e. Were all the equipment and materials necessary to implement the IEP available? Were they utilized?
   f. Did staff members responsible for the implementation of this student's IEP have sufficient time to carry out all their responsibilities to this student as well as other students' for whom they were responsible?

6. Were specified services delivered?
   a. Were services on the IEP actually delivered to the student?
   b. Did services begin on time? Were they delivered as often as specified?
   c. Were special education services coordinated so as to ensure that one service did not offset another service?
   d. Were special education services coordinated with regular education services received by the student?

7. Was progress adequately monitored?
   a. Was pupil progress checked for each short-term objective? Was it checked often?

**Checklist for Determining Pupil Progress**  continued

|   | YES | NO |
|---|---|---|
| b. Is progress data adequately documented? Is there enough detail? | ___ | ___ |
| c. Are parents advised of student progress? How often? Is this sufficient to keep the parents well enough informed so they can be active IEP team participants? | ___ | ___ |
| d. Was sufficient data provided to the team? | ___ | ___ |
| e. Is the documentation used by staff to record what is being taught, methods used, and the results of teaching, adequate to effectively monitor IEP implementation? | ___ | ___ |

This checklist is not only a useful device in an Annual Review meeting but can also be used by the team as a checklist to develop an adequate IEP in the first place.

## Study Questions and Activities

1. A physically handicapped student will be integrated into your classroom. The parents are concerned about the placement and your understanding of their child's needs. Refer to the section called "Understanding the Handicapped" and list some possible points you could make to allay their fears:
    a. How will the other kids treat him?
    b. Can a regular class setting really be better for him than the special class he's been in?

2. List specific examples of how lessons in an academic area such as math could be adapted for one of the following students:
    a. a visually handicapped student
    b. a hearing handicapped student
    c. a learning handicapped student
    d. a physically handicapped student

3. Visit a resource room. Discuss with the teacher how s/he adapts lessons and materials for handicapped students. Visit a regular class teacher who teaches handicapped students and ask the same question. List the differences and similarities in their responses.

4. Discuss the advantages of and the arguments against developing an individual implementation plan.

5. Identify your own best learning style. Describe what difficulties you remember having in school and how you compensated for them. Share your thoughts in a class discussion.

# References

Bateman, B. D. *The essentials of teaching.* San Rafael, Calif.: Dimensions, 1971.

Bigge, J. & Sirvis, B. *Children with physical and multiple disabilities.* In N. Haring, (Ed.), *Behavior of exceptional children.* Columbus, Ohio: Charles E. Merrill, 1978.

California State Department of Education. *California master plan for special education.* Sacramento, Calif.: Office of State Printing, 1974.

Champagne, D. W., & Goldman, R. M. *Handbook for managing individualized learning in the classroom.* Englewood, Cliffs, N.J.: Educational Technology Publications, 1975.

Cohen, S. Improving attitudes toward the handicapped. *Educational Forum.* November, 1977, *42,* 9–20.

Gearheart, B. R. & Weishahn, M. W. *The handicapped child in the regular classroom.* St. Louis: The C. V. Mosby Co., 1976.

Gentry, D. & Haring, N. G. Essentials of performance measurement. In N. G. Haring & L. J. Brown, (Eds.), *Teaching the severly handicapped* (Vol. I). New York: Grune and Stratton, 1976.

Hammill, D. D. & Bartel, N. R. (Eds.) *Teaching children with learning and behavior problems* (2nd edition). Boston: Allyn and Bacon, 1978.

Haring, N. (Ed.) *Behavior of exceptional children* (2nd ed.). Columbus, Ohio: Charles E. Merrill, 1978.

Heward, W. L. & Orlansky, M. D. *Exceptional children.* Columbus, Ohio: Charles E. Merrill, 1980.

Honeycutt, J. *Technical assistance package for determining reasonable pupil progress.* Los Angeles, Calif.: California Regional Resource Center, 1980.

Lerner, J. W. *Children with learning disabilities: Theories, diagnosis and teaching strategies.* Boston: Houghton-Mifflin, 1971.

Meyen, E. L. *Developing units of instruction: For the mentally retarded and other children with learning problems.* Dubuque, Iowa: William C. Brown, 1972.

Mills, B. C. & Mills, R. A. *Designing instructional strategies for young children.* Dubuque, Iowa: William C. Brown, 1972.

Pasanella, A. L., Volkmor, C. B., Male, M., & Stem, M. *Individualized educational programming: Emphasizing IEPs for very young and for severely handicapped learners.* North Hollywood, Calif.: Foreworks, 1977.

Reid, E. Seven years of research in reading (Mimeo). Salt Lake City, Utah: Exemplary Center for Reading Instruction, n.d.

Reid, E. Teacher behaviors for reading instruction (Mimeo). Salt Lake City, Utah: Exemplary Center for Reading Instruction, May, 1974.

Siegel, E. & Siegel, R. Ten guidelines for writing instructional sequences. *Journal of Learning Disabilities,* 1975, 8(4), 15–21.

Smith, J. E. & Payne, J. S. *Teaching exceptional adolescents.* Columbus, Ohio: Charles E. Merrill, 1980.

Spinazola, C. Application of the diagnostic teaching model to social emotional development. In Ward, M. E., Cartwright, G. P., Cartwright, C. A., Campbell, J., & Spinazola, C. *Diagnostic teaching for preschool and primary children.* University Park: The Computer Assisted Instruction Laboratory, College of Education, Pennsylvania State University, 1973.

Towle, M. *Resource specialists training program (Vol. V).* Instructional Strategies (Part 1). Eugene, Oregon: Regional Resource Center, University of Oregon, n.d.

Turnbull, H. R. & Turnbull, A. *Free appropriate public education: Law and implementation.* Denver, Colorado: Love Publishing Company, 1978.

Ward, M.E., Cartwright, G. P., Cartwright, C. A., Campbell, J. & Spinazola, C. *Diagnostic teaching of preschool and primary children.* University Park, Pa.: The Computer Assisted Instruction Laboratory, College of Education, The Pennsylvania State University, 1973.

Worell, J. & Nelson, C. M. *Managing instructional problems: A case study workbook.* New York: McGraw-Hill, 1974.

# Resources

## General Resources

Affleck, J. Q., Lowenbraun, S. & Archer, A. *Teaching the mildly handicapped in the regular classroom.* Columbus, Ohio: Charles E. Merrill, 1980.

This very practical book presents the components of a systematic instructional model for mainstreaming and mildly handicapped from assessment to selection of instructional activities and ongoing assessments (evaluation) of performance. Includes a section of techniques for classroom management. Many specific examples are included.

Hammill, D. D. & Bartel, N. R. *Teaching children with learning and behavior problems* (2nd ed). Boston: Allyn and Bacon, 1978.

Another very practical book for specific assessment techniques and teaching strategies for all basic subjects.

Haring, N. G. & Schiefelbusch, R. L. *Teaching special children.* New York: McGraw-Hill, 1976.

Mills, B. C. & Mills, D. D. *Designing instructional strategies for young children.* Dubuque, Iowa: William C. Brown, 1972.

Myers, P. I. & Hammill, D. D. *Methods for learning disorders.* New York: John Wiley, 1969.

Smith, R. M. *Clinical teaching: Methods of instruction for the retarded.* New York: McGraw-Hill, 1974.

Turnbull, A. P. and Schultz, J. B. *Mainstreaming handicapped students: A guide for the classroom teacher.* Boston: Allyn and Bacon, Inc., 1979.
Includes chapters on educational characteristics of handicapped students, developing and implementing IEPs, and individual chapters on basic subject areas.

## Behavioral Objectives and Task Analysis

Baker, E. *Analyzing learning outcomes.* Los Angeles, CA.: Vimcet Associates.
In this program, techniques of task analysis are applied to learning objectives. Practice is provided so that an operational objective can be analyzed into subtasks (designated as either entry or en route skills). Filmstrip, tape and manual ($12.50).

Gronlund, N. E. *Stating behavioral objectives for classroom instruction.* New York: Macmillan, 1970.
This short paperback book is a detailed and very helpful guide to the writing of appropriate instructional objectives.

Kibler, R. J., Cegala, D. J., Miles, D. T., & Barker, L. L. *Objectives for instruction and evaluation.* Boston: Allyn and Bacon, 1974.

Mager, R. F. *Preparing instructional objectives.* Palo Alto, Calif.: Fearon, 1962.

## Behavior Management

Becker, W. C. *Parents are teachers: A child management program.* Champaign, Ill.: Research Press, 1971.

Hall, R. Vance. *Managing behavior (Part 1) Behavior modification: The measurement of behavior.* Lawrence, Kan.: H and H Enterprises, 1974. ($2.25)

Hall, R. Vance. *Managing behavior (Part 2). Behavior modification: Basic principles.* Lawrence, Kan.: H and H Enterprises, 1975. ($2.25)

Hall, R. Vance. *Managing behavior (Part 3) Behavior modification: Applications in school and home.* Lawrence, Kan.: H and H Enterprises, 1974. ($2.25)

Homme, L., Csanyi, A. P., Gonzales, M. A., & Rechs, J. R. *How to use contingency contracting in the classroom.* Champagne, Ill.: Research Press, 1970.

Krumboltz, J. & Krumboltz, H. *Changing children's behavior.* Englewood Cliffs, N.J.: Prentice-Hall, 1972.

Langstaff, A. L., & Volkmor, C. B. *Contingency management.* Columbus, Ohio: Charles E. Merrill, 1975.

Panyan, M. C. *Managing behavior (Part 4). New ways to teach new skills.* Lawrence, Kan.: H and H Enterprises, 1975. ($3.25)

Sulzer B. & Mayer, G. R. *Behavior modification procedures for school personnel.* Hinsdale, Ill.: Dryden Press, Inc., 1971.

**Criterion-Referenced Instruction—General**

Drew, C. J., Frestom, C. W., & Logan, D. R. Criteria and reference in evaluation: An evaluation model for the special education teacher. *Focus on Exceptional Children*, 1972, 4(1), 1–10.

Fremer, J. *Handbook for conducting task analyses and developing criterion-referenced tests of language skills.* (P.R. 74–12) Princeton, N.J.: Educational Testing Services, 1974.

Gronlund, N. E. *Preparing criterion-referenced tests for classroom instruction.* New York: Macmillan, 1973.

Housden, J. L., & LeGear, L. An emerging model: Criterion-referenced evaluation. In Georgiades, W., & Clark, D. C. (Eds.), *Models for individualized instruction.* New York: MSS Information Corporation, 1974.

Klein, S. & Kosekoff, J. P. *Determining how well a test measures your objectives.* Report No. 94, Center for the Study of Evaluation, Los Angeles, Calif.: U.C.L.A., 1975.

**Criterion-Referenced Instruction—Systems**

*Prescriptive Math Inventory.* New York: CTB/McGraw-Hill. P.M.I. is a criterion-referenced test system for measuring mastery of math objectives for grades 4–8. It is intended as a diagnostic and prescriptive tool providing a student profile of strengths and weaknesses with suggestions for learning activities to facilitate mastery at each objective. Also included are an individual study guide for the student, an activity guide for the teacher, and interim evaluation tests for ongoing assessment.

*Prescriptive Reading Inventory.* New York: CTB/McGraw-Hill. P.R.I. is a criterion-referenced test system for measuring reading ability per behavioral objectives for grades 1.5–6.5. It is intended as a diagnostic-prescriptive tool for individualizing reading. Individual student profiles describe strengths and weaknesses in terms of behavior objectives for each of the process objectives, e.g., recognition of sound and symbol, phonic analysis, and structural analysis.

*System FORE*, Los Angeles: Foreworks, n.d. This is a developmentally oriented, criterion-referenced test system to be used as a diagnostic-prescriptive tool for obtaining a student-abilities profile in language, reading, and mathematics skills. The teacher is provided with an extensive listing of companion or reference materials and tests. Kit 2 offers the Complete System FORE package of sequences, materials, inventories, a resource teacher guide, and a learning center guide. Kit 1 is identical, but made less expensive by excluding the introductory materials for those already familiar with System FORE material. The Extension Kit expands upon resource and materials listings, and includes the new "age-equivalent pupil profile."

## Environment

Petreshene, S. S. *Complete guide to learning centers.* Palo Alto, Ca.: Pedragon House, 1978.

Smith, R. M. Neisworth, J. T., & Greer, J. G. *Evaluating educational environments.* Columbus, Ohio: Charles E. Merrill, 1978.

Volkmor, C. B., Langstaff, A. L. & Higgins, M. *Structuring the classroom for success.* Columbus, Ohio: Charles E. Merrill, 1974.

## Peer Tutoring

Christopolos, F. Keeping exceptional children in the regular class. *Exceptional Children*, 1973, 40(6), 569–572. This article provides a summary of teacher education priorities from a project in Baltimore elementary school designed to help teachers develop approaches for teaching learning disabled students in regular classes. Peer tutoring is discussed as an integration technique; record keeping and task analysis are presented in the context of tutoring procedures.

Gartner, A., Kohler, M., & Reissman, F. *Children teach children.* New York: Harper and Row, 1971.

Gibbons, B. *Hosts: Help one student to succeed—Training volunteer tutors in your reading program. A complete guide.* New York: Random House, n.d.

Lippitt, R., Eiseman, J. W., & Lippitt, R. *Cross-age helping packet.* Ann Arbor, Mich.: Center for Research on the Utilization of Scientific Knowledge, University of Michigan, 450 City Center Building, Ann Arbor, Michigan 48108.

Melaragno, R. J. *Tutoring with students.* Englewood Cliffs, N.J.: Educational Technology Publications, 1976.

## Precision Teaching

Council for Exceptional Children. *Let's try doing something else kind of thing—Behavioral principles and the exceptional child.* Reston, Va.: The Council for Exceptional Children, 1972.

Haughton, E. Great gains from small starts. *Teaching Exceptional Children*, 1971, 3(3), 141–146.

Kunzelmann, H. P. (Ed.), Cohen, M. A., Hulten, W. J., Martin, G. L., & Mingo, A. R. *Precision teaching: An initial training sequence.* Seattle, Wash.: Special Child Publications, 1970.

Starlin, C. Peers and precision. *Teaching Exceptional Children,* 1971, 3(3), 129–139.

White, O. R., & Haring, N. G. *Exceptional Teaching.* Columbus, Ohio: Charles E. Merrill, 1980.

### Reading

Exemplary Center for Reading Instruction. Ogden City and Granite School Districts, 4905 South 4300 West, Salt Lake City, Utah 84118. Director: Dr. Ethna Reid. The Center offers inservice training in reading instruction and instructional packages which can be purchased. The topical range of these packages is broad and includes "Teaching Letter Names and Sounds," "Teaching Creative Writing," and "Teaching Critical Comprehension." Write to the Center's director for further information.

### Math

Reisman, F. K., & Kauffman, S. H. *Teaching mathematics to children with special needs.* Columbus, Ohio: Charles E. Merrill, 1980.

### Social/Affective

Gordon, T. *P.E.T.: Parent effectiveness training.* New York: Peter H. Wyden, 1970.

Gordon, T., with Burch, N. *T.E.T.: Teacher effectiveness training.* New York: Peter H. Wyden, 1974.

Palomares, U., & Ball, G. *The human development program (Magic Circle).* Human Development Training Institute, 7574 University Avenue, La Mesa, Calif. 92041, or 200 West 79th St., Penthouse F, New York, New York 10024.

Raths, L. E., Harmin, M., & Simon, S. *Values and teaching: Working with values in the classroom.* Columbus, Ohio: Charles E. Merrill, 1966.

Simon, S. N., Howe, L. W., & Kirschenbaum, J. *Values clarification: A handbook of practical strategies for teachers and students.* New York: Hart, 1972.

Volkmor, C. B., Pasanella, A. L. & Raths, L. E. *Values in the classroom: A multi-media program.* Columbus, Ohio: Charles E. Merrill, 1977.

### Vocational/Career Education

Brolin, D. E. (Ed.) *Life-centered career education: A competency based approach.* Reston, Va.: Council for Exceptional Children, 1973. This publication includes information on instructional materials, resources, and student competency.

California State Department of Education (Wilson Riles). *Junior high-high school group instruction for work experience education.* Sacramento, Calif.: California State Department of Education, 1973. Could be used in a learning center or other small grouping. Offers overall goals, unit goals, and lesson objectives. Includes original resources/materials, such as crossword puzzle games, interview sheets, values appraisal sheets, and so on. Also, estimated time for lesson.

Drier, J. Jr., & Associates. *K–12 guide for integrating career development into local curriculum.* Worthington, Ohio: Charles A. Jones, 1972. An exquisite volume of resources, objectives, and suggestions for integration into subject curriculum. Worth having for the resource listings alone.

General Learning Corporation—Career Programs. *Career education resource guide.* Morriston, N.J.: General Learning Corporation, 1972. Excellent activity resource book for primary, middle and secondary levels. Also contains publisher's addresses and resource people in each state. Each activity includes listings for: concepts, performance objective, materials, capsulization of lesson procedures, and general comments.

Hoyt, K. B., Pinson, N. M., Laramore, D., & Mangum, G. L. *Career education and the elementary school teacher.* Salt Lake City, Utah: Olympus, 1973. General book for beginning career education. Offers K–6 activities by: major concepts, objectives, and strategies. Offers suggestions for pre- and inservice training for teachers. Includes parent and community activities and potential resources.

Ohio State Center for Vocational and Technical Education. *Comprehensive career education model (CCEM).* Columbus, Ohio: Center for Vocational and Technical Education, Ohio State University. CCEM is a developmental approach to the integration of career education into regular curriculum. A 104-cell matrix has been developed, combining twelve social/affectives and vocations related themes across grades K–12. Behavioral objectives within each cell consider cognitive, affective and psychomotor domains.

Smith, J. E., & Payne, J. S. *Teaching Exceptional Adolescents.* Columbus, Ohio: Charles E. Merrill, 1980. Includes four chapters on career provisions for secondary students as well as a listing of career preparation resource materials.

Weisgerber, R. (Ed.) *Vocational education: Teaching the handicapped in regular classes.* Reston, Va.: Council for Exceptional Children, 1978.

## Understanding the Handicapped

Barnes, E., Berrigan, C., & Biklin, D. *What's the difference?: Teaching positive attitudes toward people with disabilities.* Syracuse, N.Y.: Human Policy

Press, 1978. A book of activities for use with students. Each of the 94 activities is coded according to relevant disability and classroom event (e.g., writing, group discussion). Designed to provide information about disabilities, foster empathy and facilitate acceptance. The book also includes a guide for finding resources (books films and curriculum packets) as well as organizations.

Bisshopp, P. *Books about handicaps for children and young adults.* East Providence, Rhode Island: Meeting Street School, Rhode Island Easter Seal Society, 1978.

Bookbinder, R. *Mainstreaming: What every child needs to know about disabilities. The Meeting Street School Curriculum for Grades 1–4.* Boston, Mass.: The Exceptional Parent Press, 1978.
An outstanding and practical guide for educating students about disabilities. There are four units: blindness, deafness, physical disabilities, and mental retardation. The author describes various disabilities, sample lesson schedules, simulation activities, and follow up activities. The book also lists many resources for related materials.

Cleary, M. E. *Please know me as I am: A guide to helping children understand the child with special needs.* Sudbury, Mass.: J. Cleary Co., 1975.

# 8

# Making It All Work: Skills for Educational Decision-Makers

> People, young and old alike, succeed to the same degree that: (A) They control their own destinies and (B) Share responsibility with others, including responsibility for mutual growth and support. (Beery, *The Guts to Grow*, p. 6.)

This chapter and Chapter 9 deal primarily with *change* and various strategies and techniques to consider that will help precipitate and support the changes that must take place in order for mainstreaming handicapped children to be most effective and successful. Berry (1974) says that if a school or system wants to create needed change, a "growth environment" must be provided for all people who have a part in its life—teachers, children, principals, and parents. Instead of isolating ourselves from one another with walls, special classes, schedules, authoritarian hierarchies, and so forth, we need to create a climate of support, acceptance, stimulation, exchange, exploration, and communication with all adults and children in the school.

Mainstreaming requires that counselors, psychologists, special educators, and administrators develop some new skills to add to those they already possess. These personnel must be able to combine knowledge of assessment, counseling, and special teaching with the instructional skills of the classroom teacher who provides most of the direct instruction. This means a new emphasis on working indirectly with students—with and through regular teachers; in other words, we need more emphasis on consultation.

In addition to the consultation role, other roles must be assumed by professionals within a school building. We need child advocates, change agents, instructional specialists, and trainers—each contributing an important part to the goal of providing the best possible educational experience for all children.

There are four sections in this chapter; each section is directed toward one key member of the IEP team—the administrator, the resource teacher, the classroom teacher, and the parent. We highlight specific information on some special role-related skills and abilities each person will require in order to be an effective team-member participant in the educational process. The information included in each section is based on specific needs expressed by those IEP teams with whom we have worked and represent skills for individual team members.

## SCHOOL ADMINISTRATORS

Principals and administrators face dramatic changes and new demands in their roles and responsibilities. The school principal is the key to effectively carrying out the requirements of P.L. 94–142 at a school site. Two recent needs assessments have resulted in identifying some of the skills and abilities that principals see as critical to performing their job responsibilities. A task force set up by the California State Assembly Education Committee identified the following skills and abilities as necessary for effective school leadership today:

1. *instructional skills*—including the ability to monitor classroom instruction, the ability to work with school personnel to plan and organize the instructional program, and the ability to identify and coordinate resources for instructional improvement.
2. *management skills*—including communication, group problem-solving and decision-making skills.
3. *human relations abilities*—motivation, staff involvement, interpersonal dynamics, trust-building.
4. *political and cultural awareness.*
5. *leadership skills*—alert to major developments in the field, open to new ideas.
6. *self-understanding.* (Mangers, 1978)

In another study, for the League of Educational Administrator Development (Project LEAD), the following clusters of skills were identified as the top five priorities among administrators:

1. how to survive the management role—including time management, conflict management and stress management.
2. evaluation of instructional, administrative and classified personnel and improvement of staff performance.
3. communication skills and improving interpersonal skills.
4. needs assessment, evaluating and monitoring educational programs, and improving school climates.
5. skills in decision-making and team management, and problem-solving techniques.

A major effort must be made to assure every principal adequate support and assistance in adjusting to the many changes facing them in their jobs. Since we are concerned in this book with the principal's role as a team leader in educational decision-making for handicapped students, we will highlight some basic ideas in skill areas that relate most closely to that role. Many of the following ideas were developed, and have proved to be valuable, through our work with educational administrators and with management consultants from the business world.

## Characteristics of Work Groups

The school principal often assumes the role of the IEP meeting chairperson. As group leader, he or she needs good leadership skills, a thorough understanding of group process and an awareness of the various roles, both positive and negative, that individual group members may play. Verderber (1978) lists some important variables that characterize successful work groups. Among the variables are those related to

- *size*. The ideal size of a group is five to eight people. Interaction tends to break down if the group numbers more than eight.
- *cohesiveness*. Members of the group have common needs and interests; in cohesive groups the goals of the group appeal to all members and the individual members feel that they are liked and respected.
- *commitment to the task*.

- understanding and acceptance of individual *roles* within the group. (pp. 167–173)

There are two basic functions of a group: the *task function* or how the group gets the job done and the *maintenance function* or how the group interacts. Good group leaders must be aware that both functions must be satisfied if the group is to reach its potential. The roles that group members assume are related to these two functions. Group leaders should differentiate between those roles that contribute to *perpetuating* the team as a working unit and those roles that *inhibit* the group process. Verderber (1978) describes the *task related* roles that facilitate the group getting its work done.

1. *information or opinion giver*—provides content;
2. *information seeker*—sees needs for additional data;
3. *expediter*—helps the group avoid digressions and stick to the task;
4. *idea person*—the individual, original thinker;
5. *analyzer*—helps the group penetrate to the core of the problem (pp. 192–194).

*Maintenance* roles that participants play that facilitate good interpersonal relations include:

1. *active listener*—provides feedback to group members;
2. *game leader*—recognizes when the group is bogged down or tired and provides some release from the tension or fatigue;
3. *harmonizer*—smooths out misunderstandings, disagreements, and conflicts;
4. *gatekeeper*—assumes the responsibility for facilitating the interaction, keeping communication open;
5. *compromiser*—helps dissenting members find a middle ground;
6. *public relations—the front man*—the person who communicates or sells the group's decisions to the outside world (pp. 194–197).

There are negative roles that group members play and these roles can inhibit or stop group process. Verderber (1978) lists seven:

1. *aggressor*—the person who criticizes, blames and works for his/her own status;
2. *blocker*—the person who argues without giving up, goes off on tangents;

# Skills for Decision-Makers

3. *competer*—one who needs to get attention, competes with others but the audience is more important to him than his ideas;
4. *special pleader*—one who always argues for a cause or his favorite ideas;
5. *joker*—a person who must be the center of attention, throws things off track by clowning;
6. *withdrawer*—the person who drops out and is not mentally a part of the group;
7. *monopolizer*—the person who talks too much, always trying to impress the group with his/her knowledge. (pp. 197–198)

It is important to be aware of these negative roles and as group leader be prepared to confront them, discourage them, redirect attention, or get the group back on task. Remember, the success of the group depends on the skill of the leader and every other member of the team.

### Tips on Planning and Leading Meetings

- Provide an agenda ahead of time. List the tasks to be accomplished at the meeting and assign responsibilities to participants for information gathering, presentations, and so forth.
- Invite only those persons who are necessary to the decision to be made.
- Create a positive climate. Attend to the physical setting—heating, lighting, and seating arrangements. A round table is the most conducive to positive group interaction.
- Create an opportunity for everyone to speak or share something. An *inclusion activity* allows each member of the group to start out on equal footing, or, in other words, establishes the feeling of equal influence among members. An inclusion activity can be as simple as each member introducing themselves and sharing something significant that they did to prepare for the meeting. The basic rule is that everyone has a chance to speak and equal time to say it.
- Introduce the topic. Make certain that everyone understands the task at hand and the procedures for working on the task.
- Facilitate the discussion.
- Keep the interaction and discussion balanced. Attend to the task functions of the group and the interpersonal interactions.

- Watch for interpersonal conflicts, expression of negative roles, and intervene when necessary.
- Make sure the agenda is followed. Keep the meeting on target.
- Prevent potential misunderstandings due to the use of jargon, inferences, or abstractions.
- Provide a "memory system" for the group. A common memory system is a large flip chart and a felt tip marker. The chart must be visible to all participants and accurately reflect the ideas, decisions, considerations, options of the group. The finished charts can later be typed up as the permanent record of the meeting (Daniels, 1977).
- Provide closure for the group by summarizing what has occurred. Indicate what the next steps will be, or terminate the task.

**Some Reasons Why Meetings Fail**

1. Lack of effective communication skills; failure to listen and failure to provide feedback or seek feedback.
2. An ineffective leader.
3. Conflict between the common group goal and individual members' goals.
4. Unclear or ambiguous goals.
5. Negative attitudes on the part of participants, hidden agendas, pressure toward conformity.
6. Lack of problem-solving skills.

## Problem-Solving and Decision-Making

IEP teams are specifically concerned with solving problems and making decisions. Decisions concerning the provision of exceptional students with an appropriate education are often complex. Such decisions are made best by a team of people because each person brings unique skills, expertise, and experience to the problem situation. Shared participation in decision-making leads to greater satisfaction with the decision and commitment to its implementation. Sussman and Krivonos (1979) outline a basic five step problem-solving sequence:

1. Define the problem.
2. Analyze the problem.

3. Suggest solutions.
4. Establish criteria for accepting a solution.
5. Select a solution and implement it (pp. 149–150).

Steps one, two and three involve gathering and processing information and exploring ideas. During step four, the group is concerned with establishing the criteria *and* judging each solution against the criteria. The decision-making begins with selecting a solution and choosing a plan of action.

Appropriate decision-making procedures for use by IEP teams include *majority-minority voting* and *consensus.* Using the majority-minority vote, the individual group members indicate their support or rejection of the idea or plan. The majority recommendation may prevail if the parent approves. The minority voter's opinions are documented.

Consensus decision-making is an advanced skill. Daniels (1980) suggests using this procedure:

1. when you want a highly qualified decision that will have an enormous amount of group support.
2. when you have a trained group which is capable of handling the conflict inherent to this process   (p. 13).

Members must be comfortable in dealing with conflict and willing to spend the considerable amount of time it often takes to reach consensus. Consensus decision-making involves intense discussion, providing information, analyzing the relevant information, and arguing the decision until every member of the group has agreed to one decision.

## Time Management Tips

We have found that principals, and other educational administrators are eager for tips on how to organize their time. There are several good books available on time management techniques and many professional workshops offered on the topic. Here is a summary of six basic time management skills as described by Bill Daniels, a management consultant who has taught us a great deal.

*Six Fundamental Time Management Skills*

1. *Know your Goals and Priorities.* Be clear on your goals and priorities. Prioritize your activities. Focus your energy on the 5% of all activities which are real "A" level activities—those that are directly related to your goals. Attack "B" level activities which

amount to about 15% of all activities, as time permits. 80% of your activities are really "C"s. Put these into a drawer for later—you will probably never get to them and the world won't come to an end if you don't.

2. *Keep a Calendar.* A master calendar, always at hand, that only you control. Your secretary may have a copy. Never calendar "C" activities. Leave an unscheduled hour each day for emergencies.

3. *Make a "To-Do-List".* Do this daily, keep it in reach, and prioritize it into "A"s, "B"s, and "C"s. Keep it under fifteen items and check off each item as completed.

4. *Concentrate.* Plan so you concentrate on one thing at a time, even if for short periods. Minimize distractions.

5. *Learn to Set Up and Use Memory Systems Effectively.* Memory systems include filing systems, charts, graphs, procedural manuals, logs, memos, calendars, and to-do-lists.

6. *Seek Closure.* Learn how to see events or activities to a clear ending or to a "decisive moment of transition" by using one of the basic forms of closure: termination, summarization, decision-making, tabling, or delegation.   (Daniels, 1977, p. 11)

Several excellent books on group process and time management techniques are referenced in the resource section for this chapter.

# THE ROLE OF THE RESOURCE TEACHER

Although all professionals working with children (and the children themselves) need support, those mildly handicapped children being returned to the regular class, or already in regular classes, require some special support. This specialized support is usually the responsibility of a team of people within the school (an *Assessment Team*) and, in particular, the resource teacher. The resource teacher is most often a credentialed special education teacher with prior full-time teaching experience, whose major skills are in the area of educational and behavioral assessment, individualized remediation, and development of educational plans. In addition, the resource teacher must be adept at establishing rapport and stimulating cooperation among other professionals. Some responsibilities of the resource teacher include:

1. Providing assessment and instructional planning services to handicapped children in the regular classes.

2. Conducting remedial instruction of handicapped children for regularly scheduled periods of time.
3. Providing consultative services to regular teachers and parents.
4. Participating with the school-based assessment team to coordinate services to exceptional students.

A part of the resource teacher's function consists of *direct service* to identified children via actual remedial instruction for specified time periods. Another portion of the role involves *indirect* service via teacher consultation, inservice, and coordination of educational services. It is our bias that the provision of indirect services is the more expedient and effective method of bringing about change in the quality of education for all children. The more that the resource teacher role is designed to offer *real* support to the classroom teacher, the more change is likely to occur.

Some teachers lack the necessary information and skills to cope with difficult-to-teach children. Teacher training programs often fail to provide sufficient expertise in basic assessment procedures, diagnostic/prescriptive techniques, and remedial materials and methods. Resource teachers must have expertise in these areas and help and encourage other teachers to acquire them. The end goal must be for regular teachers to take over responsibility for a great deal of the assessment and planning process for both normal and mildly handicapped children. This goal cannot be accomplished with the resource teacher spending a majority of his/her time in an isolated room working with children who have been "pulled-out" of the regular classroom, even for short periods of time. Only a teacher can make and maintain changes in the classroom; others may help but cannot do so unless the teacher himself/herself desires a change. A teacher-initiated referral is, in itself, an indication that the teacher desires help and may be open to change. Emphasis then must be placed upon establishing an open, honest communication with teachers who are ultimately responsible for implementing the individual child's program.

> Regular classroom teachers must become actively involved in providing special education since educational change can take place only if teachers implement effective programs. They also must become child advocates to ensure that these programs result in expanded opportunities for children to live more meaningful and purposeful lives. (Egner & Paolucci, 1974)

## Professional Skills and Characteristics

Some general competencies widely accepted as necessary for successful performance as resource teachers include:

1. Expertise in informal assessment procedures and techniques including observation.
2. Knowledge and understanding of the dynamics of learning and remediation of specific school problems.
3. Expertise in design and implementation of instructional plans.
4. Knowledge of a wide variety of remedial and developmental instructional approaches.
5. Acquaintance with a wide variety of instructional materials.
6. Knowledge of application of behavior management techniques.

More specific skills include:

1. Writing objectives.
2. Developing criterion-referenced tests.
3. Task analysis.
4. Pinpointing target behaviors.
5. Developing behavior-change programs.
6. Selection and application of observation procedures.
7. Adaptation of instructional programs and materials.

There are some critically important personality characteristics and attitudes that enable one to function successfully in the role of a resource teacher. A resource teacher

1. Must accept and value handicapped children as people. This is crucial in dealing with regular teachers' (and others') stereotypes and feelings and in making efforts toward achieving empathy.
2. Must possess the interpersonal skills which facilitate joint problem solving and stimulate sharing of skills and resources.
3. Must respect the confidentiality of records and use good judgment in handling information related to individual child cases.
4. Should be "hungry for change."
5. Should have a high energy level.
6. Must be able to face problems directly.

7. Must be politically sensitive; aware of formal and informal power structures.
8. Must possess a strong personal and professional commitment to the needs of children.
9. Must have a self-directed attitude, including acceptance of the necessity for record keeping and accountability requirements.
10. Must possess an understanding of some basic techniques that can be used in successful inservice training.

## Communication Skills

A major part of the resource teacher's role involves consultation and communication with regular teachers and other professionals directly involved with planning and implementing programs for children. Good consulting depends on effective communication, and there are some important points to consider in order to sharpen skills in communicating with others. As a consultant, trainer, and teacher, it is important to work on increasing our ability to send clear messages that cannot be misinterpreted by the receiver, and increasing our ability to listen carefully so that further communication will occur.

Worell and Nelson (1974) suggest three steps and include some tips for increasing effective communication with children. Their points apply equally as well to adults.

1. *Establish trust*—try to convey an attitude of acceptance and respect; let others know that you will not talk about them to others or betray confidences; don't be a phony; make sure your words match your actions—don't say one thing, and do another; be real, admit your mistakes and that you don't have all the answers.
2. *Send clear messages*—be specific; make sure your non-verbal behavior matches your verbal—for example, giving a compliment while staring out the window transmits two different messages.
3. *Listen actively*—active listening means:
   a. Giving undivided attention.
   b. Waiting until the speaker's thought is completed before you begin talking.
   c. Thinking about what the speaker's message really means (decoding).
   d. Indicating when you understand what the speaker is saying via eye contact, nods, verbal statements of agreement, and questions to clarify meaning.   (p. 36)

Jung, Howard, Emory and Pino (1972) outline some additional techniques and tips for facilitating interpersonal communications:

*Paraphrasing* is any means of showing the other person what his statement means to you and can be used to make sure you understand what another person is trying to communicate. Repeat in your own words what the speaker has said to you. Do not assume you understand what the speaker intended.

*Behavior description* is "reporting specific, observable actions of others without placing a value on them as right or wrong, bad or good, and without making accusations or generalizations about the other's motives, attitudes or personality traits" (Jung et al., p. 49). Not "Jim, you are rude," but "Jim, you've talked more than others on this topic."

*Feelings*—communicate your feelings to others accurately—that way nonverbal and verbal expressions will not be misinterpreted. We need to let others understand how we feel and try to understand other people's emotional reactions. One way to do this is to practice identifying or naming feelings. Try making statements, such as "I feel embarrassed," instead of blushing or "I feel pleased," instead of saying nothing, or "I am worried about this," instead of becoming suddenly silent.

*Perception check* is a check to see if you understand another's feelings accurately. It conveys that you *want* to understand what another is feeling. This involves attempting to describe another's feelings by saying, "I get the impression you are angry with me?" Always describe feelings, never express disapproval or approval, such as "Why are you so angry?"

In summary, a resource teacher must successfully combine two major sets of skills; skill in assessment and instructional planning for handicapped students and communication/consultation skills. The resource teacher needs skills to work directly with students but, at the same time, needs skill in broader indirect helping processes. A resource teacher must combine direct and indirect service skills in order to meet the needs of students and to respond to the abilities and personalities of each teacher. A resource teacher must manage a greater variety of relationships—child, teacher, and total staff.

## Support Strategies

> Be flexible and be a problem-solver. There will never be a *single* process that solves all problems, although we are forever searching for one. Expect change and a wide variety of skills and interests and adapt! (Hammill and Bartel, 1975)

"Support" can be many things, from demonstration of a particular technique or material for an individual teacher, to providing inservice for a group of teachers. In this section we will concentrate on tips and techniques for use as a consultant in a one-to-one situation.

**Some General Tips to Establish Rapport**

- Be aware of the key people in the system and look for allies or potential allies; first seek out those teachers who are most open to change and new ideas.
- Practice "good politics"—this includes an attitude of friendliness by making eye contact. Make it a habit to look for something positive about the teacher, the room, and so on, and say so.
- Do something early that will be perceived as helpful or useful, such as distributing a useful article, pamphlet, lesson plan, or technique.
- Be a good listener. Demonstrate this by nodding if you understand, and asking questions if you don't.
- Establish realistic expectations—don't set yourself up as a "miracle worker"—don't oversell yourself.
- Don't set expectations too low. Build your own knowledge and help teachers to see and *experience* the benefits of change.
- Do all you can to minimize the perception of threat. Build an open relationship based on two-way communication and sharing of ideas and solutions. Admit you don't know all the answers.

**As a Consultant**

Consulting is the procedure through which teachers, parents, principals, and other adults significant in the life of the child communicate. Consultation involves sharing information and ideas, coordinating, comparing observations, providing a sounding board, and developing tentative hypotheses for action. In contrast to the superior-inferior relationship involved in some consultation with specialists, emphasis is placed on joint planning and collaboration. The purpose is to develop tentative recommendations which fit the uniqueness of the child, the teacher, and the setting (Dinkmeyer, 1968).

Savage (1959) has identified three types of consultants:

1. *The Expert*—Directs his efforts at arriving at the right answer for a particular problem in a particular situation.
2. *The Resource*—Directs his efforts toward providing an abundance of information so that the persons can have a choice of a wide range of alternative *pragmatic* solutions to the problem.
3. *The Process Person*—Directs efforts toward developing a method of working with all persons concerned which will bring about behavioral changes and these changes will enable them to solve their own problems and become competent in handling similar problems in the future. A consultant who leans toward being "the process person" probably has a better chance of actually facilitating some lasting change.

As a resource teacher/consultant your major functions will be to help teachers to: (a) Recognize and define needs, (b) Diagnose problems and set objectives, (c) Acquire relevant resources, (d) Design solutions, (e) Implement solutions, (f) Evaluate solutions.

Most people have trouble both asking for and giving help. Success in this area demands special skills in communicating and building relationships. Two-way communication must occur before "helping" can be relevant. As a consultant you must actively listen to the teacher's problem and hear what has already been tried. Without open-knowledge sharing, you will never know just how much help you can be. If you appear to be evaluating or judging, you will generate defensiveness. Don't give the teacher a feeling of inadequacy.

Consultation often begins with receipt of a referral. It continues with observation of the child in the classroom after referral. It may be necessary to help the teacher articulate and pinpoint needs more clearly. Spend some time identifying strengths and areas of greatest potential change in both the child and the teacher. Be certain to involve the teacher in diagnosing her own problems and solutions—this cannot be overemphasized. The level of teacher participation in the decision making and planning is directly related to level of adoption later on!

The following hints have been suggested as being helpful to one in a consultative role:

1. Listen, hear, and understand what is being said by the regular classroom teacher.
2. Acknowledge openly the skills held by the regular classroom teacher.

3. Be cognizant of the problems faced by the regular classroom teacher.
4. Adjust and modify suggestions you may have to the atmosphere of this particular regular classroom.
5. Be honest.
6. Seek the exchange of ideas and suggestions (Region V Educational Services Center, 1975, p. 9).

There are some pitfalls to avoid in consultative situations.

1. Don't over-diagnose. Select one or two things to begin changing.
2. Be objective. Do not impose your own specialty on the teacher. Be sensitive to your client's personality and teaching style. Take off your blinders and widen your perspective. There is no cure-all method or material that can be applied to all teachers and students across the board.
3. Generate several alternate solutions—and examine how practical each is, how it fits into this particular classroom and how much time is involved to implement.
4. Don't overlook reinforcement for the teacher's knowledge and efforts.

Two additional skill areas perceived to be critical for resource teachers are related to inservice training and staff development and parent education. Inservice training and staff development are discussed in Chapter 9; parent education appears later in this chapter.

Following is an inservice training checklist designed to assess training needs among resource teachers. It was developed and used by the Humboldt-Del Norte Master Plan Office in Eureka, California. A similar checklist could be developed to assess the needs of regular class teachers.

**In-Service Training Checklist**

RESOURCE TEACHER

The following list includes most of skills needed to be a Resource Teacher. Please review each skill and decide if (1) you need more training in this skill, or (2) you have sufficient training in this skill to serve as a consultant to train others. A program specialist will be available to review your needs with you.

## In-Service Training Checklist  continued

| Current Level of Knowledge | Need More Training | | Can Train Others |
|---|---|---|---|
| Low 1 2 3 4 5 Hi | | | |

### PROCESS

| | | | |
|---|---|---|---|
| _____ | _____ | Know which District staff member to contact to get support services. | _____ |
| _____ | _____ | Know how to fulfill due process procedures (i.e., send out notices, obtain signatures, time lines, etc.) | _____ |
| _____ | _____ | Understand purpose of Management Information System (computer forms) and can fill out forms correctly. | _____ |
| _____ | _____ | Know how to use referral form and referral log. | _____ |
| _____ | _____ | Ability to use Assessment Team process. | _____ |
| _____ | _____ | Know how to work with community agencies. | _____ |

### IDENTIFICATION

| | | | |
|---|---|---|---|
| _____ | _____ | Implement a screening and/or referral system to identify learning handicapped children. | _____ |

### ASSESSMENT

| | | | |
|---|---|---|---|
| _____ | _____ | Know how to select, administer, and interpret formal tests such as: Keymath, Spache, PIAT, PPVT, MVPT, other (Please list) _____ | _____ |
| _____ | _____ | Know how to construct informal assessment procedures. | _____ |
| _____ | _____ | Can administer informal inventories of academic skills. | _____ |
| _____ | _____ | Can assess readiness skills. | _____ |
| _____ | _____ | Can determine reading levels. | _____ |
| _____ | _____ | Can specify areas of reading difficulty (decoding, oral reading fluency, phonics, etc.). | _____ |
| _____ | _____ | Can determine level of academic performance. | _____ |
| _____ | _____ | Can interview appropriate staff and parents. | _____ |
| _____ | _____ | Can assess social/emotional problems in learning. | _____ |
| _____ | _____ | Can do career aptitude and attitude evaluation. | _____ |
| _____ | _____ | Can assess cultural factors influencing students' learning problems. | _____ |
| _____ | _____ | Can perceive and record behavioral patterns in classroom observation. | _____ |

## In-Service Training Checklist  continued

|  Current Level of Knowledge | Need More Training |  | Can Train Others |
|---|---|---|---|
| Low 1 2 3 4 5 Hi | | | |
| _____ | _____ | Can identify and record significant educational and affective behaviors in classroom observation. | _____ |
| _____ | _____ | Can develop a readily understood behavioral information summary. | _____ |
| _____ | _____ | Can plan and sequence assessment activities necessary for a particular child. | _____ |
| _____ | _____ | Can identify needed resources (time, space, materials). | _____ |
| _____ | _____ | Can develop learning styles profile of student. | _____ |
| _____ | _____ | Can select appropriate instructional strategies. | _____ |

### INSTRUCTIONAL PLANNING

|  |  |  |  |
|---|---|---|---|
| _____ | _____ | Can organize assessment data for study of child's problem(s) into recommendations for an educational program. | _____ |
| _____ | _____ | Can understand and use pertinent psychological test data for educational planning. | _____ |
| _____ | _____ | Can break down an instructional task into simple, sequential learning steps and match task to child. | _____ |
| _____ | _____ | Can write behavioral objectives. | _____ |
| | | Can set up and document behavior modification program. | |
| _____ | _____ | Can discuss alternative remediation strategies with Assessment Team. | _____ |
| _____ | _____ | Can select, locate, or construct materials for remediation strategies. | _____ |
| _____ | _____ | Knows how to set criteria for plan modification and exit. | _____ |

### IMPLEMENTATION

| _____ | _____ | Can implement an individualized program for each student based on written plan. | _____ |

### EVALUATION AND REASSESSMENT

| _____ | _____ | Knows how to determine progress and success of student's educational program. | _____ |
| _____ | _____ | Knows how to modify instructional plan and program if necessary. | _____ |

### In-Service Training Checklist  *continued*

| Current Level of Knowledge | Need More Training | | Can Train Others |
|---|---|---|---|
| Low  1 2 3 4 5 Hi | | | |

**CONSULTATION**

_____  _____  Can demonstrate techniques to regular _____
classroom teachers.

_____  _____  Can demonstrate appropriate listening _____
skills.

_____  _____  Use of clarifying and information- _____
gathering questions.

_____  _____  Use of nonjudgmental, nonpunitive _____
responses.

_____  _____  Can use problem-solving/conflict- _____
resolution skills.

_____  _____  Ability to conduct parent conferences _____
and counseling sessions for students.

**COORDINATION**

_____  _____  Can establish communication and _____
coordination with support personnel,
agencies, parents, etc., and keep
appropriate records of key persons
and contacts made.

**ADMINISTRATION AND MANAGEMENT**

_____  _____  Can establish necessary record- _____
keeping systems to include:
    Calendar of RST activities
    Minutes of Assessment Team
    meetings
    Records of available resources and
    materials in district
    Pupil files with necessary forms.

_____  _____  Can schedule time schedule to _____
accommodate students and support
services.

_____  _____  Can conduct needs assessment. _____

_____  _____  Can design and provide inservice _____
based on the results of needs
assessment.

_____  _____  Can budget and record expenditures of _____
management and support monies and
RST funds.

# THE REGULAR CLASSROOM TEACHER

Every classroom teacher is a change agent. . . . As a classroom teacher, you hope that the final product of your efforts will be an individual who has achieved competence, self-esteem, and self-actualizing capabilities. To the extent that you succeed in approaching these goals, you are an agent of change. (Worell & Nelson, 1975, p. 3)

## Techniques for Regular Teachers

Hammill and Bartel (1978) suggest some things that regular teachers can do to make mainstreaming easier and beneficial to all children—both normal and handicapped.

Regular teachers can

1. utilize individualized instruction, activity centers, and other techniques which allow children to work at their own pace on various levels. (See the Resources at the end of Chapter 7.)
2. design group activities in which all children can participate.
3. provide human resources to allow for more individual attention—solicit parent volunteers, high school students, and peer and cross-age tutors.
4. teach values as a regular part of the curriculum. Help children care about each other and learn to respond to others in need. (See the Resources at the end of this chapter.)

In an extensive review of the literature of current programs in mainstreaming across the nation, the following techniques rise to the surface as being critical skills for *all* teachers.

- Behavior management techniques, including Precision Teaching (charting student progress) and self-management.
- Instructional materials—selection and adaptation.
- Peer and cross-age tutoring.
- Room environment—activity centers directed toward individualized instruction.

Available data seem to indicate that teachers who refuse to accept responsibility for "exceptional" children also tend to avoid the responsibility inherent in the very concept of personalized instruction. (Farrald, p. 112, in Kreinberg & Chow, eds., 1974)

Individualizing instruction is the *key* component in an overall educational program that meets the needs of all children. In summary, the major need areas for teacher inservice seem to center around

1. *Assessment:* Selecting an appropriate informal testing technique, application of testing, and analysis—including construction and use of criterion-referenced tests.
2. *Planning:* Setting objectives, scheduling, selection of materials, and evaluation.
3. *Instruction:* Small, large group presentations; continuous assessment; individual interactions, room environment and activity centers.
4. *Behavior Management Techniques.*
5. *Use of Aides:* monitoring student completion of assignments or contract; administering diagnostic evaluations; monitoring continuous assessment procedures.
6. *Use of Volunteers or Parents:* listening to reading; correcting papers with students for immediate feedback; dictating spelling; and charting student progress.

Chapter 7 is entirely devoted to ideas, methods and techniques aimed at regular classroom teachers. In this section, we will discuss some strategies and skills teachers can use during parent conferences and IEP meetings to promote a closer, more productive working relationship with parents.

## The Parent-Teacher Conference*

The advent of P.L. 94–142, and increased awareness on the part of parents as to their rights, has created a greater desire on the part of parents to know more about their child's progress and school program. Increased parental interest and involvement in the educational process may require teachers (and other professionals) to sharpen their parent conferencing skills. Certainly the idea of parent-teacher conferences is not new; however, our approach to parent conferencing must change as we take on new roles in our work with parents. Reynolds and Birch (1977) list some "new" (and some "not so new") roles that teachers are being asked to assume in their relationships with parents. These roles include:

1. Evaluating the educational progress of pupils and reporting and interpreting that evaluation to parents.

---

*This section is reprinted from Pasanella, A. L. Trainer's *manual for Module Four: Effective parent-teacher interaction.* Sacramento, Calif: State Department of Education, Office of Special Education, 1979.

# Skills for Decision-Makers

2. Participating with parents in planning and decision-making regarding school policies and practices.
3. Consulting with parents about the problems of and with their children.
4. Explaining the work of the schools and school-related processes to parents (helping them understand "the system").

To function effectively in these roles, we must move beyond the traditional parent-teacher conference and the school "Open House." Regular parent conferencing and ongoing, two-way communication is necessary. It can make all children's educations more effective, not just the education of the handicapped.

## Purpose and Content of Parent Conferences

There are two important roles for regular classroom teachers in relationship to special education students.

1. The *referring* teacher identifies a student who should be referred for assessment for possible special education placement;
2. The *receiving* teacher receives a special education student, either full-time or part-time, in the regular class.

Both of these roles call for parent conferencing and interaction skills.

# The Regular Teacher as the Referring Teacher

*Informal conferences.* Frequent contacts between the parent and the school for the purpose of discussing student strengths and weaknesses should be the rule rather than the exception. Parents should *not* be taken by surprise and approached "out of the blue" to consent to an assessment for possible special education placement. Informal conferences between parents and teacher should be held *well* before problems reach the point where a referral may be necessary. The goal at this point is to plan adjustments in the student's regular class program that may solve the student's learning problem. Keeping parents informed as to what program modifications are being tried in the classroom, *before* referral is even considered, is the regular teacher's responsibility.

Successful parent-teacher conferences are more likely when the teacher plans and prepares carefully, and when the teacher displays a genuine willingness to state concerns honestly and openly, cutting through the superficialities and defensiveness. Several follow-up conferences may be necessary to report on pupil progress and for mutual sharing of insights and successes from both school and home.

*Preparing parents for referral.* If, after exhausting all alternatives for handling the student's problem through modification of the regular program, it becomes necessary to refer a student for educational assessment, the teacher's role may shift to that of a liaison between the parents and the educational assessment team. At this point the teacher is the professional who knows the student and parent(s) best and can help explain the process and procedures, and facilitate active participation by the parent as a team member. Parents have traditionally been observers; now they are participants in the educational planning process. The teacher, as the parents' ally, can do much to help pave the way for active parental participation by helping to explain *why* and *how* the student is being tested, by helping parents to understand how special services can help, and by helping to ensure that parents experience a positive relationship with the school.

The regular teacher, through previous contact with the parents, is also more likely to be aware of special circumstances that exist which need to be taken into account in explaining the referral and assessment procedures to be used (for example, parents who have a hearing impairment, poor reading skills, or who are non-English or limited-English-speaking).

*Preparing parents for the IEP meeting.* Hostility and fear on the part of parents can be reduced if they have already been informed of, and involved in, their child's school program for some time. There should be *no* surprises for the parent at the IEP meeting. A list of suggestions designed to help regular classroom teachers prepare parents to be more active, aware participants in the IEP meeting appears later in this section.

## The Regular Teacher as Receiving Teacher

The parent's signature on the IEP does not signal the end of parent involvement. As a *receiving* teacher you are responsible for implementing specific IEP objectives and evaluating the student's performance. The law says that child progress shall be reviewed "at least annually" but this is the minimum!

Objectives stated on the IEP should form the basis for continuing dialogue with parents. Planning conferences between the parents and teacher should continue during the IEP implementation in the classroom to work out home follow-through activities (parent-shared objectives) as well as to report progress.

*Planning for home follow-through.* Encourage parents to visit the classroom to become familiar with your schedule, curriculum and materials, methods, and activities. Discuss and plan with parents ways they can help at home to implement appropriate objectives on the student's IEP. It can be helpful to discuss with parents the importance of designating a time and place at home where follow-through activities might take place, but keep in mind the parents' schedules, other children in the home, and so forth. Make sure the student and parents have a *clear* idea of what is to be done. Make certain the work is relevant, interestholding, and well within the student's capacity to do.

*Informal progress checks.* Progress conferences should be held regularly (at least quarterly) and be scheduled at times convenient to both parties. Progress data should be written down so that the teacher can refer to it when meeting with parents. Progress checks can take many forms. Some methods that teachers use are:

- observing what the child does (if s/he plays with others on the playground, for example), and keeping a running log of (in this case) social contacts.
- keeping charts on the student's performance in certain skill areas—how many words read aloud in five minutes this week, as compared with two weeks ago; how many assignments turned in on time, and so on.
- keeping a record of how many attempts, over a specific time period that it takes the student to learn a task, concept, and so on.

It is not necessary to keep charts on *everything* the student does in the classroom, but it is necessary to keep track of progress on the specific IEP objectives being implemented. Comparison of work samples is also a progress check. Be prepared to explain clearly and thoroughly the instructional materials and teaching methods you are using with the students.

In addition to face-to-face meetings with parents, there are many other ways to keep communication going with parents. Teachers can devise and use a variety of techniques.

- weekly work samples sent home.
- written notes on progress/achievements, special problems.
- happy face notes, good day awards, and so forth.
- telephone calls.

Holding regular informal progress check conferences can lead to making needed adjustments in methods, activities, and materials that are not working, before it's too late. Such conferences help to ensure that parents are well informed about their child's performance in the classroom and also to prepare parents to be active participants in the Annual Review Meeting.

### General Tips for Holding Conferences

> What needs to be established is the fact that while professionals have certain skills and training, they cannot know the child as well nor in as many ways as the parents do—hence the need to consult together. (Losen & Diament, 1978, p. 67)

1. Meet with both parents if at all possible.
2. Encourage parents to come to the conference with their own questions and concerns.
3. Try to put parents at ease; know their names. (The parent's name may be different from the child's.)

# Skills for Decision-Makers

4. Plan comfortable, nonthreatening seating arrangements. (Don't sit behind your desk, separating yourself from the parent; use a table or easy chairs.)
5. Using the classroom as the meeting place may be an advantage—work samples, materials, records are easily accessible.
6. Establish mutual trust—get to know the parent, and let the parent know you.
7. Start by sharing what each of you know about the student.
8. If the student seems to have a problem, define the problem as you see it. Ask parent for input and reactions. Remember to use active listening techniques. Continually strive to refine the interviewing, recording, and reporting skills you're already using.
9. Together, brainstorm solutions. Don't feel that you have to come up with all the answers to the problem.
10. Cooperatively develop a plan to deal with the problem. Shared planning usually results in a better plan, and greater commitment from those involved.
11. Listen, listen, listen—guard against being perceived as the authority; respect the parents' knowledge and understanding of their child.
12. Ask questions that will open the way to further discussion.
13. Be considerate of the parents' potential vulnerability regarding their child's problems. Being a parent of a handicapped child is quite a challenge, and sometimes it is difficult for parents to learn to live with a "different definition of success, or to alter their aspirations for their child" (Kroth & Scholl, 1978, p. 14–15).
14. Expect criticism—many parents are frustrated, and "at their wit's end." Try not to take criticism personally; instead, work toward becoming the parent's ally.
15. Don't expect too much from one conference. It may take several to really establish a good cooperative relationship.
16. Organize work samples, test papers, and progress data in advance. Prepare the student's desk as it would ordinarily look and have the student's textbooks and other materials handy.
17. Prepare a fact sheet about your daily, weekly, and monthly schedules.

18. Have conference objectives in mind and list points to be covered, but keep flexible; allow parents a chance to discuss their own agenda.
19. Avoid double talk—no jargon.
20. Avoid generalities—get to specifics.
21. Be prepared with suggestions for follow-up at home; parents don't always think of the usefulness of calculators, typewriters, chalkboards, newspapers, and so forth.
22. Evaluate the outcomes of the conference.

**Suggestions to Help Parents Be More Active Team Participants**

1. Encourage parents to make an appointment to observe their child in the classroom.
2. Encourage parents to set up a notebook on their child that includes materials such as:
   - a developmental history
   - an educational history
   - a list of school and community agencies they have contacted for help in the past, and/or are receiving services from now.
   - medical reports
   - records of child's behavior at home.
3. Encourage parents to talk to their child, to be fully aware of the child's self-perceptions and how s/he feels about the school program.
4. Help parents formulate a list of questions, concerns and any thoughts or feelings to share with team members. Encourage parents to think through, and to write down, the goals they feel are important for their child, and to bring these to the IEP meeting.
5. Encourage parents to ask questions, or to ask for explanations at the meeting. Let them know that this is OK! Let them know it's also OK to take notes at the meeting.
6. Make certain parents are thoroughly familiar with terms related to the assessment and the IEP form itself.
7. Answer parents' questions about instructional planning procedures and their rights and responsibilities throughout the process.
8. Remember that the resource teacher, and other special edu-

cators, will be working with you to carry out these suggestions.

**Tips for Receiving Teachers**
1. Don't underestimate parents. Some parents of handicapped students will already have read widely concerning P.L. 94–142, be in an advocacy group, or be teachers themselves.
2. Keep in mind that many parents work, have other children, and may be undergoing tremendous pressures and scheduling difficulties. Be empathetic and work out the best arrangement for both you and the parent when making suggestions; think of ways to help parents organize and make things more manageable (for example, making notebook, scheduling time for an older sibling to work with the child, and so on).
3. Encourage sharing of concerns.
4. Listen to parents—parents are with child daily and know the child best.
5. Encourage parents to share with each other.
6. Encourage parents to keep written notes of child's progress at home; this practice helps with questions at conferences and in tying together home and school activities.
7. Keep parents informed of program and current issues in special education; xerox pertinent articles to send to them.
8. Remember the team approach! Work closely with the special educators who share with you the responsibility for effective parent involvement.

# PARENTS AS TEAM MEMBERS— WHAT THEY SHOULD KNOW

> For too many years, school districts have been contributing to the credibility gap by making promises to parents without delivering on these promises. The first thing a school district can do to close this gap in credibility, and at the same time show good faith in meeting the mandate of P.L. 94–142, is to encourage the active participation of parents of exceptional children in the education of their child. (Fanning, 1977, p. 3)

Active participation by parents in educational decision-making is no longer merely a preferred practice; it is a fundamental requirement. There is a lot that parents need to know in order to maximize their opportunities to be involved in the educational process. Parents should:

1. *know how to obtain services for their children.* Some children are not receiving any special education services and some are not receiving appropriate services.
2. *know the procedures used by local schools.* Parent consent in writing is required for both assessment and placement of students in special education programs.
3. *know their rights.* They can ask to see the school's records and files relating to their child.
4. *know their children's rights.* An individualized educational plan must be developed and written for each student identified as having exceptional needs.
5. *know how they can participate in making educational decisions.* They must be invited to participate in the meeting when their child's educational plan is being developed.
6. *know what progress their child is making and how the school measures progress.* The educational progress of students with exceptional needs must be reviewed at least once a year.
7. *know how to exercise their rights.* Parents who disagree with the findings or recommendations of the school have the right to request a review.
8. *know what types of educational settings are available to meet their child's needs.* Students with exceptional needs have the right to receive services in the setting that is most suitable to their needs, and that does not separate them from normal children more than is absolutely necessary.
9. *know about other agencies which can provide services to their children and to themselves.* Special education programs must be coordinated with other programs and services in the community.

Helping parents to exercise their right to participate in the educational process in a meaningful and productive way involves more than merely providing them with fact sheets about the law and their rights and inviting them to the IEP meeting. It involves helping them to organize themselves, and providing consultation and training so that they can feel secure enough to participate actively, side-by-side, with educators. We have used the information provided in this section as presentation material and handouts in a variety of parent training sessions. Our training programs for parents have been focused around the following content areas:

- The major rights and protections established under P.L. 94–142.
- Providing a framework for parents to use to organize and maintain information and records on their child;
- The IEP team, the IEP and its required components, and setting educational goals for students; and
- How to look at an IEP—questions to ask at the team meeting, and ways to be involved in the IEP implementation.

## Basic Facts Parents Should Know

Free Appropriate Public Education (FAPE)

- is the most fundamental and important right.
- means education must be provided to meet each handicapped child's needs.
- means that education must be provided at *no cost* to parents
- means that each child must receive an educational program that is adequate and specially designed to meet their unique learning needs.
- stipulates that if there is no appropriate public school program available, a private school program must be provided at public expense.

Least Restrictive Environment (LRE)

- means that school districts must make avaliable a variety of program and placement alternatives.
- that each handicapped child must be educated in a program that can best meet his/her needs, and that allows the child the greatest possible amount of contact with nonhandicapped children.
- is the environment in which the child can learn best; this *may* or *may not* be a regular classroom.
- only children who can benefit from regular education placement will be assigned to regular classes.
- there will still be special classes, special centers, hospital or institutional placements for children who require intensive services in protected settings.

- means that special classes and services should be located in close proximity to classes for nonhandicapped students (for example, on a regular school campus).
- means that placement is not forever; as the child's learning needs change, so should the type of placement change (a child may move from an all-day special class to a regular class or resource room program).
- means that parents must give consent for placement.

Supplementary Aids and Services

- Instructional and supportive services which assist the handicapped child to benefit from special education must be provided.
- These services include: physical therapy; counseling; speech therapy; transportation, and so on, depending on individual needs.
- Some of these services may be provided by other agencies in the community, creating a need for close communication between the school, agencies and parents.

Fair Assessment

- Educational assessment is conducted to identify a child's learning needs and to determine whether the child requires special education (and if so, what type).
- The assessment must be conducted *before* a child is placed in special education, and at least every *three* years following the initial placement.
- Parents and teachers may request assessment at more frequent intervals.
- Assessment for possible special education placement may be conducted only with parental consent. (This does not apply to routine assessment or testing carried out with every student in a class or school.)
- Parents must be notified when the school plans to conduct an assessment.
- Parents must be informed about which assessment methods will be used.
- It is important that parents fully understand the purpose and the nature of the proposed assessment before giving consent.
- Schools may not use tests that discriminate on the basis of

# Skills for Decision-Makers

racial or cultural group, or on the basis of child's handicap. (Testing a deaf child by purely auditory methods would be discriminatory.)
- The assessment must be conducted by persons who are appropriately trained and/or credentialed.
- Educational placement decisions cannot be based on the results of one test alone; the assessment must be comprehensive and must take into account the child's developmental and performance levels in several areas.
- Test scores and results must be interpreted by a team of professionals who are knowledgeable about the child *and* the assessment methods.
- Parents must be informed of their right to obtain an independent assessment (another opinion from a qualified person), and the school must consider the independent assessment results in planning the child's program and placement.
- The independent assessment may be obtained at public expense *if* the parent disagrees with the assessment done by the school *and* the school does not call for a hearing to show that its assessment is appropriate.

## The Individualized Education Program (IEP)

- For every child receiving special education services, a written IEP must be developed and reviewed each year at a meeting in which parents are invited to participate.
- The IEP specifies present performance levels, educational goals, objectives, type of placement, services, annual evaluation procedures, and review date.
- It serves as the management tool that links the child to a necessary and individually designed education program.

## Due Process Safeguards

- Due process protects the rights of each person—the student, the parents, and the school staff—and ensures that each person is treated fairly.
- Important facts about due process and procedural safeguards are listed in Chapter 2.

## Hearings

- The intent of the fair hearing provision is to provide a forum

or opportunity for appropriate educational decision-making, *not* to set up an adversarial situation.
- Hearings should be viewed as an opportunity for parents, educators, other specialists, and child advocates to review educational decisions in terms of their appropriateness for the *child*.
- Before a formal hearing is requested, attempts should be made, by both parents and educators, to reach an acceptable resolution of their differences through informal channels.

## Record Keeping

Most parents of children with exceptional needs (with the possible exception of those whose children are very young) have a substantial history of contacts with various professionals and service agencies. As the years go by it becomes more and more difficult to recall and to sequence the pertinent information about their child's progress. Yet each time parents seek services from a new agency they are typically asked to fill out forms which call for general information about the child, his or her service history, as well as developmental, medical, and educational history. Many parents express frustration at having to answer the same questions repeatedly.

One way that parents can become better prepared to participate constructively in the decisions that are made about their child and to be the guardian of their child's rights is to begin a record keeping system. Parent training sessions can include helping parents develop a systematic approach to gathering, organizing, recording, and maintaining information on their child. Commonly used forms such as *background information, developmental history, medical information/health history,* and *educational history* can be put into a notebook with tabbed dividers. Additional sections of the notebook can be set up for filing medical reports, educational, psychological, and therapy reports, copies of the child's IEP and school progress reports, copies of letters parents have written and received, and records or parent contacts (visits and/or phone calls) with service agencies.

## Goal Setting

The following goal setting guide was developed to help parents become actively involved in planning for their child.

### An Educational Goal-Setting Guide for Parents*

One of the most—if not *the* most—important thing that you, as a parent, can do to help school and other professionals do a good job is to assist in the identification of goals for your child. When teachers and other professionals have some idea of what you would like to see happen to your child, they will be more able to provide services and programs that help meet your expectations. There is no one better qualified to write a goal for your child than you, the parent. You know your child better than anyone else and you are legally in charge of his/her life. It is more than reasonable that you suggest goals for your child.

Goals are not that hard to write and you will require little special training. The short program that follows will help you to identify realistic goals for your child.

If you are writing these goals to assist school officials in planning an individual education program for your child, you should hand in your list of goals to a member of the school planning team *before* the assessment process is completed so your suggestions can be fully considered in the design of your child's IEP.

*Goals—What Are They?*

Goals are statements about things we are aiming to do, get or become. Setting goals for ourselves, and systematically working toward them, is a way of turning an ambition or desire into a reality. If you know what you want, you're more likely to get it.

Setting educational goals for children is an important part of planning an appropriate instructional program. Educational goals are statements that tell what skills or behaviors the teacher and child are aiming for. They are usually written for one school year at a time. Annual goals, such as "will be able to dress himself," may be steps along the way to life goals like, "will be independent," and represent a specific set of skills that the child will hopefully master over the school year.

*Setting Goals*

Parents can make a real contribution to the design of their child's educational program when they take some time to think about goals that they would like to see their child reach. These goals can then be discussed at meetings with school personnel. The following exercise is designed to give you practice in identifying essential, realistic, reachable goals for your child.

---

*From: Pasanella, A. L. *Working together for quality education: Seminars for parents of children with exceptional needs.* Sacramento, Ca.: California State Department of Education, Office of Special Education, 1979.

Originally developed for: *Directions II: A Workbook for families.* Los Angeles: Western Los Angeles Direction Service, 1978.

*A Step-by-Step Guide to Educational Goal Setting*

Read each section below, and take a few minutes to respond to the questions asked.

1. An educational goal describes a skill or behavior we would like to see a child learn, or do better.
2. Since educational goals are usually written for one year, they are sometimes called *annual goals.* Many different kinds of goals can be set, but most of the educational goals you will want to aim toward with your child fall into one of the following five areas:

    *Academic Skills*—e.g., reading, writing/spelling, math.
    *Self-Help Skills*—e.g., eating, dressing, shopping.
    *Motor Skills*—e.g., riding a bike, climbing stairs.
    *Social/Emotional Skills*—e.g., sharing, making friends, saying "thank you", trying new things, smiling.
    *Vocational/Prevocational Skills*—e.g., following directions, completing jobs, using tools.

3. Now, think of *one* thing you would like your child to be able to do by the end of the school year. Write it here:

    _____ will _____
    (Child's Name)

    _____

    Did you write something like: "be able to read faster"; "be able to spell better"; "improve his math skills"; or "be able to play baseball"? If you wrote something like the examples above, you have written a goal for your child.

4. Look at the goal you wrote; next, look back at Step 2, and check the skill area that is most like the goal you wrote. For example, if you wrote, "Jamie will have better coordination", you would check motor skills. If you wrote, "Alicia will be able to pick out her clothes and put them on," you would check Self-Help Skills.

5. Before going on to the next step in goal-setting, let's look at a few more examples of goals in each of the five areas.

    *Academic Goals*
    Reading:

    - read traffic safety signs
    - improve sight vocabulary
    - read at a fifth grade level
    - understand what is read
    - read a book

    *Self-Help Goals*

    - eat with a knife and fork
    - go to the store on errands
    - bring belongings home from school
    - use the stove safely
    - ride the bus
    - use the telephone

# Skills for Decision-Makers

Writing/Spelling:
- print name and address
- spell name and address
- write a book report
- make fewer spelling mistakes
- print more neatly

Math:
- get a passing grade in algebra
- count by 10s
- make change
- tell time
- learn multiplication tables

Motor Goals
- swim
- cut with scissors
- play on the basketball team
- drive a car
- play the piano

*Social/Emotional Goals*
- have good manners
- enjoy playing with age-mates
- sleep without a light on
- play table games with the family
- participate in group activities

*Vocational/Prevocational Goals*
- be on time (for school, etc.)
- learn to type
- listen and follow instructions
- do chores around the house
- fill out a job application
- work independently

Notice these things about the sample goals above:
- *They are stated positively*
- *They tell what skill the child will have* (play the piano vs. taking piano lessons).

Also notice that some goals seem to fit into more than one area. "Learn to type" could be seen as a vocational skill *or* as a motor skill. Knowing which area a goal should fit into is not really that important; the skill areas merely help to think of all the kinds of things you'd like your child to learn, to do better, and to do more often.

6. On the next page, there is space for you to write some more goals for your child. Remember, goals should be realistic and reachable within a reasonable amount of time (otherwise, both you and your child may be frustrated and disappointed). You may want to review the sample goals before you go on to the next step.

7. Try to list as many things as you can that you would like your child to be able to do. Don't worry about what language you use. Write what comes into your head. Try to keep your pencil moving!

Goals List For  _____
            (Child's Name)

Priority
Number:

_____
_____
_____
_____
_____
_____
_____

8. Now look back at Section 2 and see if you have forgotten anything important from any of the skill areas. Don't feel you *have* to have all areas covered. Add any new goals you might think of to the above list.

9. Now take your list of goals and talk them over with someone else in your family, a friend or your child, if appropriate. Can you or the other person think of anything else to add to the list? Ask yourself these questions about each of the goals: (a) are they realistic? (b) are they stated positively? Revise your goals if necessary.

10. The next step is to look at all of the goals you have written and decide which one is the most important to *you* and *to your child*. Think carefully about each goal. Now put a *1* beside the goal that is the most important, a *2* beside the next most important one, and so on until you have them all numbered. Use the space marked "Priority Number."

11. In Step 10, you *prioritized* the goals for your child—indicating their order of importance. Now you're ready for a meeting with your child's teacher(s) to talk about how these goals, and others identified by the educational team, can be included in your child's IEP. Keep in mind that it is most effective to concentrate on only a few major goals at any one time.

*Be prepared to:*

(a) add to the goals you have written those goals that the school thinks are important too;
(b) explain why a particular goal is important—why you think your child should work on it;
(c) adjust your goals to reflect additional information about what is realistic and/or critical for your child at this time;
(d) find out what you can do at home to help your child reach the goals that are finally set for him/her.

The typical sequence followed by school planning teams is to conduct an assessment, or evaluation, of your child's skills and performance, and then to use the resulting information to identify instructional or learning needs. Based on estimates of your child's rate of progress, goals are then spelled out. This goal setting guide is presented *before* the assessment section to emphasize to parents that they should convey their stated goals for their child to the planning team before the assessment process is completed.

**The Quality Individualized Education Program***

The following checklists represent one alternative by which parents can attempt to gauge the quality of the individualized education program that is being designed for their child. It is important to note that the checklists represent a demanding ideal for the development of the IEP. Very few, if any, school systems are presently able to effectively implement all of the criteria suggested here as effective practices. It is important for parents to realize that school systems have been under unusual pressures to implement the requirements of P.L. 94–142 in a very short time and that it would be unfair to expect local schools to have all the "bugs" worked out of the system.

It is also important to add that many of the best special education teachers and programs that are presently operating do not as yet always follow many of the requirements outlined below. The kind of planning required by the law takes a great deal of time—sometimes (if this time is taken away from providing consistent quality instruction) planning frustrates many good teachers and they may opt to meet the minimum requirements of the law and devote larger amounts of time to teaching children. This is not always a bad decision. But we believe that quality individual education programming will eventually result in a better education for children, so we have presented the following guidelines to assist parents in helping to make the law a reality. The law will only work if the rules and regulations are given a genuine try. We urge you to help insure that the requirements of the law are fulfilled by using the following checklists to help school professionals move forward in designing IEPs that really work.

ASSESSMENT

*What Does Educational Assessment Include?*

Educational assessment is the process of gathering information about how a child performs in various skill areas, for the purpose of determining the type of instructional program and services that will best suit the child. Assessment really involves finding out what a child

---

*These checklists were originally developed for a series of parent seminars conducted by Mr. Thomas Justice, Director of the Western Los Angeles Direction Service. The checklists are now included in an awareness program developed for the California State Department of Education.

knows, what skills s/he has, what s/he *can* do and what s/he *needs to learn to do*.

The kinds of concerns about specific behaviors or developmental lags, which led to the child being referred for assessment in the first place, should largely determine how the assessment is conducted, and what behavioral areas are assessed. Some basic areas include vision and hearing; academic skills (reading, writing, spelling, math, language); social/emotional, psychomotor, self-help, and vocational skills. Some children will also require an evaluation of intellectual ability, medical assessment, and so forth. Assessment should result in identification of the child's present skill levels, learning needs, and style of learning.

There are two basic stages in the assessment process. The first stage usually involves the administration of a series of tests and observations of your child to determine whether s/he is eligible for special services. If such an assessment reveals that your child is eligible for special services, the second stage of assessment procedures should be initiated. This will identify in more detail what your child can and cannot do, and will provide the basis for your child's individualized education program design that is closely tied to more specific identified needs.

*Role of Parents in the Assessment Process*

Before the school can begin an individual assessment for a child, parents must be informed about the purpose for which it is being done, and the method or techniques which will be used. Parents must consent, in writing, before the assessment begins.

As a parent, you can contribute to the assessment process by relaying specific information about how your child functions at home and in the community. You can also suggest areas that you think might be investigated. The following checklist may assist you in being productively involved in the assessment process and in the discussion of assessment outcomes for your child.

## An Assessment Checklist for Parents
*Questions*                                                                                           YES    NO

1. Did you provide specific, accurate information about your child's skill levels and behavior?    ___ ___

2. Did you cooperate by releasing requested information—medical reports, etc.?    ___ ___

3. Did you request that any specific areas be included in the assessment?    ___ ___

4. Were you informed about what assessment was to be done, and what methods were to be used?    ___ ___

5. Were the areas that you were concerned about in the assessment included?    ___ ___

6. Did you understand the purpose of the assessment methods used?
   If not, did you ask for an explanation?
   Did you receive meaningful answers?

7. Were you invited to attend a meeting to discuss the results of the assessment?
   Did you go to the meeting?

8. Based on what you already know about your child, and the information you needed to find out, was the assessment thorough?
   Did the results "fit" with what you know about your child?
   Did you get meaningful, helpful information?

9. Did the assessment provide a clear picture of how your child performs in critical skill and/or developmental areas? (Did it tell you what your child needs to learn?)

10. Were you informed of your right to see your child's school records, test scores?

11. Did the assessment make mention of your child's area of strengths as well as his weaknesses?

12. Did the assessment reveal particular ways your child learns best, his or her learning style?

13. Were the assessment findings reported to you clearly in understandable language?

14. Did the assessment findings pinpoint specific *behaviors* needing improvements?

15. Did the assessment findings clearly specify behaviors needing improvement in a way that progress can later be *measured* in a clear cut fashion?

16. Was the teacher who will be working with your child involved at some point in the assessment process?

If you checked "YES" for most of the questions on the checklist, you may be ready to go to the next section. If many of your answers fell in the "NO" column, it can mean one or both of the following:

    (a) You are not exercising your right and responsibility to be involved in the assessment process.

    (b) The school is not doing everything that you can expect it to do.

Assessment is sometimes a complex and rather technical process. Competent professionals will welcome your input and your perception of your child's strengths and weaknesses and will help you to understand, accept, and use the assessment findings. They should also be able to direct you to additional assessment resources, when necessary. The presence of these attributes in the person, or team of persons, who conduct an educational assessment of your child is perhaps your best guide for judging the extent to which the assessment was accurate and appropriate for your child.

## CHECKLIST FOR QUALITY IEPS

After your child has been determined eligible for special services, the school district is responsible for developing a written education plan that should constitute the basis for your child's daily instructional program. The following checklist is designed to assist you in evaluating the quality of the IEP that is being developed for your child.

*Annual Goals*                                                                                                     YES   NO

Are stated goals clear and understandable?                                                                         ___   ___
Not overly vague or too specific?

Are stated goals reasonable and verified as realistic by assessment findings?                                      ___   ___

Did you, as a parent, input to the development of such goals before they were presented to you?                    ___   ___

Are the stated goals the same as the goals you feel are most important?                                            ___   ___

Are the goals few enough in number to be reasonably accomplished in one year?                                      ___   ___

Is the teacher who will be working with your child in agreement with the stated goals?                             ___   ___

Have *all* the people who will be working directly with your child participated in goal-setting?                   ___   ___

Do stated goals look like a coordinated, thoughtful plan of action that avoids duplication?                        ___   ___

*Short-term Objectives*

Does the list of objectives for your child give you a clear idea of what work is to be done during the school year? ___   ___

Can you answer each of the following questions for each objective?                                                 ___   ___
    What is to be done?                                                                         ___   ___
    By when will it be done?                                                                    ___   ___
    By whom will it be done?                                                                    ___   ___
    How will you know when the objective is completed?                                          ___   ___

Does the teacher working with your child agree that all objectives are reasonable?                                 ___   ___

## Skills for Decision-Makers

Are data now available that say where your child presently functions in relation to each objective? \_\_\_ \_\_\_

Are objectives written so that they reflect more precisely each of the stated goals? \_\_\_ \_\_\_

Does it appear that the individual needs of your child are reflected in these objectives? \_\_\_ \_\_\_

Do you understand stated objectives are "aims" statements, a "game plan," and that no one should be expected to guarantee you such objectives will be accomplished as presently written? (Objectives may need to be changed.) \_\_\_ \_\_\_

Has a review date been established to review progress toward objectives? \_\_\_ \_\_\_

*Descriptions of Related Service Needed*     YES   NO

Have you thought about related educational services that your child needs? \_\_\_ \_\_\_

Check any services you think your child may need:

| | NEEDED | NOT NEEDED | NOT SURE |
|---|---|---|---|
| Physical Therapy | \_\_\_ | \_\_\_ | \_\_\_ |
| Occupational Therapy | \_\_\_ | \_\_\_ | \_\_\_ |
| Speech Pathology | \_\_\_ | \_\_\_ | \_\_\_ |
| Audiological Services | \_\_\_ | \_\_\_ | \_\_\_ |
| Vocational Counseling | \_\_\_ | \_\_\_ | \_\_\_ |
| Vocational Programming | \_\_\_ | \_\_\_ | \_\_\_ |
| Counseling | \_\_\_ | \_\_\_ | \_\_\_ |
| Parent Counseling and Training | \_\_\_ | \_\_\_ | \_\_\_ |
| Adaptive or Special PE | \_\_\_ | \_\_\_ | \_\_\_ |
| Transportation | \_\_\_ | \_\_\_ | \_\_\_ |
| Psychological Services | \_\_\_ | \_\_\_ | \_\_\_ |
| Recreation | \_\_\_ | \_\_\_ | \_\_\_ |
| Medical Diagnostic or Evaluation | \_\_\_ | \_\_\_ | \_\_\_ |
| School Health Services | \_\_\_ | \_\_\_ | \_\_\_ |
| Social Work Services in Schools | \_\_\_ | \_\_\_ | \_\_\_ |
| Other | \_\_\_ | \_\_\_ | \_\_\_ |

    YES   NO

Have the services that you have checked as needed been written on your child's individual educational program, or at least considered at the meeting? \_\_\_ \_\_\_

Is the frequency and estimated duration of such services specified? \_\_\_ \_\_\_

Have other major agencies or persons providing services to your child been notified of the IEP meeting, if you feel such an invitation is appropriate? Such agencies or persons might be:

*Coordination Needed*

| | |
|---|---|
| County Mental Health Department | _____ |
| Department of Vocational Rehabilitation | _____ |
| Department of Public Social Services | _____ |
| The Easter Seal Society | _____ |
| Crippled Children's Society | _____ |
| Pediatricians and other doctors | _____ |
| State Department of Health—Continuing Care Services | _____ |
| County Health Department | _____ |
| Tutors | _____ |
| Other Specialists or Therapists | _____ |

                                                                                                                                                           YES  NO

Have you signed release forms and requested that copies of your IEP be mailed to other persons or agencies serving your child?   ___ ___

Has some effort been made by members of the school team to coordinate the school plan with other outside agencies providing service to your child?   ___ ___

*Assignment to School Programs/Placement*

Have all appropriate school placement alternatives been considered (local school, school district, county, or other regional programs)?   ___ ___

Have you visited the classroom(s) that are being recommended for placement for your child? Or, have you made some effort to assess the quality of the recommended placement?   ___ ___

Does the recommended placement maximize the opportunity for your child to interact with children in regular classrooms? Or with children who are less handicapped?   ___ ___

Has a specific plan of communication been developed among the professionals who will be working with your child to insure that instruction is coordinated and not duplicated?   ___ ___

Will the recommended placement enable your child to reach stated goals and objectives?   ___ ___

*Specific Assignments of What Persons are Responsible for Each Objective*

Has one person been designated as being in charge of coordinating the efforts of school personnel and related service providers?   ___ ___

Is the responsibility for achieving stated objectives assigned?   ___ ___

Is *one* person designated as primarily responsible for achieving each stated objective?   ___ ___

Is the person(s) assigned responsibility for achieving the objectives the most logical choice for that responsibility?   ___ ___

Have you asked or thought about any ways you might contribute to ___ ___
the achievement of stated objectives?

If you have agreed to some part of the responsibility for achieving a ___ ___
stated objective, are you clear as to exactly what is expected of you?

Is every person providing service to your child responsible for at least ___ ___
one objective?

*Methods by Which Progress Toward Stated Goals and*
*Objectives will be Measured*

Have the methods for evaluating your child's progress been specified ___ ___
(e.g., achievement tests, teacher-made tests, observations, criterion-
referenced tests)?

Have the particular tests, methods of observation, etc. been specified? ___ ___

## Study Questions and Activities

1. Select two groups, of three persons each, from the class to debate the pros and cons of: "Resolved—the mildly handicapped can be served more effectively by *indirect* as opposed to *direct* services from special education resource teachers." (See also Chapter 7.)

2. Have one class member assume the role of Ms. Vera Destraught, a first-year teacher with an overabundance of students with learning and behavior problems, and have another class member assume the role of a resource specialist responding to Vera's request for help. Role play one or more of a series of conferences: (a) The first conference to define the problem(s), (b) the second conference to report the results of classroom observations and other informal assessments, (c) the third conference to plan joint responsibilities for instruction, and (d) the fourth conference to evaluate pupil progress. To lend variety, have class members take turns role playing different "teachers" (for example, Mr. Manley Makismo, who hates to admit to his problem pupils, or Mrs. Ima Intellect, who already has the "answers" to her pupils' many problems). Good luck!

3. Identify an organized group of parents of handicapped in your community. Attend one of their meetings. Interview some of the parents about their role and experiences concerning parental involvement in educational programming.

# References

Bauer, H. The resource teacher—A teacher consultant. *Academic Therapy,* 1975, *10* (3), 229–304.

Beery, K., Brokes, A. L., Howlett, H., Jiguor, J. W., Lobree, V. A., Marshall, D. A., McCurdy, R. E., Racicot, R. H., Rolle, R. E. W., Stuck, R. L., Wardlaw, J. H., & Wiley, E. M. *The guts to grow.* Sioux Falls, S. D.: Dimensions (Adapt Press), 1974.

Berlin, I. N. Preventive aspects of mental health consultation to schools. *Mental Hygiene,* 1967, *51* (1), 34–40.

Daniels, W. R. *Take your time: Tactics for time management.* Mill Valley, Calif.: American Consulting and Training, 1977.

Daniels, W. R. *The manager's playbook: Procedures for effective teamwork in meetings.* Mill Valley, Calif.: American Consulting and Training, 1980. (Mimeo)

Dinkmeyer, D. The counselor as consultant: Rational and procedures. *Elementary School Guidance and Counseling.* 1968, *2,* 187.

Dinkmeyer, D. & Carlson, J. *Consultation: A book of readings.* New York: John Wiley, 1975.

Dollar, B., & Klinger, R. *A systems approach to improving teacher effectiveness: A triadic model of consultation and change.* Houston, Tex.: Houston Independent School District, n.d. (Mimeo)

Educational Research Consultants. *Project LEAD, Leadership Development Center Needs Assessment.* Sacramento, Calif.: California State University, Department of Educational Administration, March, 1978.

Egner, A., & Paolucci, P. For the sake of children: Some thoughts on the rights of teachers who provide special education within regular classrooms. In R. Johnson, R. Weatherman, & A. M. Rehmann (Eds), *Handicapped youth and the mainstream education.* Minneapolis: Audio Visual Library Service, University of Minneapolis, 1975, 29–47.

Fanning, R. The new relationship between parents and schools. *Focus on Exceptional Children,* 1977, *9* (5), 3.

Hammill, D. D., & Bartel, N. R. *Teaching children with learning and behavior problems* (2nd ed.). Boston: Allyn and Bacon, 1978.

Haughton, D., & Enos, D. *Project and pert design for PREM.* Austin, Tex.: University of Texas, School of Education, Preparing Regular Educators for Mainstreaming Project, 1975. (Mimeo)

Heward, W. L., Dardig, J. C., & Rossett, A. *Working with parents of handicapped children.* Columbus, Ohio: Charles E. Merrill, 1979.

Jung, C., Howard, R., Emory, R., & Pino, R. *Interpersonal communications: Leader's manual.* Portland, Ore.: Northwest Regional Educational Laboratory, Tuxedo, N. Y., Xicom, 1972.

Klinger, R. *The KPLC as a model for individualized instructional support.* Houston, Tex.: Houston Independent School District, n.d. (Mimeo)

Kreinberg, N., & Chow, S. (Eds.). *Configurations of change: The integration of mildly handicapped children into the regular classroom.* Sioux Falls, S.D.: Adapt Press, 1974.

Kroth, R. L. & Scholl, G. T. *Getting schools involved with parents.* Reston, Va.: The Council for Exceptional Children, 1978.

Lambert, N. *Similarities and differences between school-based and community-based consultation.* Berkeley: University of California, n.d. (Mimeo)

Losen, S. M., & Diament, B. *Parent conferences in the schools.* Boston: Allyn and Bacon, 1978.

McGinty, A., & Keogh, B. *Needs assessment for inservice training: A first step for mainstreaming exceptional children into regular education.* Los Angeles: Graduate School of Education, University of California, Los Angeles, 1975. (Mimeo)

Mangers, D. *The school principal: Recommendations for effective leadership.* A report of the Assembly Education Committee Task Force for the improvement of pre- and in-service training for public school administrators. Sacramento, Calif: State Capitol, 1978.

Reynolds, M. C., & Birch, J. W. *Teaching exceptional children in all America's schools.* Reston, Va.: The Council for Exceptional Children, 1977.

Savage, W. Consultation services in local school systems. In K. Holly, *Consultant Handbook.* Duarte, Calif.: Duarte Unified School District, ESEA Title III Prospect: Clarity, 1975. Chicago: Midwest Administration Center, University of Chicago.

South Carolina Region V Educational Services Center. *The resource room: An access to excellence.* Lancaster, S.C.: Region V Educational Services Center, 1975. (out of print)

Sussman, L. & Krivonos, P. D. *Communication for supervisors and managers.* Sherman Oaks, Calif.: Alfred Publishing Co., Inc., 1979.

Verderber, R. F. *Communicate!* (2nd ed.). Belmont, Calif.: Wadsworth Publishing Co. Inc., 1978.

Worell, J., & Nelson, C. M. *Managing instructional problems: A case study workbook.* New York: McGraw-Hill, 1974.

# Resources

## Time Management

Daniels, W. R. *Take your time: Tactics for time management.* Mill Valley, Calif.: American Consulting and Training, 1977.

Lakein, A. *How to get control of your time and your life.* New York: Peter Wyden Inc., 1973.

## Groups and Group Process

Potter, D. & Anderson, M. *Discussion in small groups: A guide to effective practice* (3rd ed.). Belmont, Calif.: Wadsworth Publishing Co., 1976.

Shaw, M. E. *Group dynamics: The psychology of small group behavior.* New York: McGraw-Hill, 1971.

## Parents

*P.L. 94–142 Implementing procedural safeguards—A guide for schools and parents.* Reston, Va.: The Council for Exceptional Children.
Three sound filmstrips, cassette tapes, a discussion guide, and ditto masters. This how-to package focuses on due process aspects as they pertain to P.L. 94–142 regarding the rights and protection of educators, parents, and their children.

*Those other Kids.* Minneapolis, Minn.: University of Minnesota, Audio-Visual Library Service.
A 26-minute film covering right to education, due process, and continuum of delivery services.

*More than a Promise.* Columbus, Ohio: Charles E. Merrill, 1978.
A 10-minute film which provides an overview of the provisions and intent of P.L. 94–142 and includes the views of parents and educators.

Pasanella, A. L. *Trainer's manual for module four: Effective parent-teacher interaction.* Sacramento, Calif.: State Department of Education, Office of Special Education, 1979.

Pasanella, A. L. *Trainer's manual for working together for quality education: Seminars for parents of children with exceptional needs.* Sacramento, Calif.: California State Department of Education, Office of Special Education, 1979.

## Resource Rooms

Cohen, S. *Resource teachers simulation training packet.* Columbus, Ohio: Charles E. Merrill, 1978.

Hawisher, M. F. & Calhoun, M. L. *The resource room: An educational asset for children with special needs.* Columbus, Ohio: Charles E. Merrill, 1978.

Wiederholt, J. L., Hammill, D. D., & Brown, V. *The resource teacher: A guide to effective practices.* Boston: Allyn & Bacon, 1978.

# 9

# Making It All Work: Inservice Training, Service Delivery, and Program Evaluation

In this chapter we describe some successful training techniques that have worked for us. We discuss some of the system policies and procedures that must be in place in order to assure full services to handicapped students. And finally, we outline some models that have been used to evaluate the effectiveness of services and programs.

## INSERVICE TRAINING

In the process of affecting change in the education of handicapped children, common needs for group inservice may arise. Awareness level inservice will be needed for parents and community agencies. Teachers may need inservice in such areas as identification and assessment, observation and screening, instructional planning, classroom environment, behavior management techniques, and curriculum modification. Resource suggestions for inservice content are presented at the end of this chapter. Here, we will concentrate on the process and methods for presenting the content, including some tips on making inservice successful.

There are a variety of methods for conveying information, knowledge, and skills to others. Some of these methods include demonstrations, consultation, and workshops. It is important, as a trainer, to be aware of each and of their advantages and limitations. The following methods are adapted from Havelock (1973).

1. *Lecture* is overused and is mainly an awareness level and interest creator. It is a one-way medium in which the presentor sends a message and receives no counter message.
2. *Film or Slides* can be "lectures on celluloid" and used for awareness, interest, and introductory purposes.
3. *Demonstrations* build interest, awareness, and "pretrial" evaluation.
4. *Consultation or person to person interaction* forces the teacher to think about change immediately. It is a two-way approach that increases reality and allows expression of feelings of doubt or difficulty.
5. *Group Discussions* increase feelings of safety and willingness to take risks, enable feelings to be discussed, provide opportunity to move toward concensus, and allow cooperative involvement.
6. *Conferences or Workshops* can incorporate all of these methods and, in addition, can include use of tasks to allow participants to practice new skills and commitment to implement new skills in classroom with resource teacher support.

## Types of Training Experiences

The first type of training is informational in nature, where the objective is for the trainee to gain a greater *awareness* of a product, an idea, or a new approach. An example of this would be an "Introduction to Mainstreaming" meeting for parents. The second type of training has as its objective greater *skill* or *knowledge* on the part of the trainee. Most workshops are of this second type. Participants leave knowing more than when they came, but often lack a systematic approach or plan to enable them to actually implement the newly acquired ideas or skills back in their classrooms. The third type of training has as its objective, *visible, observable change* in the trainee's classroom. The major thrust of this training is implementation by trainees in classrooms with students. In the following sections, we are primarily addressing ourselves to the second and third types of training: skills acquisition and training toward implementation.

States and local school districts have been planning and implementing massive training efforts to meet the P.L. 94-142 mandate. Many of these workshops have been awareness type training in which large groups of professionals come together in large auditoriums to spend the major portion of their time listening. We have participated in this type of training. We have also participated, with much more personal satisfaction, in developing and conducting inservice workshops that are aimed at adoption or implementation of ideas. The training process we prefer to use is an adaptation of the Dissemination/Change Agent Model.

## Dissemination/Change Agent Model*

The Dissemination/Change Agent Model or D.C.A. model is an idea-dissemination model. Over time, the criteria for success are based on whether the idea or content area is eventually implemented in the home setting of the participants. The model involves (a) training educators in a given idea or skill, and (b) facilitating a spread-of-effect by having participants return to their school districts and train a predetermined number of other educators in the idea or skill.

The model follows a general format described below.

- Change agent teams are selected. Each team consists of a classroom teacher, psychologist or resource person, and an administrator from the same school district or school site.
- An Idea-Insertion Conference is held during which the teams are instructed in the idea to be disseminated. Each team develops a plan to implement the idea in the classroom of the teacher-member of the team. Each team also develops a plan to train a specified number of other teachers in their district to implement the idea.
- Then the idea is actually implemented in the teacher-member's classroom for a specified minimum period of time.
- Teams train other people to implement the idea in their classrooms.
- The implementation of the teachers and others who have been trained is evaluated.
- A Spread-of-Effect Conference is held during which each team describes how implementation, training, and evaluation were

---

*This training model was originally developed, field-tested and refined by Bruce Weston and other staff members of the Instructional Materials Center for Special Education and later the California Regional Resource Center, University of Southern California, Los Angeles.

accomplished. Each participant completes an evaluation of the dissemination model.

The DCA Model includes the following stages:

STAGE 1. Initial letter mailed to a number of potential users announcing the training process and content briefly, application is included.

STAGE 2. In response to applicants, a screening letter and response form is sent; includes specific information on training process, content area, and information for self-selection of teams.

STAGE 3. Self-Identification of applying teams. Teams pre-commit to train others and implement content.

STAGE 4. Selection of teams by the training agency.

STAGE 5. Training of teams at the Idea-Insertion Conference.

STAGE 6. Development of training plans by teams.

STAGE 7. Implementation of idea or content area in teacher-member's classroom.

STAGE 8. Training of other persons by teams.

STAGE 9. Feedback or evaluation of team's implementation and training efforts.

STAGE 10. Spread-of-Effect Conference in which each team presents their implementation and training experiences.

*The Initial Letter*

Purpose: To inform the target population of the opportunity to participate in the training.

The initial step in the recipients' self-selection process.

Content: Brief description of the DCA process including the required team composition. (e.g., teachers, psychologists, administrators).

Brief description of content area.

Dates of both the training conference and spread-of-effect conference.

Indication of teams' commitment to train others.

Information on responsibility for expenses.

Application procedures: Who may apply, deadlines, and forms.

An invitation to pass the information on.

# Training, Delivery, and Evaluation

Mailing: Send 300 or more letters for each three-person team desired. (This number has worked best)

Schedule one month between initial mailing and application deadline.

*The Screening Letter*

Purpose: To more fully describe the demands of participating in the training.

To provide the applicant an opportunity to screen herself or himself out.

Content: Detailed list of project objectives.

An individual response form.

Date and site of the training conference and spread-of-effect conference.

Information on activities of the training and spread-of-effect conferences.

Date on which teams will be notified of their selection/rejection.

Information on responsibility for expenses.

Delineates the nature of the teams' commitment to train and facilitate the implementation in their home district or county.

Mailing: Mailed only to those who replied to initial letter.

Allow one month between mailing and deadline for response.

There are many excellent training programs and examples of some of them are listed at the end of this chapter. We urge you to learn about existing training programs and try adapting materials to meet your local needs *before* you set about designing your own training program.

However, we would also like to share some tips with our readers that we have found valuable in adapting existing training materials to fit local needs and in creating new training materials.

## Content Preparation

The boundaries of any concept or content are broad. If you are after awareness-type training, provide a survey and be inclusive, if that is your objective. If your objective is implementation, you must be willing to simmer a large body of information down into several major actions which the participants can actually perform. This increases the chances that participants will experience initial success and increases the probability that participants will expand their knowledge later.

To develop content with *implementation* as the objective, first attempt a small sequence of concepts or substeps. Then take it, debug it, and polish it. Elicit responses and criticism from experienced experts—include those who may already be implementing the ideas. Once you have a draft of the content sequence, substeps, and skills to be learned, try dividing content up into *presentation* chunks and *task* chunks. Keep in mind that the sequence must be carefully paced, provide appropriate amounts of practice for learners, and work in ways of providing immediate feedback and knowledge of results. Delete anything that is irrelevant or extraneous, or anything that would be nice to teach but is not critical at this stage of training.

## Task Design

The next step is to develop tasks for participants so they can practice what they learn. Tasks should be fairly short and focus on one, maybe two, small pieces of the total content. The most effective tasks actively involve the participants in responses and provide feedback on adequate performance. Tasks can be written and involve recall or application of information, or they can be directed toward implementation (actual live practice of skills learned). Tasks A through E which follow are samples taken from a variety of workshops.

### Task A

*Note:* This task is an example that calls for simple recall of information presented during a large group presentation.

List at least five steps, which you feel are important, from the initial referral of a child to placement of that child in a Resource Program.

### Task B

*Note:* Another example of task that involves simple recall of information.

A. In the spaces below, list the four basic steps involved in Precision Teaching:
   1. _____

# Training, Delivery, and Evaluation

      2. _____
      3. _____
      4. _____

B. Now list the three criteria for pinpointing a behavior. A pinpointed behavior must be:

      1. _____
      2. _____
      3. _____

**Task C: Part 1**

*Note:* This example illustrates a method for involving participants in *applying* information received to themselves and their situations. This task was used at a principals' workshop.

*Problem:* You are back in your own school situation. Your Appraisal Team is operational. You have a Resource Teacher and an aide.

    1. Fifteen students from five classrooms have been placed by the Appraisal Team in the Resource Program.

    2. Four of the above 15 students are also assigned for auxiliary services.

    3. Six other students have been referred and are waiting to be processed.

    4. Two Appraisal Team meetings have been scheduled for one week.

Based on the above information and the list of required Resource Teacher job activities (part 3), design a hypothetical schedule for a week of Resource Teacher time in your school.

*Note:* If you are in a rural school, assume that your Resource Teacher is assigned to three schools.

**Task C: Part 2**  *Resource Teacher Hypothetical Weekly Schedule*

|      | MON. | TUE. | WED. | THUR. | FRI. |
|------|------|------|------|-------|------|
| A.M. |      |      |      |       |      |
|      |      |      |      |       |      |
|      |      |      |      |       |      |

|  | MON. | TUE. | WED. | THUR. | FRI. |
|---|---|---|---|---|---|
| P.M. |  |  |  |  |  |
|  |  |  |  |  |  |
|  |  |  |  |  |  |
|  |  |  |  |  |  |
|  |  |  |  |  |  |

Check the list in part 3 to be sure you have included all job activities.

**Task C: Part 3**  *Resource Teacher Job Activities*

- ☐ Attendance at Appraisal Team Meetings
- ☐ Consultation with Parents
- ☐ Consultation with Regular Teachers
- ☐ Observation in Regular Classroom
- ☐ Conducting Assessments
- ☐ Coordination of Auxiliary Services for Referred Children
- ☐ Coordination of Referral and Assessment Information and Findings
- ☐ Professional Growth (Including Visits to IMC, Reading Literature)
- ☐ Remediation (Direct Service)
- ☐ Demonstrations
- ☐ Supervision of Resource Teacher Aide
- ☐ Assistance in Writing Individual Instructional Plans

**Task D**

*Note:* This activity illustrates the use of hypothetical situations. The task was used in a workshop for parents on Parent Rights and Responsibilities.

**Directions**

Read the three "situations" below and respond to the questions. Work *independently* or in pairs. Refer to your handouts. Add to your responses following the group discussion.

**Situation A**

Mrs. Burns, the principal of the elementary school where Michael, a handicapped 10-year-old, is in a special class, says to Michael's mother, "Mrs. Green, we've tried everything and your son does not

# Training, Delivery, and Evaluation

progress. We feel that you should place him in a private institution for the physically handicapped. Really, it would be the best for you *and* Michael. Public school is just not the place for a child like Michael."

1. Are Michael's rights being violated? ____ Yes ____ No
2. What are Michael's (and his parents') rights in this situation?

   _____
   _____
   _____

3. What court cases(s) and/or legislation supports your response to question 2 above?

   _____
   _____
   _____

**Situation B**

A school superintendent says to Mr. Palmer, the father of a school-aged retarded daughter, "I understand your point. You want us to serve all handicapped children. I too think this is a fine goal, but we simply can't afford to open another special class. We don't have the money. Why, the last time we added a class for 'trainable' kids over there in Orchard District, we had to let an art teacher and a P.E. teacher go. I'm truly sorry, Mr. Palmer, but that's just the way it is right now."

1. On what legal grounds might Mr. Palmer challenge the statement of the superintendent? _____

   _____

2. What court decisions support your responses to the above question?

   _____
   _____
   _____

**Situation C**

Mr. and Mrs. Avila, following a conference with the school principal and psychologist, reluctantly agree to the placement of their son, Jose, in an EMR class. They are puzzled by what the school officials have told them about their son's performance on certain tests of mental ability, but conclude that the school knows best. In the

Chicano community where they live, Jose has always appeared normal and well adjusted.

1. On what basis does it appear that the EMR placement decision has been made?
   _____
   _____

2. What court decisions have been handed down in California which address the problem faced by the Avilas? _____
   _____
   _____

3. How do the provisions of P.L. 94–142 relate to this problem?
   _____
   _____

### Task E

*Note:* This task focuses on actual implementation with students. The workshop content here was Precision Teaching.

### Implementation

By now you will have gathered sufficient *baseline data* for your first project. The next step is to discuss the project with the student. Complete and check off the following steps with the behaver.

- ☐ 1. Discuss the project with the student. Show him or her the baseline data and together decide whether the pinpointed behavior should be *accelerated* or *decelerated*.
- ☐ 2. With the student, decide on a realistic aim and a target date for reaching that aim. Mark the *aim* on the chart.
- ☐ 3. Draw a *Phase Change Line* to indicate the end of the *before* Phase on the chart.
- ☐ 4. Discuss possibilities for the first *Intervention* with the child.
- ☐ 5. Begin the first *Intervention Phase* of the project as soon as possible and continue it for at least one week. Chart the data.

*Remember:*

- that behavior changes slowly; small steps are more easily and comfortably accomplished by the learner than are giant leaps. Sometimes it is necessary to esablish subgoals or aims so that the final target will not seem impossible to the child.

# Training, Delivery, and Evaluation

- to try the Intervention for at least a week. If the Intervention does not bring about a change in the first day or two, don't give up!

## Developing a Schedule

A carefully designed and well-thought-out schedule is a necessity for a smooth running workshop. Particularly in that part of the workshop or conference where the content or idea is being presented, we like to use a large group/small group cycling process that goes something like this:

1. The presenter (ideally someone who is presently using the ideas or skill being presented) presents one major point to the total group being trained. This presentation is limited to 15 minutes.
2. The group goes immediately to pre-announced small groups where they are given a brief written task to do that relates directly to the presentation they have just heard in the large group.
3. After most of the people in the small group have completed this task, their responses are discussed. Since the written task is intended to be a learning device, as contrasted to a test, participants are encouraged to make any changes or additions to their task sheets that they wish.
4. At the completion of this discussion, at the time indicated on their schedule, the participants return to the large group setting for another chunk of input. The large/small group cycles take about one hour to complete 15 minutes for presentation, 35 minutes for task and discussion, and 10 minutes to move from large to small group and back.

This large group/small group format and the time segments alloted to each accomplishes several things.

First, it forces the presenter to plan presentations carefully and get to the point almost immediately. Second, it provides for physical movement on the part of the participants. It requires the participants to become actively involved (through the task sheets) rather than just passively involved (listening). It provides a setting (the small groups) which is more conducive to risk taking, that is, admitting the need for further information or clarification; and, it provides instant feedback to the presenter(s) in the form of the completed task sheets—as to where s/he is "hitting the mark" and where s/he is missing it. Thus, the presenter can correct his or her course and give feedback to the participants.

Schedules A–C illustrate the combination and alternation of large group presentations with small group activities and tasks. The array of schedules includes examples for half-day, one-day, and two-day workshops.

**Schedule A**

PARENT WORKSHOP

Parent Rights and Responsibilities in
the Education of Exceptional Children

WORKSHOP SCHEDULE

LG = Large Group    SG = Small Group

| | | |
|---|---|---|
| (LG) | 9:00–9:15 | Coffee; Name Tags |
| (LG) | 9:15–9:30 | Introductions; Workshop Schedule and Objectives |
| (LG) | 9:30–9:50 | *Presentation:* "Legal Rights of the Handicapped: Educational Change Via Litigation and Legislation." |
| (SG) | 9:50–10:15 | *Activity I:* Discussion |
| | 10:15–10:20 | Break |
| (LG) | 10:20–10:40 | *Presentation:* "Due Process" |
| (SG) | 10:40–11:05 | *Activity II:* Discussion |
| | 11:05–11:10 | Break |
| (LG) | 11:10–11:20 | *Presentation:* "Action Strategies for Parents" |
| (SG) | 11:20–12:00 | *Activity III* (Personal Commitment: Group Strategies) |
| (LG) | 12:00–12:30 | Group Sharing; Evaluation; Wrap-up. |

**Schedule B***

BEHAVIOR MANAGEMENT

**Workshop Objectives**

1. at the conclusion of the workshop, participants will be able to identify the major concepts of, and rules for, a Contingency Management System.
2. By the end of the workshop, participants will be able to plan each step necessary in setting up a Contingency Management System in the classroom.

---

*This schedule (and Schedule C following) is based on A. Langstaff and C. Volkmor, *Contingency Management* (Columbus, Ohio: Charles E. Merrill, 1975). A sound filmstrip package and book.

3. Three weeks after the workshop, participants will have implemented a Contingency Management System. To be considered successful, the system designed by the teacher will include *all* of the following observable characteristics:
    3.1 Classroom divided into task area (where students work on academic tasks and assignments) and an *RE area* (where children go after task completion to engage in self-chosen reward activities).
    3.2 A posted *RE menu* or list of activities from which students can choose for their free time (RE time).
    3.3 Nonverbal signal(s) which: (a) individual students can use to indicate need for teacher attention, (b) the teacher uses to signify the time for students to return to task area.

**Sample Program**

| | | |
|---|---|---|
| 1. | Presentation | Pretest |
| | | Introduction to Contingency Management |
| | | Filmstrip 1 |
| | | Contingency Management: Basic Principles. |
| 2. | Small Group Activity | HPB's: Pinpoint "natural reinforcers." Task 1. |
| 3. | Presentation | How Contingency Management works in the Classroom |
| | | Filmstrips 2 and 3 |
| | | Discussion on Planning a Contingency Management Program. |
| 4. | Small Group Activity | LPBs and HPBs. |
| | | Creating a Menu and Room Arrangement. |
| | | Tasks IV, V, VI, VII, Activity I. |
| 5. | Presentation | Planning schedule and developing tasks for a Contingency Management Program. |
| | | Filmstrip 4 and discussion. |
| 6. | Small Group Activity | Developing a schedule and listing tasks. |
| | | Activities II, III, IV. |
| 7. | Presentation | Getting the Program started: Signals, explaining program to students, helpful hints. |
| 8. | Small Group Activity | Task X on heading off problems. |
| 9. | Presentation | On to implementation! Adaptations, refinements. |
| 10. | Small Group Activity | List steps for first day implementation. |
| 11. | Small Group Activity | Posttest. |
| 12. | Presentation | Questions and answers. |

**Schedule C***

SAMPLE WORKSHOP SCHEDULE
TWO DAY WORKSHOP

(L) = Large Group    (S) = Small Group

**Day 1**

| | |
|---|---|
| 8:30–9:00 (L) | Pretest |
| | Overview of Workshop |
| 9:00–9:30 (S) | Communication Game |
| 9:30–9:50 (L) | Filmstrip 1 |
| | "Basics of Contingency Management" |
| |   HPB/LPB |
| |   Reinforcers (RE) |
| |   Menu |
| | (Short presentation taken from Chapter 1) |
| 9:50–10:10 (S) | Task I HPB/LPB |
| | Compare answers in group |
| 10:10–10:20 | RE |
| 10:20–10:30 (L) | Filmstrip 2 |
| 10:30–11:00 (S) | Read Chapter 2 and discuss issues |
| 11:00–11:20 (L) | Filmstrip 3 |
| | Chapter 3—Short presentation by teacher-presenter |
| |   student LPBs + HPBs |
| |   Examples of menus |
| 11:20–11:40 (S) | Task IV and V |
| | Compare answers in group |
| 11:40–12:00 (L) | Room Arrangement (Chapter 3) |
| | Examples: Teacher-presenter |
| 12:00 | Lunch |
| 1:00–1:20 (S) | Task VI Diagram Classroom |
| | Compare answers in group |
| 1:20–1:40 (L) | Filmstrip 4 |
| | Chapter 4—Signals |
| |     Schedules: Teacher-Presenter |
| |     Examples |
| 1:40–2:00 (S) | Activity II—Compare answers in group |
| 2:00–2:15 (L) | Chapter 4 |
| | Explaining the system: Teacher-Presenter |
| | Student Tasks—Examples |
| 2:15–2:35 (S) | Activity III |
| | Compare answers in group |
| 2:35–2:45 | RE |

---

*This schedule is adapted from one originally designed and used by Bruce Weston, Director, California Regional Resource Center.

| | |
|---|---|
| 2:45–3:00 (L) | Routines: |
| | Cleanup, Approximations, and so forth |
| 3:00–3:40 (L) | Questions and Answers |

**Day 2**

| | |
|---|---|
| 8:30–8:50 (L) | Chapter 5—Short presentation |
| | First day preparation |
| | Teaching the System to students |
| 8:50–9:10 (S) | List steps for first day implementation |
| 9:10–9:50 (L) | Variations (taken from Chapter 6 in text): |
| | Individualization. |
| | Saving up time. |
| | Checkmarks. |
| | Second week. |
| 9:50–10:00 | RE |
| 10:00–10:30 (L) | "Dealing with Undesired Behaviors" |
| | (taken from Chapter 5 in text) |
| 10:30–10:50 (S) | Task X |
| | Compare and discuss answers in group |
| 10:50–11:10 (L) | Contracting for Implementation |
| | Follow-Up Plans |
| | Back-Home Support |
| 11:10–11:30 (S) | Posttest |
| | Teacher Contracts |
| 11:30–12:00 (L) | Questions and answers |

## Small Groups

We have some strong feelings about the use of small groups at conferences or workshops. Careful attention to the dynamics of the small-group process can "carry" a conference even when some of the other elements are less than perfect, such as the large group presentations, the setting, and so forth. Here are some basic principles, developed by Bruce Weston, director of the California Regional Resource Center, which seem to hold for us:

1. Choose your group leaders carefully. Their skill at facilitating someone else's learning is more important than their expertise in the skill or idea being taught.

2. The ideal size for a small group seems to be between 5 and 10. Less than 5 seems to make the participants feel uncomfortable. More than 10 becomes cumbersome and slows the process.

3. Except at times when the conference process calls for a team interaction, assign people to small groups with people other

than those from their own district or school if possible. This seems to forestall the natural tendency of persons of lesser status to defer to people of higher status in their district.

4. When appropriate to the content being presented, ask all of the nonteacher-members of the group to assume the role of the teacher of a hypothetical class (if this is the focus on the content being presented).

5. Don't switch people from one group to another once the groups have begun. It is important that each group assumes responsibility for its own success as a group. If you step in and remove or add people to a group that has already begun to operate, you threaten this process.

6. After you have made it clear that you and the presenter(s) are available at any time for further information or clarification, stay out of the small groups unless specifically invited to come in. Group process seems to stop when an "outsider" comes in, even if the outsider's presence is well intended.

7. Keep others from entering the small groups. This can be particularly hard on "visiting firemen" who simply want to get an idea of how things are going.

**Time Commitment**

If you have looked at the schedules on the previous pages, you have probably noticed how carefully they are timed. We have been repeatedly reinforced for holding to such a schedule. Though it may look compulsive at first glance, our commitment is not to the clock, which is only a mechanical device, but to people. When we hold to the schedule (as long as it is reasonable) we are saying by our behavior that we are willing to be predictable.

**Some Tips for Planning and Carrying Out Inservice**

1. Remember, there are different levels of inservice—those aimed at awareness or information imparting, and those aimed at teaching a concept to be implemented in classrooms.

2. Plan carefully down to the last detail: equipment, location, content presentations, tasks, and handouts.

3. Communicate your inservice objectives to participants ahead of time.

4. If you are aiming toward adoption and implementation of a technique, arrange for participants to be actively involved in

small group tasks requiring development and planning of how they will implement it.

5. Plan "helps" for participants after they leave the training session. This can be in the form of printed presentation summaries, handouts, bibliographies of selected readings, lists of sources for needed materials, and referrals to teachers and/or schools where the participants can see the idea or technique in action.
6. Prepare handouts—give participants something to take with them.
7. If there is prerequisite material, distribute it ahead of time so participants can come prepared.
8. Tasks should be fairly short and focus on one, maybe two, small pieces of the content. Allow practice of skills learned.
9. Allow discussion time.
10. Keep to your time commitment.
11. Design opportunities for participants to apply new information and skills. (See examples of implementation tasks.) We have often brought a group of students to the workshop settting (or arranged for participants to go into a classroom) in order to try a new skill.
12. Provide immediate feedback to participants regarding their success.
13. Arrange for individual consultation and assistance until participants reach criterion on tasks.
14. Remember, teachers teach like they were taught. If we want teachers to change the way they teach children, we must change the way we teach teachers. This means *modeling* techniques and changing from the traditional presenter-dominated group lecture to a participant-centered mastery learning program.
15. Don't forget the importance of reinforcing teachers. Consider and try to arrange for such "rewards" as release time, inservice points, college credit, resource books, instructional materials, added support by resource teacher, and praise and compliments for a job well done!
16. Try to involve principals in your training efforts. They can be a *major* reinforcer to keep things going back home.
17. Attend to the location or setting for your workshop. Try to

arrange for a comfortable, quiet site away from phones and other interruptions.

On the next few pages you will find a topical outline for a series of workshop sessions covering many aspects of a comprehensive service plan for handicapped children. Each segment could be presented as an overview in a half-day session or expanded to involve a week or more of indepth inservice. This outline is based on a plan for inservice training which was conducted over a two-week period by the Master Plan Humboldt State University Inservice Consortium, Eureka, California. Session content is aimed at various personnel: administrators, program specialists, resource teachers, regular teachers, and parents.

**Topical Outline of a Comprehensive Inservice on Instructional Programming**

### I. Identification and Referral
  a. Current issues in placement of students in special education
  b. Formal and informal screening systems
  c. Referral procedures
  d. Analyzing the referral information
  e. Due process/parent involvement

### II. Support Services and Community Resources
  a. Identifying services and resources within the community
  b. Establishing and maintaining contact, communication, and cooperation.

### III. Assessment—Formal and Informal
  a. Identifying tools/instruments to assess and to evaluate student strengths and weaknesses
  b. Selecting appropriate testing strategies
  c. Reliability, validity, and item analysis
  d. Analysis, developing, and using criterion-referenced tests
  e. Using evaluation data to make educational hypotheses

### IV. Assessment—Learning Style/Teaching Style/Environmental Considerations
  a. Defining learning styles and teaching styles and matching the two

b. Identifying assessment techniques for determining learning and teaching styles
c. Selecting instructional strategies to suit the learning styles of case students

V. **Informal Assessment and Observation**
   a. Techniques to sequence and document informal assessment
   b. Different types of observation as assessment
   c. Techniques to chart progress
   d. Using this data to plan effectively
   e. Interviewing

VI. **Assessing Career Attitudes and Developing Career Education Experiences**
   a. Using interviewing and career interest inventories to assess career attitudes
   b. Instructional strategies for career education
   c. Coordinating with other agencies

VII. **Teaching Methods and Techniques—Reading**
VIII. **Evaluating Commercial and Teacher-Made Materials—Reading**
IX. **Teaching Methods and Techniques—Math**
X. **Evaluating Commercial and Teacher-Made Materials—Math**
XI. **Classroom Management**
   a. Organizing materials
   b. Charting progress
   c. Reward systems
   d. Tutoring programs

XII. **Individualizing Instruction**
   a. Key features of individualized instructional programs
   b. Management strategies used in individualized programs
   c. Comparing instructional formats used in managing individualized instruction:
      Job sheets

Learning stations
Programmed instruction
Contracts

XIII. **Behavior Management**
 a. Pinpointing student behaviors in specific terms
 b. Applying contingency management principles
 c. Identifying "problem" behaviors and determining appropriate response

XIV. **Instructional Plans**
 a. How to write
 b. Specifying objectives and success criteria
 c. Selecting methods/techniques
 d. Specifying materials

XV. **Implementation and Evaluation**
 a. Task analysis
 b. Curriculum relevance
 c. Supporting the classroom teacher
 d. Evaluating student outcomes
 e. Revising/updating the plan
 f. Due process/parent involvement

XVI. **Parent Involvement**
 a. Methods of encouraging parents to share feelings, problems, and concerns
 b. Communication techniques
 c. Activities for use at home

XVII. **Due Process Rights and Responsibilities**
 a. School
 b. Parents

XVIII. **Consultation Skills: Communication and Team Planning for Parents and Teachers**
 a. Active listening
 b. Problem solving/conflict resolution

# PLANNING A FULL SERVICE DELIVERY SYSTEM

## Developing System Policies and Procedures

School districts have been planning for delivery of full services since 1975. They have been developing the necessary procedures and forms in order to comply with federal and state laws. The following are lists of some of the policies and procedures that should now be in effect in most districts.

*Parent Involvement and Public Participation* are procedures for including parents and other interested parties in the planning process. This would include the establishment of an Advisory Task Force or Community Advisory Committee composed of parents, handicapped individuals, regular class teachers, special education teachers, other public school personnel, and representatives from other public and private agencies.

*Program Operations* are comprehensive search procedures for actively seeking out all persons in need. Program operations include: Referral procedures, procedures for administration and supervision of IEP development and implementation. A continuum of placement options and a policy on maximum interaction of handicapped students with normal peers in both academic and nonacademic settings exists. A list of programs and services that are provided directly by the district or county, and those available through other agencies, such as the State supported schools, should be available.

*Procedural Safeguards* are comprised of confidentiality procedures; culturally appropriate assessment procedures; procedures on informing parents of their rights; assessment guidelines for child study teams and the responsibilities of team members; and procedures for initiation of due process hearings, including procedures for informal resolution of disagreements.

*Personnel Development* includes both plans for ongoing staff development, and procedures for conducting needs assessment, identifying resources, and evaluating impact.

*Evaluation* is a plan for collecting and annually reporting state required data. This data should reflect pupil performance, least restrictive placement, the degree to which services identified in IEPs are provided; and the parent, pupil, teacher, and administrator attitudes toward the services and processes provided.

*Regional Service Coordination* means procedures to communicate with and refer to other agencies and/or state special schools, policies for accepting referrals from other agencies; procedures for communication and cooperation with regular vocational and career education programs; a plan for adequate physical education programs; procedures for equal access to programs such as music, homemaking, education, industrial arts, recreational activities, and so forth; and a plan for coordination of services with regional occupational programs, post-secondary and adult programs, private agencies, and other public agencies. More detail on planning for full services may be found in *The Prince William Model: A planning guide for the development and implementation of full services for all handicapped children.* Washington, D.C.: National Association of State Directors of Special Education, 1976.

## Interagency Collaboration

> The idea that human service agencies should work together to meet the needs of handicapped people is not new. It is, however, an idea which is rapidly coming of age. Service system inefficiencies, political and fiscal conservatism, federal initiatives, and heightened expectations on the part of consumers are all forces which demand interagency collaboration. (Regional Resource Center Task Force on Interagency Collaboration, 1979, p. 1)

The current emphasis, now that many of the basic policies and procedures necessary for implementing P.L. 94–142 are in place, is interagency collaboration—the articulation of efforts across agencies providing services to the handicapped. One of the major thrusts behind the move toward interagency collaboration is the concern about remedying the problems of waste, redundancy and overlap of services, and the desire to encourage sharing of resources to maximize federal and state dollars. The IEP is one example of an area where there is overlap. Many service provider agencies require that IEPs be written for every individual served. It is a duplication of effort for each agency to develop a separate plan when a single plan could be developed jointly. Besides joint development of IEPs, a few additional examples of desirable outcomes of interagency collaboration are:

1. single instructional plan format
2. cooperative identification procedures
3. coordination of common case data requirements
4. sharing resources to maximize dollars.

Some barriers that may exist to interagency planning are:

1. variations in client eligibility criteria
2. lack of understanding of and about the law
3. professional jargon
4. turf protection
5. difficulty in pinpointing decision authority.

Federal agreements are in effect and written interagency agreements are operational at the state level in many states. Interagency collaboration is being pursued, as it relates to providing services to the handicapped, with Vocational Education, Vocational Rehabilitation, Special Education, and Mental Health and Crippled Childrens' Services. Many local agencies are now following suit. The Regional Resource Center Task Force on Interagency Collaboration (1979) presents nine major strategy areas on an approach to interagency agreement development. The strategies in their process outline for interagency planning are:

- *determine* needs and rationale for initiation of interprogram collaboration project;
- *define* service delivery population of interest;
- *identify* agencies and programs serving or authorized to serve the target population(s) and contact agency administrator;
- *define* current program policies and services, responsibilities of identified programs;
- *compare* local programs and procedures across agencies to identify gaps, overlaps, constraints and other linkages;
- *identify* local policy and procedures wherein modifications would enable satisfaction of need and rationale for collaboration and *specify* the needed modifications;
- *determine* which modifications can be made on the local interprogram agreement;
- *enable* implementation of interprogram modifications;
- *implement* local evaluation functions. (p. 3)

## Characteristics of Local Interagency Agreements*

It is assumed that a functional interagency agreement would specify, at minimum, the parties to the agreement; service responsibilities; authorities; and time lines. Following are several areas in which

---
*From: Santa Barbara County Schools, Comprehensive Plan for Special Education, Interagency Workshop, June, 1980.

collaborative effort has the potential for improving the delivery of services to handicapped children.

**Types of Interagency Agreements**

1. Standards—agreement on terms, vocabulary, and nature of services.
2. First Dollar—who pays first when a client is mutually eligible?
3. Complementary Dollar—you pay for this and we'll pay for that.
4. Shared Personnel—our staff will assist your staff or vice versa.
5. Shared Facilities—we'll meet at your place this time/ours next.
6. Shared Equipment—our bus/your Xerox.
7. Uniform Procedures—forms, due process.
8. Coordinated Administration—staff development, client monitoring, funding, state and local planning, and reporting.

In summary, local agreements should be *signed* by *authorized* representatives of each agency and *shared* with all staff.

**Sitting Down Together**

Before sitting down to plan, it helps if agency personnel have done some homework and if each representative:

- has an awareness of the rationale for and benefits of interagency collaboration,
- has analyzed any existing state-level agreements between agencies serving the handicapped for implications for local agreements,
- is familiar with the other agency and its local functions, procedures and services in its area of responsibility.

The following "Local Agreement Checklist" is an example of a mechanism for getting agencies to sit down and begin planning together. The checklist was prepared for use by special education and mental health representatives. Other agencies may require different goals and checklist items. The complete checklist includes program goals and related questions in the areas of Referral, Assessment, IEP, Placement, Program, and Inservice. The Assessment and IEP sections are reproduced here as samples.

# Assessment*

**Definition:** *Each individual with exceptional needs who is assessed for special education services shall have the benefit of a multi-disciplinary team of persons, and no single procedure shall be used as sole criterion for assessment.*

| LOCAL EDUCATION AGENCY | LOCAL MENTAL HEALTH | POSSIBLE AREAS TO CONSIDER FOR DEVELOPING AGREEMENTS |
|---|---|---|
| 1. May contract for services from local mental health to conduct appropriate educationally relevant assessments. | 1. Shall make available fee information and may contract with local education agencies for assessments. | 1. Fee for Mental Health assessment? How are parents informed? How is fee determined? Does this pose a problem to interagency collaboration? |
| 2. Shall develop, with local mental health programs, criteria/guidelines for appropriate referrals to local mental health agencies for assessment. | 2. Shall develop, with local education agencies, criteria/guidelines for appropriate referrals to local education agencies for assessment. | 2. Procedures for parent/guardian consent to assessment. |
| 3. Shall provide educational assessments, with parental consent, as required by California Administrative Code Title 5, Education, for those pupils who may require mental health services. | 3. Shall provide information regarding educationally relevant assessments, with parental consent, as appropriate when requested by the local education agency to complete a client's or individual's data base. | 3. Established timelines for assessment and reassessment. |
|  |  | 4. Guidelines for preparing written report on all children/clients evaluated. |
|  |  | 5. Procedures, including confidentiality for sharing assessment results with other appropriate agencies/individuals. |
|  |  | 6. Procedure for interpreting assessment finding and recommendations to parents/guardians/clients. |
|  |  | 7. What is the range of assessment services provided by each agency? |
|  |  | 8. What constitutes educationally relevant assessments as conducted by Mental Health? |
|  |  | Other: |

---

*Developed by Joseph J. Pasanella, Santa Barbara County Schools, Comprehensive Plan for Special Education, 1980.

# IEP*

**Definition:** *The individual with exceptional needs shall have a right to an appropriate education and related services in accordance with his or her IEP, including full education opportunity in the least restrictive environment.*

| LOCAL EDUCATION AGENCY | LOCAL MENTAL HEALTH | POSSIBLE AREAS TO CONSIDER FOR DEVELOPING AGREEMENTS |
|---|---|---|
| 1. (a) Shall provide education services to individuals with exceptional needs and shall refer individuals with exceptional needs and his or her parents to mental health for appropriate mental health services, as needed.<br><br>1. (b) If a pupil's assessment indicates that there is a need for Mental Health services to be initiated or continued, the Eligibility and Planning Team or Educational Assessment Service or School Appraisal Team shall invite the mental health professional or his or her representative to participate in or submit written information at any meeting for the purpose of discussing or developing an individual IEP.<br><br>1 (c) Should work with local mental health agencies to identify indirect service needs which might be provided by local mental health. | Shall provide mental health services in accordance with the local county mental health plan, utilizing the Uniform Method of Determining the Ability to Pay to individuals with exceptional needs and their parents as provided for in Title 9, California Administrative Code, Articles 4 and 5.<br><br>Shall designate a staff member to participate in or to submit written information at any meeting for the purpose of discussing or developing an individualized education program for an individual with exceptional needs who is a client of mental health.<br><br>May provide indirect services as described in California Administrative Code, Title 9, Article 4. Section 545 to local education agencies. | 1. How are education services noted on the treatment plan?<br>2. How are Mental Health services noted on the IEP?<br>3. Define IEP and Treatment Plan. What are the areas of similarity/difference/duplication between these forms?<br>4. How often are IEP/Treatment Plan meetings held? Are both agencies represented at each others' meetings? What is policy on notification and attendance at meetings for mutual clients?<br>5. What is the responsibility for contributing information at IEP/Treatment Plan meetings?<br>6. What procedures are established for monitoring client progress?<br>7. Is there a duplication of services (e.g., guidance/counseling?).<br>8. Is there a multi-discipline approach to program planning?<br>9. How are parents/clients involved in program planning?<br>10. What procedures exist for coordinating individual program plans with those developed by other agencies? |

*Developed by Joseph J. Pasanella, Santa Barbara County Schools, Comprehensive Plan for Special Education, 1980.

## IEP continued

| LOCAL EDUCATION AGENCY | LOCAL MENTAL HEALTH | POSSIBLE AREAS TO CONSIDER FOR DEVELOPING AGREEMENTS |
|---|---|---|
| 2. Shall release information according to Section 431 (c), Title 5, California Administrative Code, which implements Education Code Section 49060 and 45 CFR 121a.560-573, including a provision ensuring rights of those individuals, defined as a parent pursuant to 45 CFR 121a.10 and Title 5, California Administrative Code, Section 3301. | Shall release educationally relevant confidential patient information only with written parental consent according to Section 5328 of the Welfare and Institutions Code. | 11. What procedures exist for evaluating client progress? Written procedure for sharing client progress data with other agencies providing service to that client? |
| | | 12. How are indirect services provided? |
| 3. Shall notify mental health personnel of the date and location of the annual review for a known mutual client. | Shall designate a staff member to participate in or contribute written information to the periodic review of an individualized education program of a known mutual client, as appropriate. | 13. What procedure is used for releasing confidential information on an ongoing basis? (Mental Health to Education and vice versa.) |
| | | 14. In the event that Mental Health representatives cannot attend an IEP meeting, what is the follow-up procedure? |
| | | Other: |

Using the checklist as a guide, the planning process involves each agency representative (a) to judge the relevance of the questions in the column labeled "Possible Areas to Consider for Developing Local Agreement" and to eliminate or add items for discussion as appropriate and (b) to discuss each program goal in the left column and arrive at one of three decisions:

1. An informal agreement already exists. (Proceed to document it);
2. An agreement needs to be developed in this area. (Define a process and a timeline for developing such an agreement); or
3. An agreement needs to be developed in this area but a *roadblock* exists. (Describe roadblock and examine strategies for overcoming it).

It is not always easy to break through the bureaucratic barriers, political tangles, turfdom, and differences in terminology and definitions that exist between agencies. But through honest attempts at open communication, perseverance, patience, and negotiation, it can be and is being done. Figure 11 illustrates one format for local agreements.

**Figure 11** *Sample Local Agreement Format*\*

Program Goal:

| LEA RESPONSIBILITIES | JOINT RESPONSIBILITIES | AGENCY RESPONSIBILITIES |
|---|---|---|
| 1. | 1. | 1. |
| 2. | 2. | 2. |
| 3. | 3. | 3. |
| Authorized Signature | | Authorized Signature |

\*Developed by Andrea Carroll for Santa Barbara County Schools, Comprehensive Plan for Special Education, Interagency Workshop, June, 1980.

# EVALUATION OF THE INSTRUCTIONAL PROGRAM

> It is not a child's performance on a standardized test which renders him eligible for special education services, but rather the discrepancy between his rate of acquiring skills and the minimum rate required of all children to achieve essential education within the usual 12 or 13 years of public schooling. (Christie & McKenzie, 1974, p. 16)

An established continuum of the essential minimum objectives that each child must demonstrate to criterion at the elementary level, the junior high school level, and the high school level is critical. Within each span of grades, minimum objectives for all children at each grade level or subject area must be clear. It is only when objectives are clear for all children that we are alerted to those children for whom special services are warranted; and it is only when minimum objectives for all children are clearly specified that we can determine when it is time to *phase out* special services for those children with special needs.

There are no handicapped children under this criterion-referenced system. There are only children who are eligible for some level of specialized service because the "levels of their current behavior are less than the levels of the minimum objectives applicable to the child with his years of schooling" (Christie & McKenzie, 1974, p. 5). A child is eligible for special services when he or she is not acquiring essential skills at a minimum rate. S/he is ready for total integration into the regular classroom when s/he is acquiring essential skills at a minimum rate.

## Evaluating the Effectiveness of the Services

One of the biggest dangers of special education is that once a child has been identified and placed, s/he tends to stay there indefinitely. Inadequate provision for "phase out" is a severe weakness in the system. When a child receives specialized services designed to accelerate mastery of minimum objectives established for all children within the school, evaluation of those special services is essential. If a child's achievement rate is not accelerated by those services, the child has not been served and the services have not been effective.

The special educator shares accountability with the regular classroom teacher in a mainstreaming situation. When the child meets minimum objectives set for all children in his or her grade level, s/he is ready to be phased out of the special service program. Establishing minimum objectives for students at each grade level and relating remedial objectives to the objectives of the regular curriculum provide a means for determining an exit point for the child from special service support to maintenance by the regular classroom teacher.

The efficacy of special support services is determined by examining the results produced. The most important result is growth in student achievement. Other results are more difficult to assess. The following pages represent some sample forms for generating feedback on the effectiveness of resource services for handicapped students.

**Regular Faculty Evaluation of Resource Model***

1. How many of your students have you referred to the resource teacher?
   a. _____ (1–3)   b. _____ (4–5)   c. _____ (6–10)
   d. _____ more than 10   e. _____ none
   (If *none* (e), respond only to questions # 16 thru # 19.)

Rate the quality of service you have received from the resource room teacher for the following eight questions (thru #9). The questions will be answered on your separate answer sheet using the following rating scale.

    a—excellent
    b—good
    c—fair
    d—poor
    e—no help at all

2. Testing students
3. Offering suggestions and ideas
4. Preparing materials for your use
5. Tutoring your student in the resource room
6. Tutoring your student in your classroom
7. Observing students in your classroom
8. How would you rank the overall service the resource unit has been to your school?
9. How would you rank the overall service the resource unit has been to yourself?

**Instructions**

Use this scale to rate the next six questions (#10 thru #15):
Though all situations may not be precisely described by *one* of the three possible responses, please select the *one* most closely approximating your situation.

    a. I needed much more assistance
    b. I needed more assistance
    c. Assistance has been adequate

---

*Taken from South Carolina Region V Educational Services Center, *The Resource Room: An Access to Excellence*, 1975, pp. 177–83.

**Regular Faculty Evaluation of Resource Model**   continued

The resource room teacher could have provided more assistance in the following areas:

10. Tutoring students in resource room
11. Tutoring students in my room
12. Preparing materials for students to use in my room
13. Offering ideas and techniques that were of assistance to me
14. Demonstrating materials for specific remedial needs
15. Testing students
16. Have you participated in a placement committee meeting?
    a. yes _____   b. no _____
17. Have you participated in meetings with the resource teacher and two or more teachers to discuss the needs of specific students (a diagnostic team meeting)?
    a. yes _____   b. no _____
18. How many years have you been teaching?
    a. 0–1 yr. _____   b. 2–3 yrs. _____   c. 4 yrs. _____
    d. 5 or more yrs. _____
19. If you have knowledge of other ways that the resource unit has been of service to you, please use the green sheet to state your opinions.

**Principal's Evaluation of Resource Units***

## I. General

1. What is the basic organization of your school?
    _____ a. Primary
    _____ b. Elementary
    _____ c. Middle
    _____ d. Junior High
    _____ e. Senior High

2. How long have resource rooms been a part of your school's organization?
    _____ a. 1 year
    _____ b. 2 years
    _____ c. 3 years
    _____ d. 4 years
    _____ e. 5 or more

If you do *not* have a resource room serving learning disabled children, stop at this point. Otherwise continue with the remaining questions.

3. What is the administrative organization pattern of the school?
    _____ a. Traditional self-contained
    _____ b. Departmentalization

---

*Taken from South Carolina Region V Educational Services Center, *The Resource Room: An Access to Excellence,* 1975, pp. 177–83.

**Principal's Evaluation of Resource Units**   continued

_____ c. Team teaching
_____ d. Unit Teacher
_____ e. Other

Which of the following curriculum organization patterns are being used in your school?

|   | YES | NO |
|---|---|---|
| 4. Wisconsin Design Materials | _____ | _____ |
| 5. Individually Guided Education | _____ | _____ |
| 6. Fountain Valley Testing | _____ | _____ |
| 7. IMS Math | _____ | _____ |
| 8. Basals and adopted texts | _____ | _____ |
| 9. Others _____ | _____ | _____ |

## II. Student Instruction in L. D. Resource Rooms

10. What is the total number of children seen by the resource teacher on an average weekly basis?
    _____ a. 26–28   _____ b. 29–33   _____ c. 34–38
    _____ d. 39–43   _____ e. 44 or more

11. What is the fewest number of children with whom the resource teacher works during any given period in the daily schedule?
    _____ a. 1
    _____ b. 2 to 4
    _____ c. 5 to 6
    _____ d. 7 to 10
    _____ e. more than 10

12. What is the largest number of children with whom the resource teacher works during any given period in the daily schedule?
    _____ a. 2 to 4
    _____ b. 5 to 6
    _____ c. 7 to 10
    _____ d. 11 to 15
    _____ e. 16 or more

13. Are the children willing to work with the resource teacher?
    _____ a. yes   _____ b. no   _____ c. sometimes

14. How frequently have you observed in the resource room for a period of 10 or more minutes?
    _____ a. 0
    _____ b. 1–2
    _____ c. 3–5
    _____ d. 6 or more

Principal's Evaluation of Resource Units  continued

### III. Faculty Rapport

15. Is the resource teacher willing to share her skills, knowledge, and materials with others?
    \_\_\_\_a. yes   \_\_\_\_b. no   \_\_\_\_c. sometimes
16. Is the resource teacher accepted as a peer?
    \_\_\_\_a. yes   \_\_\_\_b. no   \_\_\_\_c. sometimes
17. Is the assistance of the resource teacher sought by others?
    \_\_\_\_a. yes   \_\_\_\_b. no   \_\_\_\_c. sometimes

### IV. Records

Is the following data concerning each child served in the resource unit available in an organized manner to the appropriate persons?

|  | YES | NO |
|---|---|---|
| 18. Reason for referral | | |
| 19. Psychological evaluations | | |
| 20. Academic problems | | |
| 21. Behavioral problems | | |
| 22. Academic progress | | |
| 23. Behavioral progress | | |

Are reports of student progress made regularly to:

| | YES | NO |
|---|---|---|
| 24. child? | | |
| 25. parent? | | |
| 26. regular teacher? | | |
| 27. placement committee? | | |

### V. Scheduling

28. Are the children being seen for periods of at least 30 minutes?
    \_\_\_\_a. yes   \_\_\_\_b. no
29. Are the children being seen for periods of more than 30 minutes?
    \_\_\_\_a. yes   \_\_\_\_b. no
30. Does the resource teacher have some time (30–45 minutes) during the day for planning?   \_\_\_\_a. yes   \_\_\_\_b. no
31. Does the resource teacher have some time (three hours) during the week for student observations and instruction in the regular classroom?   \_\_\_\_a. yes   \_\_\_\_b. no
32. Does the scheduling permit the pupil in the resource room program maximum opportunities to participate with his peers in as many non-academic areas as possible?   \_\_\_\_a. yes   \_\_\_\_b. no
33. Is there enough flexibility of scheduling so that scheduling is in the best interest of individual pupils?   \_\_\_\_a. yes   \_\_\_\_b. no

**Principal's Evaluation of Resource Units   continued**

34. Is scheduling frequently reassessed to determine if changes need to be made either for individual pupils or for groups?
    _____a. yes     _____b. no

35. Are there *regularly scheduled* weekly meetings held between resource and regular class teachers?     _____a. yes     _____b. no

36. Are there *regularly scheduled* monthly meetings held between resource and regular class teachers?     _____a. yes     _____b. no

## VI. General Evaluation of the Resource Model for L. D.

37. Can the supplemental instruction and support offered in a resource setting meet the needs of L. D. students in your school?
    _____a. All of the students
    _____b. Most of the students
    _____c. Few of the students

38. Have the regular classroom teachers expanded or modified the curriculum of the regular classroom so that it is also appropriate for these handicapped pupils?
    _____a. yes     _____b. no

39. Is there a need for additional resource units?
    _____a. yes     _____b. no

40. Is there a need for self-contained classroom units in your school?
    _____a. yes     _____b. no

Rank each of the following using the following scale:
   a—excellent
   b—good
   c—average
   d—poor
   e—no assistance

41. _____ Resource teacher as tutor
42. _____ Resource teacher as organizer
43. _____ Resource teacher as consultant
44. _____ Resource teacher as school asset
45. _____ Resource room service to the school
46. _____ Regular teacher as a source of referrals
47. _____ Resource room's capability of meeting needs of exceptional children
48. _____ Regular teacher willingness to work with others for benefit of exceptional child

## VII. Strengths

The resource room has been effective in:

**Principal's Evaluation of Resource Units** continued

49. _____ a. yes _____ b. no  Relieving the regular teacher of troublesome students.
50. _____ a. yes _____ b. no  Tutoring students who are having trouble
51. _____ a. yes _____ b. no  Providing expertise in the areas of classroom management
52. _____ a. yes _____ b. no  Providing expertise in the area of remediation

**Structured Observation***

_____
            Person Observed                    Observer

N = No basis for evaluation (can't observe)
1 = Attempting skill, but inadequate
2 = Adequate (minimum acceptable skill)
3 = Outstanding

_____ 1. Arrangement of class
   3 = Areas for individual work, small groups, and private discussion
   2 = Areas for individual work and small groups
   1 = No variety

_____ 2. Is the process up-to-date and complete?
   3 = Process checklist and supporting documents within time frame.
   2 = Required documents present and noted within time frames
   1 = Required documents missing.

Ask RST to select two folders at random:
   3 = Both folders consistently complete
   2 = Both folders have required documents
   1 = Some or all have missing required documents. Make comments if necessary.

|  | Folder # | Folder # | Folder # |
|---|---|---|---|
| a. notification of due process |  |  |  |
| b. release of information |  |  |  |
| c. permission to test |  |  |  |
| d. certification |  |  |  |
| e. instructional plan |  |  |  |

*This form was developed for use in the Humboldt-Del Norte Master Plan Project, Eureka, California, 1976.

**Structured Observation**  continued

_____3. Documentation to indicate assessment
   3 = Documentation of all of the following areas:

|  | Folder # | Folder # | Folder # |
|---|---|---|---|
| a. classroom observation |  |  |  |
| b. educational history |  |  |  |
| c. academic skills |  |  |  |
| d. cultural/language factors |  |  |  |
| e. health |  |  |  |

   2 = Assessment documentation in folder to support all objectives
   1 = No evidence to support objective in educational plan. Look at two folders. Comment if child is overly-assessed with no meaningful plan.

_____4. Are appropriate signatures on educational plan?
   2 = Signatures of principal or designee, resource teacher, program specialist, parent, or other if needed
   1 = Less than required signatures

_____5. The child's activities are tied to the educational plan.
   3 = Activities are directly related to the child's objectives
   2 = Some activities tie into objectives
   1 = No relationship

_____6. Indications that class activities are individualized.
   3 = Evidence of where child started, where he is now, where he is going on majority of objectives and activities that provide for varied learning rates
   2 = Same as above for only one objective
   1 = No such evidence

_____7. Evidence of a variety of materials and/or approaches.
   3 = Variety of learning alternatives listed in plan and readily available materials reflect variety of learning styles on majority of objectives
   2 = Same as above with one objective
   1 = Only one or few things for all children

_____8. Observe each student's behavior over two five-minute periods. Note on and off task behavior at the end of each thirty-second interval.

**Structured Observation** continued

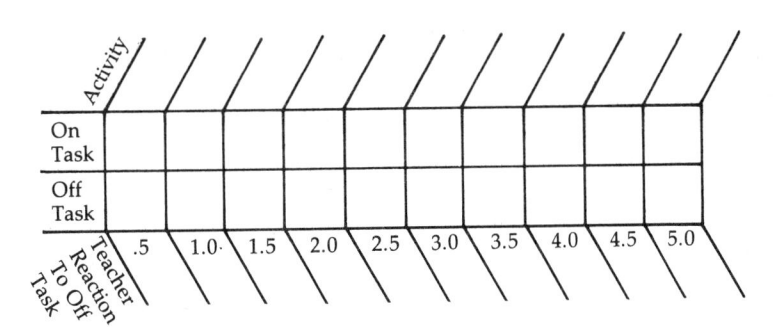

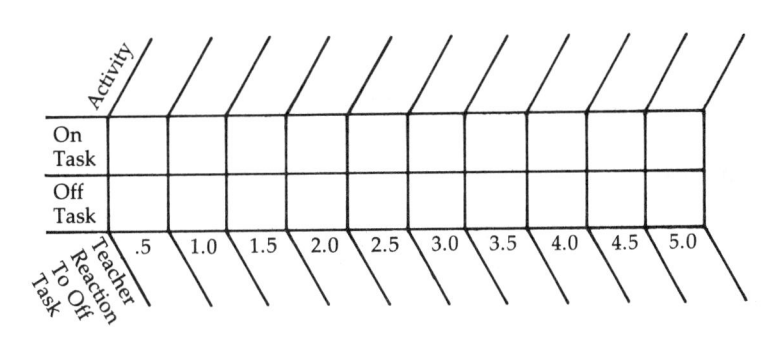

[Observation grid: Activity / On Task / Off Task / Teacher Reaction To Off Task, with time columns .5, 1.0, 1.5, 2.0, 2.5, 3.0, 3.5, 4.0, 4.5, 5.0]

[Second identical observation grid]

Circumstances of observation (do not observe during transition period)
3 = Over 75% on task
2 = 65%–75% on task
1 = Below 65% on task

_____9. What classroom management techniques are in evidence?
Yes   No
—   —   Individual children rewarded for academic behaviors
—   —   Individual children rewarded for social behaviors
—   —   Teacher rewards appropriate group behavior
Types of rewards (Check all rewards available, two checks if observed)
( ) Checkmarks          ( ) Praise, smile
( ) Activities/privileges   ( ) Tangibles
( ) Touch, pat           ( ) Stars
( ) Free time            ( ) Tokens
Yes   No
( )  ( ) Kids have opportunity to choose type of reward.

## PROGRAM REVIEW MODEL

The Program Review process described on the following pages was developed by and implemented in the Santa Barbara County Schools, Comprehensive Plan for Special Education. Program Review is necessary to monitor compliance with state and local regulations. This program review process is also concerned with program self-renewal as reflected in the following stated purposes:

1. to identify program strengths and weaknesses (needs assessment) which then provides an information base for program improvement or modificiation;
2. to generate staff motivation and commitment to planning for positive change;
3. to produce a detailed plan for program improvement or modification (if needed) (Pasanella, 1977, p. 1).

The process has three phases: *Planning, Information Gathering,* and *Follow-Up.*

## Planning

1. Identify the program to be reviewed.
2. Develop a program review checklist (See Figure 12). The checklist items include requirements of P.L. 94–142 and items generated by input from program staff and administrators.
3. Select program review team and schedule review. Review team can consist of peer facilitators, outside consultants, program specialists, and *always* parents.
4. Discuss checklist and process with program staff. Explaining program review process steps and purpose reaching a common understanding of the checklist items and introducing facilitators to the staff reduces anxiety on the part of the program staff. An essential step!

## Information Gathering

5. Self-evaluation by program staff is accomplished as each staff member completes the checklist *independently*. This step could be completed as a part of Step 4.
6. Conduct structured classroom observation. Observation is conducted by program review facilitators. Student folders are also examined and the same students are observed in classroom activities.

# Training, Delivery, and Evaluation

7. Conduct parent interviews. Interview the parents of the students observed in the classroom.
8. Conduct staff interviews.
9. Provide immediate informal feedback. Facilitators hold an exit meeting with the program staff to give an initial summary report.
10. Generate a written report. Facilitators analyze all information and prepare a written report that is disseminated to program administrator and staff. Report documents "what is," or the condition that exists at present. Staff discusses "what should be" in Steps 11 and 12.

## Follow-Up

11. Meet to identify priority need areas. The report is reviewed and discussed by staff and administrator. Consensus is achieved on priority need areas for program change and improvement.
12. Meet to design plan for program change. An administrator and staff formulate objectives, a timeline, and identify person(s) responsible for program change areas.
13. Provide ongoing support. Regularly scheduled meetings are held to review progress toward objectives.

All too often the site visit or review process ends at Step 10, and most things tend to continue the way they were before. Follow-up and support are vital to the change process, so be sure to include them. (Pasanella, 1977, p. 7)

Figure 12 includes excerpts from a review checklist developed and used to evaluate a program for the severely handicapped. The entire checklist included 10 categories: Students, staff, parents, community resources, instructional materials/media, equipment, supplies, physical facility, transportation, and administrative considerations. Existing items can be adapted or deleted to reflect the critical dimensions of other programs.

**Figure 12**  *Sample Program Review Checklist*

Date _____

Program _____  Location _____
Administrator _____  Phone _____

**Figure 12** continued

*Names/Positions of persons conducting review:*
1. _____
2. _____
3. _____
4. _____

1. STUDENTS

    1.1 Number enrolled _____ Student/Adult ratio _____

    1.2 Is a written IEP available for each student?   YES    NO
        If NO, explain _____

    1.3 Does the IEP for each student contain:

       Statement of student's present performance level? _____

       Goals to be achieved by the end of current school year? _____

       Measurable short-term objectives for each goal? _____

       Special education and other services needed by student? _____

       Type of physical education program in which student will participate? _____

       Special instructional media/materials needed by student? _____

       Date when services will begin, and length and frequency of services? _____

       Statement of extent to which student will participate in regular education? _____

       Justification of student's placement (attempted interventions/least restrictive environment)? _____

       List of person(s) responsible for implementing the IEP? _____

       Objective criteria, evaluation procedures, and schedule? _____

       Comments:

    1.4 Has each student been assessed by the School Appraisal Team or the Educational Assessment Service within the last three years? _____

    1.5 Based on actual classroom observation, are IEPs being implemented through:

       Assessment of individual baseline performance? _____

       Systematic observation and daily recording? _____

       A planned instructional environment? _____

       Instructional methods appropriate for individuals? _____

       Instructional methods *observed*: _____

          Large Group _____            Small Group _____
          One-to-one _____       Peer/cross age tutoring _____
          Modeling _____               Demonstration _____

**Figure 12** continued

      Molding _____           Drill _____

      Other _____             _____

  Instructional activities related to objectives stated for students? _____

  Frequent staff planning related to student progress? _____

  Measurement techniques appropriate to determine student gains? _____

  Documented revisions to IEPs based on data? _____

  Support services? _____

    Check services available:

| | | | |
|---|---|---|---|
| Speech & Language | _____ | Adaptive P.E. | _____ |
| Audiological Services | _____ | Aural Rehabilitation | _____ |
| Behavior Management | _____ | Braille Transcription | _____ |
| Clerical Service for the Blind | _____ | Community Liaison/ Health Service | _____ |
| Vocational Education & Work Study | _____ | Counseling & Guidance | _____ |
| Home/Hospital | _____ | Supplemental Instruction | _____ |
| Interpretation and Note-Taking Services | _____ | Mobility Training for the Blind | _____ |
| Occupational Therapy | _____ | Physical Therapy | _____ |
| Parent Education | _____ | Reading Service for the Blind | _____ |
| Specialized Driving Training | _____ | Vocational Education Training | _____ |

    Specify additional services needed:

  Are services delivered by special services personnel related to objectives stated for students? _____

  Articulation with regular and/or special education programs? _____

  Articulation with community resources? _____

  Comments:

1.6 Specify procedures used for Annual Review:

**Figure 12** continued

    1.7 Specify exit criteria:

    1.8 Specify available alternatives for students who exit from program:
        *Educational*                     *Vocational*                     *Community*

        Comments:

2. STAFF

    2.1 Describe staffing pattern:

    2.2 List support personnel and describe roles:

    2.3 Describe use of paraprofessionals:

    2.4 Describe use of volunteers (not including parents of students):

    2.5 Describe staff recruitment procedures:

    2.6 Describe inservice training provided for staff:

3. PARENTS (based on interview with parent)
    3.1 Due process safeguards are observed    _____
    3.2 Parents participate in development of IEP    _____
    3.3 Parents participate in Annual Review for student    _____
    3.4 Parents participate in classroom instruction of student    _____
    3.5 Regular student progress reports are made to parents    _____
    3.6 Information/awareness activities are provided for parents    _____
    3.7 Structured training sessions are provided for parents    _____
    3.8 Parents receive help in developing programs at home that are consistent with programs at school    _____
    3.9 Counseling is available to parents    _____

Comments:

4. COMMUNITY RESOURCES: (Check those available to students/parents in this program)

**Figure 12**  continued

| | | | |
|---|---|---|---|
| Advocacy Groups | _____ | Recreation programs | _____ |
| Baby Sitting | _____ | Respite care | _____ |
| Day Care | _____ | Legal aid | _____ |
| Medical | _____ | Parent associations | _____ |
| Others: _____ | | | |

Comments:

5. INSTRUCTIONAL MATERIALS/MEDIA

    5.1 Available media/materials are appropriate to students' needs _____

    5.2 Budget for materials _____

    5.3 Staff can articulate appropriate selection/evaluation criteria _____

    5.4 Quantity of usable materials is adequate _____

    5.5 Care, storage, and display of materials _____

    Comments:

6. EQUIPMENT

    6.1 Available equipment is appropriate to student's needs _____

    6.2 Budget for equipment _____

    6.3 Staff can articulate appropriate selection/evaluation criteria _____

    6.4 Quantity of usable equipment is adequate _____

    6.5 Care, storage, and display of equipment _____

    List available special equipment:

    Comments:

## Study Questions and Activities

1. Form discussion groups and share experiences with inservice workshops in which you have participated. Describe those workshops you have found to be the most beneficial and/or enjoyable. To what extent where the recommendations for effective inservice workshops (presented in the text on design of tasks, schedules, and small group involvement) validated by the group's experiences?

2. As a class project, class members should form work groups to develop inservice training workshops for regular class teachers. Each group should propose: (a) A topic for an inservice workshop, (b) the workshop objectives, (c) the schedule to be followed, (d) the media and materials for presentations, (e) the tasks for group involvement, and (f) a rating sheet for evaluation of the workshop relative to stated objectives. The workshop should be evaluated by either presenting it to a group of cooperating regular teachers and obtaining their feedback, or presentation of the developed materials (objectives, media, tasks, rating sheet, and so on) to a panel of experts (for example, regular teachers, principals, and resource specialists) for feedback. Develop a revised workshop design on the basis of the feedback obtained. Revised workshop materials may be reproduced and combined into a booklet which may be distributed to class members for future reference.
3. Design an awareness workshop for parents of handicapped students based on information in the section called "Parents as Team Members" in Chapter 5.
4. Visit the central office of a local school district and secure and review copies of procedural manuals and information related to the education of handicapped students. Examples include assessment team procedures, resource program manuals, parent involvement, and due process procedures.

## References

Christie, L. S., & McKenzie, H. S. *Minimum objectives: A measurement system to provide evaluation of special education in regular classrooms.* Burlington, Vt.: University of Vermont, College of Education and Social Services, Spring 1974. (Mimeo)

Havelock, R. G. *The change agent's guide to innovation in education.* Englewood Cliffs, N.J.: Educational Technology Publications, 1973.

Pasanella, A., Volkmor, C., McIntyre, R., Watts, C., Weston, B., & Williams, T. *An odyssey: Success strategies for educational change agents.* Unpublished manuscript, 1975.

Pasanella, J. *A prototype program review model for special education.* Santa Barbara, Calif.: Santa Barbara County Schools, Comprehensive Plan for Special Education, August 1977.

Regional Resource Center Task Force on Interagency Collaboration. *Volume II. Interagency collaboration on full services for handicapped children and youth: A guide to local implementation.* Washington, D. C.: Department of Health, Education, and Welfare, Office of Education, Bureau of Education for the Handicapped, August 1979.

South Carolina Region V Educational Services Center. *The resource room: An access to excellence.* Lancaster, S.C.: Region V Educational Services Center, 1975. (Out of print)

# Resources

## Introduction to Mainstreaming

Barnes, E. *Children learn together: The integration of handicapped children into schools.* Syracuse, N.Y.: Human Policy Press. (Slide-show) A powerful statement on mainstreaming including a discussion of the history of exclusion and segregation of disabled children and the recent forces—court decisions, parent power, changing attitudes—that are encouraging mainstreaming. It presents arguments for integration and responds to the concerns typically raised by teachers and parents. The slides demonstrate what is necessary for integration to succeed, including preparation, individualization, and range of specific supports and services to teachers. The slide-show consists of 132 slides and is available for $30.

Hales, S., McClain, N., & Samson, J. *SERT: Special education for regular teachers.* Special Education Services Department, Education Service Center, Region 10, and Special Education Department, East Texas State University, n.d. Eight modules in soft booklet form are designed to assist regular class teachers in dealing with special needs students mainstreamed into regular classrooms via the comprehensive special education plan for Texas. Each module is designed with pre- and posttests. The eight modules are:

1. Comprehensive Special Education
2. Formal Appraisal
3. Team Planning for Student Program Management
4. Informal Assessment
5. Organizing Content for Individual Differences
6. Materials Selection
7. Classroom Management
8. Evaluation of Instruction

Lexington, Massachusetts Public Schools. *Lexington teacher training program.* San Mateo, Calif.: Agency for Instructional Television, 1973. (Video tape) *Diagnosis and educational planning* is the first in a series of 10 video tapes which comprise *The Lexington teacher training project: Integration of children with special needs in the regular classroom,* available from the

Agency for Instructional Television. The project is designed to help regular classroom teachers deal with the vast differences between individuals in their classrooms, and to help special educators blend their skills into the regular classroom setting. The programs do not reveal indepth information about instructional plans for particular problems, but the roles of psychologists, MDs and learning specialists are clearly portrayed. Some of the other programs in the series are:

*Early assessment: Steps to planning:* A teacher carries out activities which reveal differences in children's development in kindergarten. *After assessment:* Observations of a kindergarten classroom where activities are individualized to meet children's needs. *Every child can learn:* Math and reading teachers, working in a team with third and fourth graders, together with a learning specialist, demonstrated specific principles for adapting lessons for children with learning problems in an integrated classroom. *Together they learn:* Retarded primary level children, almost indistinguishable in the regular classes, work in different types of groups in an integrated program. The cassette is planned to show that the educable retarded can work with other children. *Every student is different: The high school.* This cassette suggests various ways by which a high school can provide for individual differences of students.

The programs are available in quadruples, 1 inch, ¾ inch cassette, and ½ inch video formats. Each program costs $200, and A.I.T. writes that, "Previews of representative lessons are available on request at no charge to those interested in considering this series for in-school use." Requests for information should be directed to the Agency for Instructional Television, Western Office, 1670 S. Amphlett Blvd., San Mateo, Calif. 99402.

Lott, L. A., Hudak, B. J., & Scheetz, J. A. *Strategies and techniques for mainstreaming: A resource handbook.* Monroe, Mich.: Monroe County Intermediate School District, 1975.

Region III Education Service Center. *Principals training program.* Austin, Tex.: Region III Education Service Center, 6504 Tracor Lane, Austin, Texas 78721. *What it is:* An extensive training package that develops the "rationale for returning the handicapped child to the regular classroom, alternate administrative and instructional arrangements for programming for handicapped students in the regular classroom" (including filmstrip presentations of the different models of the Resource Specialist concept) and "how to administer a building special education program," which discusses the team assessment procedure, instructional planning, and organization for delivery of services. *Contents:* This is a multi-media pacakge. It contains two 16 mm films, eight filmstrips with cassettes, seven transparencies, a *Book of Readings*, a *Leader's Manual and Particpant Manuals. Strengths:* Well organized. Task sheets are practical and oriented to the role of the principal in mainstreaming. Good introduction to mainstreaming and ways to deal with problems of implementation.

Fosters understanding of the roles of all those involved in the mainstreaming process. The program is flexible and can be adapted to local needs ($350). Books and parts can be purchased separately.

Region XIII Education Service Center. *Teacher training program: Mainstreaming mildly handicapped students in the regular classroom.* Austin, Tex.: Region XIII Education Service Center, 1976. Price per kit is $375. A multi-media training package which focuses on skills, concepts, and attitudes necessary to successfully mainstream, including: areas of individualizing instruction, utilizing alternate behavior management strategies, and interfacing the regular and special education. The program contains Facilitator Manual, Participant's Manual, 7 filmstrips and tapes, games and puzzles, 6 audiotape cassettes, 41 transparencies, and 2 16mm films. The program phases (Mainstreaming Group Activities, Skill Building, Individualized Activities and Implementation Take Home Reinforcement) comprise 45–50 hours of instruction.

## Classroom Management

Buckhalter, G., Presbie, R., & Brown, P. *Behavior improvement program.* Chicago, Ill.: Science Research Associates, 1975. An extensive and lucid presentation of classroom management and record keeping, using behavioristic principles, is presented in this inservice training package for teachers. There are 24 lessons (about 10 minutes each) involving defining, observing, counting, charting, increasing, and decreasing classroom behaviors. The lessons are recorded on audio cassettes, accompanied by picture books which the participants view in "sync" with the tapes. Three of the tapes have accompanying filmstrips.

The package is programmed to meet the individual needs of the participating teachers. They are instructed in gathering baseline data on behaviors of their students. Then according to the frequency of the behaviors, the teachers are directed to those units of the program relevant to their problems. The program provides spirit masters for individual improvement charts and a large "class improvement chart" for the portrayal of group data.

The package would be helpful, through its organization and examples, for the resource teacher's inservice program for the regular education teacher. The package provides examples from K-12 classrooms and can readily accommodate actual school problems into the program.

In addition to the classroom behavior, there are lessons on bus, playground, and lunchroom behaviors. There is also a lesson on involving parents in behavioral management systems.

The package may be purchased for $240.75 from Science Research Associates, 259 E. Erie St., Chicago, Illinois 60611. A filmstrip/cassette program used to introduce the program may be purchased for $21.40.

Center at Oregon for Research in the Behavioral Education of the Handicapped. *The PASS program.* Eugene, Ore.: Center at Oregon for Research in the Behavioral Education of the Handicapped, 1974. An inservice program, with consultant's manual, teacher's manual and a filmstrip/cassette program. The program is directed towards consultants, psychologists, counselors, or resource specialists able to conduct an inservice training program for four teachers. It is a 45-day training period, involving 6 two-hour meetings with the teachers and extensive classroom observation and consultation by the resource person.

*The program for academic survival skills* (PASS) concerns group management of academic-related skills. It is for an entire class, having a general problem of work and study skills during one or two periods of the day. The resource person first observes the class to record the percentage of time all the students are showing academic survival skills (e.g., listening to directions, attending to tasks, and so on). And the general objective is to have the kids acting academically 80% of the time that they should be.

The teacher is trained in defining the skills to the class, observing and timing their occurrence, charting the data, and reinforcing the class as its academic survival skills improve. The gradual withdrawal of extrinsic reinforcements is also covered. The resource person is, more or less, caretaker of the inservice program using a "Manual for Consultants" as a guide. The teachers receive a training manual. There is a filmstrip/cassette program included which clearly explains the steps of the program and the roles of the resource person and the participating teachers. That program may be borrowed from CORBEH. The teacher's and consultant's guides cost $3 each. CORBEH is located at the University of Oregon, 1590 Willamette Street, Eugene, Oregon 97401.

Center at Oregon for Research in Behavioral Education of the Handicapped. *The class program.* Eugene, Ore.: Center at Oregon for Research in the Behavioral Education of the Handicapped, 1975. *Contingencies for learning academic and social skills:* a procedures manual, two filmstrip/cassette programs, is a program for "acting-out" children. It is designed to help teachers reduce the amount of time spent coping with disruptive kids. The teacher-consultant (psychologist, counselor, and resource specialist) is responsible for a behavior rating scale on the child, and the consultant does classroom observations. Children observed to be "on-task" less than 80% of the time qualify for the *CLASS* program. The consultant acquires written agreements from the teacher, principal, parents, and child before the program can be implemented. The program requires rewards and punishments to be consistent at home and school.

During Phase I (five days), the consultant spends time with the child in the classroom, so that the teacher isn't required to neglect the rest of the class while the problem child is beginning a behavior modification program. Phase II (25 days) requires the gradual withdrawal of the consultant from the program.

A procedures manual for the consultant is included in the kit, along with two filmstrip/cassette programs. The first filmstrip offers an overview of the *CLASS* program, and the second is a fictionalized case study of a child going through it. The filmstrips offer sufficient information for psychologists, counselors, and resource specialists to determine if the program would be beneficial to their caseloads. They may be borrowed from CORBEH. The manuals for the consultants the teacher manuals cost $3 each.

Langstaff, A. L., & Volkmor, C. B. *Contingency management.* Columbus, Ohio: Charles E. Merrill, 1975. This program is designed to train preservice and inservice teachers, in both regular and special education, how to implement a Contingency Management System. The complete program consists of a book and four sound-filmstrips:

1. "Contingency Management: Basic Principles"
2. "Contingency Management in the Classroom"
3. "Planning a Contingency Management Program—I"
4. "Planning a Contingency Management Program—II"

All of the information needed to successfully implement a Contingency Management System is presented in the book and the filmstrips. The program is self-instructional; it can be used by individuals or with groups. Chapters 1–4 of this book provide further exploration of the ideas presented in the accompanying filmstrip through:

1. Structured tasks and activities that develop skill in applying the principles of Contingency Management.
2. A short self-test on the filmstrip and text content.

Also included in the book are samples of classroom materials and suggestions for adaptations and further reading on Contingency Management.

## Social/Affective and Communication Skills

Gordon, T. with Burch, N. *T.E.T: Teacher effectiveness training.* New York: Peter H. Wyden, 1974. This book, like Gordon's *P.E.T. Parent effectiveness training*, concentrates on developing communication skills for better interpersonal relations (in this case, between teacher and student) and for facilitating conflict resolution. In addition to the T.E.T. inservice trainers' courses and teachers' courses are available from Gordon's organization, Effectiveness Training:

> Effectiveness Training Incorporated
> 531 Stevens Avenue
> Solana Beach, California 92075
> (714) 481-8121

Palomares, U. *Human development program (Magic circle)*, LeMesa, Calif.: Human Development Training Institute, 1975. The H.D.P. is a complete curriculum for grades K-12, designed to encourage (a) awareness, (b) mastery, and (c) social interaction. The developmentally sequenced curriculum of topics is for use in the carefully structured setting of the "Magic Circle." The ground rules for Magic Circle include: no "put-downs," equal speaking time, optional verbal participation, among others. In upper grade settings the curriculum is referred to as *Inner change*, not *Magic circle*. H.D.P. workshops are highly recommended prior to use of curriculum:
> Human Development Training Institute
> 7574 University Avenue
> LaMesa, Calif., 92041

Volkmor, C. B., Pasanella, A. L., & Raths, L. E. *Values in the classroom: A multi-media program*. Columbus, Ohio: Charles E. Merrill, 1977. A set of six filmstrips and a work-test about the process of valuing and values clarification. The entire program is based on the earlier work of Raths, Harmin, and Simon.

## Precision Teaching

White, O. R., & Haring, N. G. *Exceptional teaching* (2nd ed.). Columbus, Ohio: Charles E. Merrill, 1980. A multimedia program for teachers, concentrating on specific assessment and prescription procedures which can be used with a wide variety of exceptional learners. The diagnostic-prescriptive approach is demonstrated by *real teachers in actual classrooms*. The program consists of films, either 16mm or Super 8; audio cassette tapes; and work text.

## Individualized Instruction

Mager, R. F., & Pipe, P. *C.R.I: Criterion-referenced instruction: Analysis, design and implementation*. Training workshop of materials available from:
> 13245 Rhoda Dr.
> Los Altos Hills, Calif. 94022

Volkmor, C. B., Langstaff, A. L., & Higgins, M. *Structuring the classroom for success*. Columbus, Ohio: Charles E. Merrill, 1974. This program shows how to function as a teacher and guide of an open classroom—how to create a more stimulating and more productive learning environment. Film, tapes, and text provide realistic experience with tested and proven techniques.

Behavior management principles are blended with ideas for decentralizing the physical room environment and setting up activity centers for individualized instruction.

The program provides a wide variety of semistructured activities to allow the reader to interact with the material. The text provides self-checking exercises to assist the student in understanding the concepts presented by the film and audio tapes. The filmstrip and book contents are:

1. Overview of Open Education
2. Room Environment
3. Creating Activity Centers
4. Behavior Management Principles
5. Behavior Management in the Classroom
6. Individualized Instruction.

# Index

Abeson, A., 3, 8, 28
Academic skills, 134
  arithmetic, 136–37, 218–19
  reading, 134–35, 216–17
  written language, 217
Adamson, G., 9
  fail-save model, 9–10
Administrators, 242–48
  important skills of, 242–43
  leading work groups, 243–45
  planning meetings, 245–46
  problem-solving, 246–47
  time management, 247–48
Affective education, 219–22
Affleck, J., 119, 134, 137, 155, 202–3, 204–5, 211, 234
Agard, J. A., 5, 8, 24, 29, 146, 157, 179
Almy, M., 94, 98–99, 108
Anastasiow, N., 135
Anderson, J., 222
Anecdotal records, 57, 98
Archer, A., 119, 134, 137, 155, 202, 204, 234
Arithmetic, 136–37
  Cuisenaire Rods, 219
  Key Math, 218
  Montessori, 219
  programmed, 219
  structural, 218
Assessment, 91–154
  affective behavior, 145–47
  case studies, 153–54
  format of, 150
  report of outcome, 152–53
  social behavior, 145–47
  system approach, 147–48
Axelrod, S., 108

Babikan, E., 159
Bagley, M. T., 18, 28
  consultant teacher model, 19
Baker, E., 235
Ball, H. H., 160

Ballard, J., 8, 162
Bancroft, Richard A., 15, 28
Barber, L., 159
Barker, L. L., 235
Barnes, E., 331
Bartel, N. R., 119, 122, 134, 136–37, 155, 215, 234, 252, 259, 284
Basal reading series, 216
Basic Test of Reading Comprehension, 135
Bateman, B. D., 233
Bauer, H., 284
Baxter, I., 159
Becker, W. C., 235
Beery, K., 5, 28, 241, 284
Behavior description, 252
Behavior management, 210
  changing behavior, 211
  classroom rules, 211
Bender, L., 138, 155
Bennett, G. K., 155
Bently, G. I., 216
Berlin, I. N., 284
Berman, P., 23, 28
Bersoff, D. N., 120
Bessel, H., 222
Bigge, J., 191, 233
Birch, J. W., 5, 29, 260
Bloom, B. S., 127
Boyd, J. E., 134–35, 155
Brabner, G., 134, 135, 156
Brandt, R. M., 56, 57, 88
Brantley, J. C., 179
Brokes, A. L., 284
Brolin, D. E., 140, 156
Brown, P., 333
Brown, V., 17, 286
Buchanan, A., 159
Buckhalter, G., 333
Burch, N., 238, 335
Bureau for Education of the Handicapped (1979), 166, 170

Burgdorf, R. L., 3, 28
Buss, W., 30
Buswell, G. T., 136–37, 156

Calhoun, M. L., 17, 29, 286
California Test, 137
Campbell, J. D., 18, 135, 145, 158, 199, 234
Career education, 222–23
Career needs, 140–45
Carlson, J., 284
Carroll, A., 314
Cartwright, C. A., 18, 29, 52, 70, 88, 94, 98, 107, 108, 135, 145, 156, 199, 234
Cartwright, G. P., 18, 29, 52, 70, 88, 94, 98, 107, 108, 135, 145, 156, 199, 234
Cascade diagram, 3–4, 9
Casey, R. J., 3, 28
Cegala, D. J., 235
Champagne, D. W., 233
Chow, S., 259, 285
Christie, L. S., 315, 330
Christopolos, F., 237
Civil Rights Act of 1964, 1
Classroom teacher, 258
  role in parent conferences, 260–61
  techniques for, 259–60
Cloward, R. D., 135
Cohen, S. A., 121, 135, 233, 286
Collaboration
  of special and regular education, 47
Communication skills, 251–52
Conferences, parent-teacher, 260–66
  for IEP meeting, 263–64
  informal, 261–62
  for referral, 262–63
  tips for having, 264–66
Consultation, 59–61
  in mainstreaming, 241–42
  provisions of, 61
  as resource teacher, 253–55
Consulting teacher model, 18–19
Content preparation, 291–92
Contingency contracting, 213
Council for Exceptional Children, 237
Court decisions, 7, 10–14
  Brown v. Board of Education, 11
  Diana v. State Board of Education, 13
  Larry P. v. Riles, 13
  Lau v. Nichols, 11
  Mills v. D. C. Board of Education, 11, 13
  Wyatt v. Stickney, 11
Criterion-Referenced Measurement (CRM), 122–27
  uses of, 126–27
Cruickshank, W. M., 33
Crutchfield, M., 160
Csanyi, A. P., 235
Cuisenaire rods, 219

Daniels, W. R., 44, 246–48, 284
Dardig, J. C., 284
Decision-making for teachers
  procedural safeguards, 38
  responsibilities of personnel, 41
  responsibilities of principals, 40
  responsibilities of teachers, 40–41
  rights of teachers, 39
Deno, E., 8–9, 18, 29, 88
  cascade model, 3–4
Deno, S., 111
Diagnostic/Prescriptive Teacher (DPT) Program, 74
Diagnostic teaching model, 18
Diament, B., 264, 285
Diana v. California State Board of Education, 13, 29
Dinkmeyer, D., 222, 253, 284
Direct service models, 16–17
Direct teacher activities, 204
Dissemination/Change Agent Model (or DCA model), 289–91
Dollar, B., 284
Doris, J., 1, 30
Due process, 13, 15, 38, 93
  safeguards of, 271
Dunn, K., 145, 156
Dunn, L. M., 8, 29
Dunn, R., 145, 156
Duration recording, 57, 100–101

Educable mentally retarded (EMR), 14
Educational assessment (see Assessment)
Educational evaluation, 223
  collecting data, 225
  making decisions based on data, 225
  precision teaching, 226–29
  selecting an evaluation procedure, 223–25
Educational planning, 6
Education for All Handicapped Children Act of 1975 (see Public Law 94–142), 30
Educational specialist, 5
Egner, A., 249, 284
Eiseman, J. W., 237
Emory, R., 252, 284
Enos, D., 284
Evaluating the IEP
  annual review, 229
  checklist for, 230–32
Evaluation, 315
  effectiveness of services, 315
  sample forms of, 316
Event recording, 57, 100
Exemplary Center for Reading Instruction, 202, 238

Fail-save model, 9–10
Fair assessment, 270–71
Fair, G. W., 142, 156
Fanning, R., 267, 284

# Index

Farr, R., 135, 156
Fernald method, 217
Fink, R., 142, 156
Forness, S. R., 52, 88
Foster, G. G., 57, 88, 89
Fourteenth Amendment, 11, 13
Free Appropriate Public Education (FAPE), 269
Fremer, J., 236
Frequency recording, 57, 100
Freston, C. W., 236
Friedman, T., 15, 29
Frostig Developmental Test of Visual Perception, 119
Frostig, M., 138, 156

Gartner, A., 237
Gearheart, B. R., 233
Gentry, D., 224, 233
Gibbons, B., 237
Gilhool, T. K., 3, 10, 11, 29
Gillingham Phonics, 217
Glasser, W., 222
Goal setting guide
　for parents, 273-83
Goldman, R. M., 233
Gonzales, M. A., 235
Gooden, B. O., 159
Goodman, L., 121
Gordon, T., 238, 335
Gottlieb, J., 5, 8, 20, 22, 24, 29, 146, 157, 179
Graham, F., K., 138, 156
Greer, J. G., 237
Gronlund, N. E., 235, 236
Gross, J., 111
Gurski, G., 56, 61, 88
Guskin, S., 20, 22, 29
Guszak, F. J., 216

Hagen, E., 98
Hales, S., 331
Hall, R. V., 102, 108, 235
Halo effect, 57, 109
Halpern, A. S., 142, 156
Handicapped
　hearing, 183-85
　learning, 188-89
　physically, 189-92
　preparing classmates, 192-94
　understanding of, 182
　visually, 185-87
Hammill, D., 17, 62, 88, 95, 119, 120-22, 136, 138-39, 156-57, 215, 234, 252, 259, 284, 286
Haring, N. G., 52, 88, 136, 200, 203-4, 224, 233, 238
Harmin, M., 147, 158
Harms, T., 103, 130
Haughton, E., 237, 284
Havelock, R. G., 288, 330

Hawisher, M. F., 17, 29, 286
Hawkins, R. P., 108
Hearing problems, 54, 183-85
　facts for teachers, 183
　about hearing aids, 183-84
　in the regular classroom, 184-85
Hearings, 271-72
Heward, W. L., 52, 88, 233, 284
Hewett, F. M., 52, 88
Higgins, M., 211, 213, 226, 237, 336
Hiltbrunner, C. L., 89
Hobbs, N., 8, 29
Homme, L., 213, 235
Honeycutt, J., 229, 233
Housden, J. L., 125, 236
Howard, R., 252, 284
Howlett, H., 284
Hudak, B. J., 332
Human Relations Kit, 223
Humboldt-Del Norte Master Plan Office, 255, 321
Humboldt-Del Norte Master Plan Project, 64
Husek, T. R., 124

Identification of handicapped, 51-58
　characteristics of, 52-55
　screening process, 55-56
　screening techniques, 56-58
IEP form, 174
　evaluation of, 229
　example of, 176
　length of, 175
　as related to P.L. 94-142, 174
　time of placement, 175
　time of writing, 175
IEP team, 42
　effectiveness of, 46-49
　functions of, 44-45
　responsibilities of, 43-44
IEP team (members of),
　administrators, 242-48
　classroom teacher, 258-66
　parents, 266
　resource teacher, 248-58
Illinois Test of Psycholinguistic Abilities, (ITPA), 119, 138
Implementing IEP, 181-232
　annual review, 229
　behavior management, 210
　checklist for, 230-32
　classroom management, 214-15
　social and instructional integration, 182-83
Independent child activities, 205
Individualized Education Program (IEP), 15, 161-79, 271
　annual goals for, 167
　components of, 165
　definition of, 161-62

Individualized Education Program (cont.)
  duration of services, 171
  evaluation review date, 171
  implementing, 181–232
  levels of performance, 166–67
  placement recommendation, 172
  purpose of, 163
  short-term objectives, 168–70
  special educational services, 170
  team members, 164–65
Individualized Implementation Plan (IIP), 177, 194–202
  development of, 196–98
  example of, 195
  materials for, 200–1
  measuring progress, 201
  as part of IEP, 177
  purpose of, 195
  techniques in, 199–200
Individualized instruction, 259
Individualized reading, 217
Informal Reading Inventory, 216
Inservice checklist
  for resource teacher, 255–58
Inservice program, 17, 18, 287
  delivery of, 307–8
  planning aids, 302–4
Instruction, systematic, 203
Instructional integration, 6
Instructional specialists, 17
Integration (as part of mainstreaming), 6–7
  instructional, 6
  social, 6
  temporal, 6
Intelligence quotient (IQ), 9, 13, 14
Interagency collaboration, 308–14
  barriers against, 309
  examples of, 308
  sample of Local Agreement Checklist, 310–13
  sample of Local Agreement Format, 314
  strategies for, 309
  types of, 309–10
Interviews, 112–18
  improvement of, 115–18
  limitations of, 115
  nonverbal cues, 117
  open, 113
  open-ended questions, 116
  outcomes, 118
  structured, 113
  types of, 112–18
  uses of, 113–15
Irving, W., 22, 29, 156
Irwin, L., 142

Jiguor, J. W., 284
John, L., 136–37

Johnson, G. O., 8, 29
Jones, R. L., 7, 9, 20, 22, 29, 30
Jung, C., 252, 284

Kanfer, F. H., 113
Kanowitz, J., 115
Kauffman, J. M., 89
Kauffman, S. H., 238
Kaufman, M. J., 5–7, 8, 24, 29, 146, 157, 173, 179
Kendall, B. S., 138, 156
Kent, R. N., 115
Keogh, B., 1, 3, 10, 21, 29, 285
Key Math, 218
Kibler, R. J., 235
Kirk, S. A., 138, 157
Kirk, W., 138
Klein, S., 236
Klinger, R., 284, 285
Kobler, M., 237
Kokaska, C. J., 140–41, 156
Kosekoff, J. P., 236
Kreinberg, N., 259, 285
Krivonos, P. D., 246, 285
Kroth, R. L., 285
Krumboltz, J., 235
Krumboltz, H., 235
Kukic, M. B., 5, 7, 24, 29, 146, 157, 179
Kukic, S., 177
Kung, J. W., 3, 28
Kunzelmann, H. P., 238
Kurihoff, P., 30
Kurtz, D. P., 89

Lakein, A., 286
Lambert, N., 285
Langstaff, A. L., 145, 157, 211, 213, 226, 237, 335
Language arts
  listening, 218
  oral and written, 218
  reading, 218
Language experience approach, 217
Language problems, 53–54
  assessment, of, 137–38
Laosa, L. M., 120–21
La Pray, M., 134, 157
Larry P. v. Riles, 13–30
Larsen, S., 58, 59, 88, 139, 157
Lau v. Nichols, 11, 30
Laub, K. W., 89
La Vor, M. L., 8
Law of the Hammer, 112
LEA (Local Education Agencies)
  responsibilities of, 39
League of Educational Administrator (Project LEAD), 243
Learning, stages of,
  initial, 203

# Index

Learning, stages of (cont.)
  maintenance, 203
  proficiency, 203
Learning problems, 188–89
  facts for teachers, 188
  in the regular classroom, 188–89
Learning Style Questionnaire, 145
Learning styles, 208–9
Least Restrictive Environment (LRE), 3–5, 7, 15, 269–70
Least restrictive placement, 15
Lefever, D. W., 156
Le Gear, L., 125
Legislation, 14–15
  IEP, 164–66
  PL 94–142, 161–62
Lerner, J. W., 233
Levitt, M. L., 3, 10, 29
Le Voci, J. P., 143, 157
Lewis, J., 142, 157
Liles, R. D., 138, 157
Lilly, M. S., 5, 8, 9, 17, 18, 21, 30
Lippitt, P., 237
Lippitt, R., 237
Lister, J. L., 146, 157
Lobree, V. A., 284
Local Agreement Checklist
  assessment sample, 311
  IEP sample, 312–13
  for interagency collaboration, 310
Logan, D. R., 236
Losen, S. M., 264, 285
Lott, L. A., 332
Lowenbraun, S., 119, 134, 137, 155, 203–4, 234

MacMillan, D. L., 7–8, 9, 21, 30
Mager, R. F., 235, 336
Mainstreaming
  components of, 6–7
  and court decisions, 10–14
  definitions of, 5–9
  evaluating effectiveness of, 20
  as feature of P. L. 94–142, 22
  and implementation of change, 22–23
  implications of, 1–3
  influence of educators, 8–10
  institutional motivation, 23
  legislation, 14–15
  problem areas of, 21
  project implementation strategies, 24
  strategies for, 26–27
Maintenance function, 45, 244
Mangers, D., 285
Mann, P. H., 159
Manpower Attitudes Test, 142–43
Marsh, D. D., 23, 24, 25
Marshall, D. A., 284

Martin, Reed, 39
Mayer, G. R., 213, 236
McCarthy, J. J., 138, 157
McClain, N., 331
McClung, M., 10, 30
McCurdy, R. E., 284
McGinty, A., 285
McIntyre, R., 330
McKenzie, H. S., 315, 330
McLaughlin, M. W., 23, 24, 25, 28
McNeil, W., 3, 28
Melragno, R. J., 237
Memory for Designs Test, 138
Mercer, J. R., 120, 159
Meyen, E. L., 11, 233
Meyers, C. E., 7–8, 9, 14, 30
Meyers, E. S., 160
Miles, D. T., 142, 235
Miller, T. L., 18
Mills, B. C., 233
Mills, R. A., 233
Mills v. D. C. Board of Education, 11, 13, 30
Misclassification, 10, 13, 14
Models
  for diagnostic teaching, 18
  Dissemination/Change Agent Model (DCA model), 289–91
  for educational decision-making, 34–38
  for identification, 18
  for the resource room, 16–19
  South Carolina Regional v Educational Services Center, 153
  for teacher consultant, 79
  of Vermont Consulting Teacher, 18–19
Modified Reward Preference Assessment, 145
Molloy, L., 3
Montessori, 219
Myers, P. I., 235

National Association of State Directors of Special Education (1976), 167
Neisworth, J. T., 89, 237
Nelson, C. M., 196, 199, 221, 234, 251, 259, 285
Newcomer, P. 138, 157
Nonverbal cues, 117
Norm-referenced testing, 124–27
Nyberg, D., 147, 158

Observations, 94–111
  advantages of, 95, 146
  anecdotal records, 98–99
  duration recording, 100–101
  frequency recording, 100
  involving measurement, 100–102
  "placheck" method, 100
  skills of, 96–97
  time sampling, 101

Observations (cont.)
types of, 98–99
Occupational Awareness Test, 143
Occupational Preference Test, 143
Ohio Trade and Industrial Education Services, 144
O'Leary, K. D., 115
Open-ended questions, 116
Opinions About Work (test), 142
Organization
of classroom, 209–10
of time, 209
Orlansky, M. D., 52, 88, 233

Palomares, U., 222, 336
Panyan, M. C., 236
Paolucci, P., 249, 284
Paraphrasing, 117, 252
Parent training
goal setting, 272–83
record keeping, 272
Parents, 266
as active IEP team participants, 266–67
rights of (under PL 94–142), 268–69
Participation Chart, 108
improvement of, 109–10
limitations of, 109
outcomes of, 111
Pasanella, A. L., 42, 158, 173, 179, 233, 260, 273, 285, 286, 324–325, 330, 336
Paul, J. L., 33
Payne, J. S., 234
Peabody Language Development Kit, 218
Pennsylvania Association for Retarded Children (PARC), 11, 13, 30
Perception check, 252
Perceptual-motor problems, 53, 138–39
Petreshene, S. S., 237
Physical problems, 189–92
facts for teachers, 189–90
in the regular classroom, 190–92
Pino, R., 252, 284
Pipe, P., 336
Placement alternative
(see Least restrictive environment), 4
Placheck (Planned Activity Check), 57, 100, 102
Polin, L., 140
Popham, W. J., 124
Potter, D., 286
Precision teaching, 57, 226–29
materials used, 226
steps followed, 226–29
Presbie, R., 333
Prescriptive Instructional Activities Form, 143
Prescriptive Math Inventory, 236
Prescriptive Reading Inventory, 236
Principal
responsibilities of, 40

Problem behaviors, 52–55
hearing, 54
information processing, 54
language, 53–54
perceptual motor, 53
retrieval, 52–53
social-emotional, 54–55
speech, 54
vision, 54
Problem solving, 246–47
Procedural protection, 13
Process checklist
instructions for completing, 77
sample of, 75–76
Process testing, 119–21, 147
Program Review Model, 324–29
follow-up, 325
information gathering, 324–25
planning, 324
sample of, 325–29
Programmed reading, 217, 219
Public Law 94–142, 15, 24, 38, 91, 92, 161, 308
changes since inactment, 42
definition of IEP, 161–62
evaluating progress, 201
evaluation in mainstreaming, 22
justification of placement, 172
objectives of, 170
quotations from, 2
related to IEP form, 174
related services for IEP, 170–71

Racicot, R. H., 284
Raffeld, P., 142, 156
Rand studies
attitude of principal, 24
attitudes of teachers, 25
Raths, L. E., 147, 158, 336
Rausch, H. L., 112
Reading, 134–36, 216–17
basal series, 216
Fernald, 217
Gillingham phonics, 217
individualized, 217
language experience approach, 217
programmed, 217
Spalding phonics approach, 217
tips for teaching, 217
Receiving teacher
definition of, 261
home follow-up, 263
informal progress checks, 263–64
tips for, 267
Rechs, J. R., 235
Record keeping
by parents, 272
Reese, J. H., 57, 88

# Index

Referral analysis, 149
Referral Analysis Chart, 79–82, 85
   case studies, 83–84, 85–86
   directions for completing, 78
Referrals, 58–86
   alternatives to, 58–59
   analyzing, 77–78
   examples of, 59–60
   procedures of, 62
   qualities of, 62–63
   Referral Analysis Chart, 78–82
   sample forms, 63–75
Referring teacher, 261–63
   definition of, 261
   preparing parents, 262–63
Region III Education Service Center, 332
Region XIII Education Service Center, 333
Regional Resource Center Task Force on Interagency Collaboration, 308–10, 330
Rehabilitation Research and Training Center, 142
Reid, E., 234
Reinforcement Inventory, 145
Reinforcements (or rewards)
   activities, 213
   attention, 212
   contingency contracting, 213
   food, 212
   knowledge of results, 212
   tokens, 213, 214
Reissman, F., 237
Resource programs, 16
   direct service models, 16–17
   direct vs. indirect, 19–20
   managing of, 17
   problems of, 19
Resource teacher, 16, 248–58
   characteristics of, 250–51
   communication skills of, 251–52
   as consultant, 253–55
   in-service checklist for, 255–58
   responsibilities of, 248–49
   support strategies, 252–53
Retrieval problems, 52–53
Reward preferences, 145
Reynolds, M., 74, 260, 285
Risley, T. R., 102
Rocky Mountain Education Laboratories, 142–43, 158
Rolle, R. E. W., 284
Ross, R., 134, 157
Rossett, A., 284

Sabatino, D. A., 18, 153
Salvia, J., 147, 158
Samson, J., 331
San Diego Quick Assessment, 134
Saslow, G., 113
Savage, W., 253, 285
Scheduling (for workshops), 297–302
Scheetz, J. A., 332
Schiefelbusch, R. L., 234
Schipper, W., 174, 179
Scholl, G. T., 285
School records, 118–19
Schulz, J. B., 179, 182, 213, 216, 235
Screening process, 55
   organizing and implementing, 55–56
   purpose of, 58
Screening techniques, 56
   checklists, 56–57
   rating scales, 56–57
Semel, E. M., 138, 158
Semmel, M. I., 5, 21, 95
Shaw, S. F., 17, 18
Shaw, W., 17, 18
Siegel, E., 197, 234
Siegel, R., 197, 234
Simon, S. B., 147, 158
Simpson, D., 142
Sirvis, B., 191, 233
Skill testing, 121–27, 147
Skindrud, K., 112–18
Smith, J. E., 234
Smith, P. B., 216
Smith, R. M., 134, 136, 139, 158, 235, 237
Social-emotional problems, 54–55, 145–47, 219
Social integration, 6, 174
Social and Prevocational Information Battery, 142
South Carolina Regional v. Educational Services Center, 68, 316, 331
Spalding Phonics Approach, 217
Special educators, 17
Speech problems, 54
Spencer, E. F., 136–37, 158
Spinazola, C., 18, 135, 145, 158, 199, 220, 234
SRA Achievement Test, 137
   materials for, 223
Stanford-Binet, 119
Stanford Test, 137
Starlin, C., 238
Starr-Anderlini, L., 43
Stellern, J., 120, 145, 158
Strickland, B., 179
Structural arithmetic, 218
Stuck, R. L., 284
Suiter, P., 159
Sulzer, B., 213, 236
Supplementary Aids and Services, 270
Support personnel
   responsibilities of, 41
Support strategies, 252–55
Sussman, L., 246, 285
System FORE, 236

Task analysis, 122–23, 196–99
  example of, 198
Task design, 292–97
Task function, 244
Task related functions, 44
Teacher consultants
  tasks of, 18–19
Teachers of handicapped students
  responsibilities of, 40–41
Teaching procedure
  chaining, 206
  cueing, 206
  demonstration, 206
  effective, 202
  fading, 206
  modeling, 207
  practice, 207
  shaping, 206
  techniques for, 206–7
Team (for IEP), 164
Temporal integration, 6
Test of Language Development (TOLD), 138
Testing, 119–27
  California Test, 137
  Criterion-Referenced Measurement (CRM), 122–27
  Differential Aptitudes Test, 144
  Frostig Developmental Test of Visual Perception, 119
  Illinois Test of Psycholinguistic Abilities, 119
  Informal Reading Inventory, 216
  Key Math, 218
  Manpower Attitudes Test, 142–43
  Memory for Designs Test, 138
  Norm-Referenced Testing, 124–27
  Opinions About Work, 142
  process, 119–21
  skill, 121
  Social and Prevocational Information Battery, 142
  SRA Achievement Test, 137
  Stanford-Binet, 119
  Stanford Test, 137
  task analysis, 122–23
  Test of Language Development (TOLD), 138
  Wechsler Intelligence Scales, 119
Thorndike, R. L., 98
Thurman, S. K., 151, 158
Time management, 247–48
Time sampling, 57, 101
Token systems, 213, 214
Towle, M., 234
Tubesing, D. A., 117

Tubesing, N. L., 117
Tucker, J. A., 152, 158
Turnbull, A. P., 33, 39, 179, 181, 182, 234, 235
Turnbull, H. R., 39, 179, 181, 234

Van Etten, G., 9
  fail-save model, 9–10
Vasa, S. F., 89, 120, 145, 158
Verderber, R. F., 244, 285
Vision problems, 54, 185–87
  facts for teachers, 185–86
  in the regular classroom, 186–87
Vocational education, 222–23
Vocational needs, 140–45
Volkmor, C. B., 145, 157, 179, 211, 213, 226, 233, 238, 330, 335, 336

Walker, H., 177, 180
Ward, M. E., 135, 145, 158, 212, 219, 234
Wardlaw, J. H., 284
Watts, C., 330
Wechsler Intelligence Scales, 119
Weintraub, F. J., 8
Weishahn, M. W., 233
Weston, B., 289, 330
White, O. R., 136, 158, 200, 233, 238, 336
Whittlesey, J. R. B., 156
Wiederholt, J. L., 17, 62, 88, 121, 286
Wiig, E. H., 138, 158
Wiley, E. M., 284
Willems, E. P., 112
Williams, T., 330
Wilson, W., 174, 179
Worell, J., 196, 199, 221, 234, 251, 259, 285
Work groups
  characteristics of, 243–44
  maintenance roles, 244
  negative roles, 244–45
  planning and leading, 245–46
  task related roles, 244
Workshops
  scheduling of, 297–302
  topical outline for, 304–6
Why Work Series, 222
World of Work Kit, 223
Wyatt v. Stickney, 11

Yonkers Career Education Project, 143
Yoshida, R. K., 20, 22, 29, 30
Ysseldyke, J. E., 18, 29, 57, 88, 89, 120–21, 147, 158

Zero reject model, 9
Zettel, J., 162, 179